IRISH TERRIER

Lucy Jackson

I hope that this book will encourage and prove helpful to newcomers to the breed, while clearly presenting the ready information for breeders and professionals. Breed Standards are of vital importance and need to be a constant source of reference. I hope too that in maintaining and promoting greater understanding of the breed it will help to give all Irish Terriers the sort of lifestyle that suits them best. Their health, happiness and general well-being is and should always be our first consideration.

contents

Front Cover:
Ch Naranja Jumping Jack Flash (sitting) with Amber. Photo: Marc Henrie
Title page:
Kate and Huli. Photo: Tracy Morgan
Opposite:
Photo: Marc Henrie
Back Cover:
The author with a friend. Photo: Tracy Morgan

acknowledgements

Firstly, a salute to the breed and to all the glorious Irish Terriers I have known and loved.

Secondly, a deep debt of gratitude to Edna Howard Jones for her inspired understanding of the breed and on whose handbook *Irish Terriers* I have shamelessly relied.

This book would not have been possible without the help and encouragement of my many good friends within the breed. They have been unstintingly generous in supplying hundreds of photographs and tracking down much necessary information. My special thanks, then, to Dr Alex Noonan, Ann Bradley, Ferelith Somerfield, Lindsay Willamson, Paul Livesey, Sam Price, Eileen Batley, Joan Simcock, Lyn Fegan, Helen Crawley and Ursula Merrington. Special thanks also to May Williams, whose remarkable collection of Irish Terrier Records proved invaluable as source material. Also profound gratitude to my vet, Frank Seddon B.Vet.Med.MRVCS, whose patience and skill answered an endless stream of questions. Thanks also to May Williamson, who has a remarkable set of Irish Terrier records of breed lines and memorabilia.

I should like to thank the Irish Terrier Clubs at home and abroad who have contributed facts and figures so generously.

Last but not least, I should like to thank my son, James H Jackson, for his invaluable help with the manuscript.

Edna Howard Jones and Tom.

dedication

For **Edna Howard Jones**
who loved and understood
Irish Terriers
and whose unsurpassed knowledge
and skill
gave so much to the breed.

foreword

Edna Howard Jones, to whom this book is dedicated, once wrote: "Irish Terriers are like a drug, and once hooked there is no cure."

I count myself among those unrepentant addicts who have measured out their lives with the Irish Terriers they have owned – or rather, that have owned them!

In the early days, the editor of a book about dogs was exasperated by the endless enthusiasm expressed in their contributions by Irish Terrier breeders. "In each paragraph one learns that no better dog ever lived!" she exclaimed. This same spirit of passionate enthusiasm remains ever undimmed among the owners and breeders of today.

Yet what is it about the breed?

After all, at first glance the Irish Terrier could be mistaken for just a 'good basic brown dog', not one that captures the popular imagination as a designer item or fluffy fashion accessory. This is perhaps why they have escaped the hazards of over-breeding and remained so remarkably healthy and sound in wind and limb – the authentic descendants of their ancient terrier ancestors.

And look carefully at that outline – the body is sturdy and strong, yet racy and built for speed, the perfect ratio of size and weight, the ideal proportion of length in leg and back, the neck and head balanced and held high. Add to that a water-resistant coat, a deep-throated bark, an acute sense of hearing and the nose of a tracker dog. Irish Terriers are tough and remarkably free from general health problems and have more long-lived veterans than any other breed. You could almost say that this must be a dog that has been designed by a dog!

The character too has remained intact; the combination of qualities undiluted. Their strength as all-purpose town or country dogs has remained uncompromised.

Those who know or own Irish Terriers will recognise the attributes applied to the breed, and all will have anecdotes supporting these: the heedless pluck, the blind courage and indomitable spirit, the upbeat sunny nature and the irrepressible sense of fun. Their devotion to 'their' people is legendary and they love to be part of everything happening around them. They are watchful and gentle with even the smallest child, and their zest and enthusiasm for joining in any game make their suitability as family pets hard to equal.

They are highly intelligent – 'too clever by half', it has been said. Certainly they can be spirited, wayward and full of their own ideas. But they are never mean and, if properly handled from the beginning, they are the easiest to train of all the terriers. This is because they are deeply sensitive and cannot bear to be in trouble with those they love. They will not thrive if treated with harshness or indifference.

But more than that, they are dogs with a soul and a depth of character and generosity of spirit. Some would even say, a touch of pure mysticism.

For those of us who love them, the charm, the old Irish magic, is as strong as ever. With their supreme self-confidence, I can almost hear them saying: "Now why need you be asking? For sure no better dog ever lived!"

And, with joy and gratitude, I would have to agree with them.

Lucy Jackson

Chapter One

Origins and Early History

Terriers derive their name from the Latin *terra* meaning 'earth'. Recognised and classified as a group by the Greeks and Romans, they were dogs of any size that hunted by digging into the earth to catch rodents, badgers, foxes, rabbits or any other small animal on which they could feed.

"It crept up on me when I wasn't looking!"

The Irish Terrier is an extraordinarily old breed descended, in all likelihood, from the ancient Terrier of Great Britain. Greek writers claimed that in no other part of Europe was so much care given to cultivating this dog *as a race from generation to generation*. This rough-coated, black-and-tan terrier evolved gradually into the breed developed in Ireland whose qualities were hardiness, almost unsurpassed skill as a ratter and a temperament ideally suited to living in close proximity with human beings. The resemblance to the Wolfhound in coat, colour and outline suggests a relationship with that ancient breed. The breed was seen as the perfect all-rounder and appealed to people of all classes. Irish manuscripts refer to *the poor man's sentinel*, *the farmer's friend* and *the gentleman's favourite*.

Even when they were known as 'Irish Terriers' and had been bred for show for generations, with recorded pedigrees, it was not at all uncommon for bitches to whelp black-and-tan pups in their litters. Today, as a throw-back, many pups are born with black down, which lifts and comes off within about eight weeks.

Whenever and whatever its origin, the Irish Terrier emerged as a breed in the 1870s, although many breeders at that time claimed that the breed had existed 50 years earlier.

Various strains of the breed evolved: the large County Cork variety, the Ballymena strain from County Antrim (closer to today's racier looking show dog) and the vermin-killing, blue-and-tan, short-legged terriers of the Glen of Imael in the Wicklow Mountains. They were bred more for their working qualities and gameness than for their looks.

Standardising the Breed

Standardisation of the breed took time. A Dublin Show in 1873 was the first to provide a separate class for Irish Terriers. They were a varied lot in size and colour, some weighing as little as 4kg (9lb). The colours ranged through red, black-and-

Irish Terrier pups doing what comes naturally with a rabbit skin.

tan, grey and even brindle. However, some common characteristics were predominant even then. They all had close, wiry and water-resistant coats, good length of body and the famed Irish Terrier temperament – bonny, sensitive and courageous, already the thinking 'Daredevils'.

In 1879, the first Irish Terrier Club was called into existence and a breed standard was drawn up. The gain in popularity of the breed from this point onwards was extraordinary and, although exhibiting was still in its infancy, by the turn of the century it was not uncommon to have up to 30 dogs in any one class in the shows.

By 1905 the breed was strong enough to warrant the production of a magazine devoted entirely to its activities. The first copy of the *Irish Terrier Review* was produced in January 1905 and the publication appeared quarterly for some years. It appears that many burning issues of yesteryear flare up with the same frequency today: the quality of judging, over-trimming, size and incorrect coats. Some things have changed: the best dog biscuit then was advertised at 13s 6d (62^1/2p) per cwt (50.8kg), and the top stud fee (for Ch Mile End Barrister) was £3 3s 0d (£3.15).

People in all walks of life were becoming Irish Terrier enthusiasts and, in 1911, another Breed Club, the Irish Terrier Association, was formed with the then Marquis of Breadalbane as President and with Vice Presidents including HH The Maharajah of Jind, The Right Hon Lord Greville (3rd Baron), the Lord Dewar, Major General Sir Foster Newland and Colonel Sir Edward Ward Bt, to name but a few. The Right Hon The Earl of Lonsdale eventually became President, retaining his interest in the Association until his death in 1944.

Later, other breed societies were formed: the Northern Irish Terrier Club, the North of England Irish Terrier Club, the Southern Irish Terrier Society and the Irish Terrier Club of

Scotland. All these work wholeheartedly in their geographical areas, and there is a great exchange of ideas and spirit of cooperation between them. For more details about these societies, see chapter 13.

First World War

It was the breed's ready intelligence, ratting abilities and sheer conviviality that threw them into such a prominent role during the First World War. Shipped to France, they performed acts of extraordinary courage as guard and patrol dogs, messengers or simply as ratters, keeping the troops company in the mud of Flanders, Ypres and Paschendale. Their story inspired me to research and write *Jock of the Great War* as a tribute to the Irish Terriers who served and died on the Western Front. They were known affectionately as the 'Micks' and the 'Paddys'. Various anecdotes about their exploits can be found in chapter 15.

Slemish Sweet Honey bringing home a rabbit.

Decline in Popularity

Records show a gradual decline in popularity starting in the 1920s. This may have been due to breeding restrictions during the First World War or to a desire on the part of the dog-owning public for a change of fashion. Certainly, the appearance of more exotic types presented a wider choice to a country eager to move on and away from the bleakness of the previous decade. The heyday of the terrier was over, and steady urbanisation could not have helped. Whatever the cause, the breed was to reach a very low ebb during those years. By 1933, although many breeders were actively interested, sales were not brisk, the entries at shows were poor and many societies ceased to schedule the breed. It was then that the late Mr Gordon Selfridge made a generous gesture in an endeavour to rekindle interest in the breed he loved. He offered a department in his famous Oxford Street store to be used for an exhibition of Irish Terriers. This was held in November and was opened by His Grace the Third Duke of Atholl, who was a staunch supporter of the breed. The exhibition was beautifully arranged and 22 of the best known dogs and bitches of the day were on view. Attendants were dressed in Irish national costumes and a souvenir programme was given to all visitors. Whether the exhibition rekindled interest in the breed is moot.

Effects of the Second World War

During the Second World War the breeding of all kinds of dogs came to a standstill. The few people who were able to carry on in any breeds were responsible for their preservation. The status of those breeds today owes much to those few stalwarts who bridged the pre- and post-war period.

The Usefulness of the Breed

There has always been a purpose for the existence of the breed, and we are told that, long before Irish Terriers were officially recognised, small, red, rough-coated terriers formed an essential part of the life of the humbler Irish families who gained a precarious living off a few acres. Here was a dog with the courage and ability to guard against intruders and thieves and able to kill the rats that abounded and yet live in peace with the children, the hens and the rest of the human and animal family that shared the cabin. These very qualities are still to be found today. The Irish Terrier is a wonderful ratter, given the chance, and excels at catching rabbits. As a guard it is second to none.

Edna Howard Jones related the following story of two of her bitches working a hedge prior to the days of myxamatosis:

It was a picture of intelligence and cooperation. One waiting silently, pointing, on one side, while the other, utterly regardless of thorn and bramble, would work the hedge and drive the rabbits out to her partner who would catch and kill with great speed.

Two of Miss Paull's Irish Terriers: Ch Paymaster and Erasmic.

Irish Terriers are incredibly quick dogs and it was not uncommon for bitches with litters to kill and bring back rabbits for their pups when they reached weaning age. They would put the rabbit down for the puppies to tear to pieces, standing back and watching but never taking any themselves. Another rather surprising fact about their working ability is that, properly trained, they prove excellent gundogs; their soft mouths make them perfect retrievers, and they were used extensively to work fields for partridge and other game before the Second World War.

F M Jowett wrote that, as sporting companion, vermin killer or game-finder, the Irish Terrier had no superior.

He is very hardy, and able to stand more wet, cold and fatigue than most other Terriers, and the right kind of coat is so hard and dense on the body that wet cannot penetrate it, and not being too long, it does not hinder them in cover work. I know no breed of dog that repays careful training better.

Swimming and diving after water rats, bolting otters from drains and tree roots and drawing and holding badgers: small wonder that the breed also became the poacher's favourite. The assertation of the Irish Terrier's age-old instincts can be just the same in town-bred dogs, and the famous ratting qualities remain undimmed.

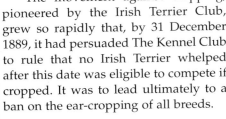

Chapter Two

Major Developments

The Late Nineteenth Century
The Irish Terrier Club

On 31 March 1879, the first meetings were held in Dublin to found a club for the protection and advancement of the breed. Mr R Erskine and Mr E F Despard, both from Belfast, chaired these initial gatherings. Draft rules were laid down and the first resolution (proposed by Mr William Graham and seconded by Dr R B Carey) *that an Irish Terrier Club be called into existence* was carried unanimously.

A general meeting of the English Section of the Club, held in London on 28 April in the same year, agreed the draft rules, and the annual subscription was set at 10s 0d (50p). While the Committee consisted of 20 members, with two Vice Presidents, the Hon Secretaries and the Treasurer elected annually by voting papers, the list of judges was not limited in number. There was only one Challenge Cup, and it was for open competition, becoming the property of anyone winning it five times.

In 1880, the general meeting drew up a scale of points for judging the breed and resolved that Irish Terriers with uncropped ears should be accepted into competition. At the time there were probably only two uncropped specimens existing, namely Ch Sport and Ch Sporter.

The movement against cropping, pioneered by the Irish Terrier Club, grew so rapidly that, by 31 December 1889, it had persuaded The Kennel Club to rule that no Irish Terrier whelped after this date was eligible to compete if cropped. It was to lead ultimately to a ban on the ear-cropping of all breeds.

The founding fathers

The founders and key supporters of the Irish Terrier Club at this time provided the building blocks for the development of the breed in the 20th century, and certainly contributed much to its

Ch Sporter.

Ch Bolton Woods Mixer.

Ch Dan'el II.

astonishing popularity before the First WorldWar. The sums offered for good specimens were remarkable: it is said that £500 was once refused for Ch Bolton Woods Mixer, and Ch Straight Tip was sold for £400.

A founder, Mr Geo Jamison of Belfast, had a strong kennel, and his beautiful bitch Ch Rum was exported to America. Another founder, Mr George R Krehl (a Londoner) bred the fine Ch Pagan II, Ch Dan'ell II, Bishop's Boy and Ch Sporter. His brother, Mr Albert W Krehl, was another well-known exhibitor of the period, as was Mr Waterhouse, a Dubliner, who owned Peter Bolger and that famed stud dog and father of the modern breed, Killiney Boy.

Dr R B Carey, the Irish Terrier Club's first Hon Secretary and one of its best judges, owned a well known kennel, its best dogs being Ch Sport, Spuds, Ch Nabocklish, Pilgrim (sold to the Earl of Shannon for £100) and Ch Sting. Other prominent figures included Mr A T Arrol, Mr R J Ridgeway of Waterford, Mr W J Cotton and Mr H A Graves, who owned Ch Glory and Ch Playboy.

But perhaps it is to Mr William ('Billy') Graham, 'the Irish Ambassador', to whom most credit is due for producing the modern show-standard Irish Terrier. Breeding from the best dogs and bitches, he more than anyone else established the breed's recognisable character, colour and characteristics. The dogs that passed through his hands are nearly all the dogs that have made history in the breed, the most important perhaps being the following:

- Ch Erin
- Ch Sporter
- Seaforde
- Ch Glory
- Ch Gripper
- Gilford
- Ch Garryford
- Garryowen
- Ch Pagan II

- Ch Breda Rattle
- Breda Star
- Breda Ida
- Breda Olive
- Breda Vixen
- Breda Iris
- Breda Florence
- Ch Breda Mixer (see over)
- Ch Breda Muddler

Ch Breda Mixer.

Ch Ted Malone.

The first real Irish Terriers

Killiney Boy, called the father of present-day pedigree Irish Terriers, bred by Mr Burke of Dublin and later owned by Mr Howard Waterhouse, was by Jack ex Jess, the latter being a wire-haired black-and-tan Welsh Terrier bitch. This explains the common appearance of broken-haired black-and-tan puppies in earlier strains descended from him. A cropped dog, Killiney Boy, was described as *a rare good, game little Terrier with a hard coat and grand Terrier head, but rather low on the legs.* He is said to have been worried and almost eaten by a litter of puppies that he sired!

If Killiney Boy was the father of the pedigree Irish Terrier, then Ch Erin must be termed the mother of the breed. A cropped bitch from Co Antrim, she was described as having *a very long clean head, with the true keen, wicked expression, and being full of type and character, with a hard red coat, grand body shape and set-on of stern, racy in build and quality all through.* Her owner, William Graham, deemed her the best Irish Terrier bitch he had ever seen, an opinion confirmed by many of his contemporaries. Her first litter to Killiney Boy produced Ch Pagan II, Ch Poppy and Ch Playboy: *a marvellous litter,* and one destined to have a great influence on the breed. By the outbreak of the First World War over 90% of show Irish Terriers could trace their descent from either Killiney Boy or Ch Erin, as a study of the extended pedigree of Belfast Rufus illustrates.

Ch Pagan II, a member of that famous first litter, sired a quality dog named Michael, who in turn, when mated to Ch Droleen (another daughter of Killiney Boy and Ch Erin) sired Ch Brickbat. Bred by Mr E A Weiner, Ch Brickbat stood out as the best dog of his day, and was dubbed the aristocrat of the breed. He won the Club's 60-guinea Challenge Cup 12 times in succession, under various judges, without suffering a defeat. A cropped dog, weighing about 12.7kg (28lb) with a long, clean head, lovely neck, perfect shoulders, the best of legs and feet, racy in build yet with plenty of bone and substance, he had a good, hard, straight yellow-red coat, moderate in length, and was described as *essentially a gentleman.* As one commentator observed: *Too much a gentleman, perhaps, for an Irish Terrier; a bit more 'devil' and fire would have improved him.*

Brickbat, in turn, sired Mr George Krehl's Ch Dan'ell, another cropped dog, who inherited the coat and quality of his sire, but was a much smaller specimen. Ch Dan'ell went on to sire the beautiful Ch Ted Malone, bred by Mrs Butcher, who was not a great success at stud.

The modern drop-eared look

Another member of Erin's first litter to Killiney Boy was Ch Playboy, whose ears were so small and well carried that they were allowed to remain uncropped although it was the fashion to crop in those days. He was probably the best show dog of his day, and he sired another drop-eared dog, Bogie Rattler, who, when mated to Biddy III, a drop-eared bitch by Ch Griper ex Cora (another bitch with perfect ears), bred two dogs that may be said to have laid the foundation of the modern drop-eared Irish Terrier: Ch Bachelor and his litter brother Benedict, bred by Mr C J Barnett. Nearly all the best show dogs trace their descent from one of these two dogs.

Ch Playboy.

Ch Bachelor was a renowned show dog, with a well-shaped head, small, perfectly carried ears, a very hard yellow-red coat, a good neck, firm loin and strong hindquarters, with tail well set. *A good hard game Terrier, but rather too much on red Fox Terrier lines, and... not quite as much liberty as is desirable in an Irish Terrier.* He was not a great success as a stud dog, but the bitches by him bred good ones, particularly Irish, who produced Ch Checkmate, Charon, Farndon Mixer, Ch Breda Muddler and several others for her owner, Mr George Mayall. Her sister, Red Inez, a cropped bitch with a lovely head and sound, hard, red coat, bred Ch Blue Nettle and several other notables.

Almost all Bachelor's stock were *game and good workers*, and usually carried their ears better than those sired by his brother, Benedict. Benedict was not a show dog, being smooth on his head, with dark shadings at the end of his muzzle. His ears, though small, folded and were badly carried. His shoulders, legs and feet were excellent, but he is thought to have been, like his brother Bachelor, too *cobby* and *lacking in liberty*. His coat was peculiar, and he grew some hard, rough hair down his neck and over his back, although his sides and legs were quite smooth. He was, however, a great success as a stud dog and, being in Mr Billy Graham's famous kennel, had a chance to mate with the best. When he was mated with the big, racy, long-headed, cropped bitches who were plentiful in Ireland before the turn of the century, the resulting specimens had smaller ears, reduced size and improvements in the colour and texture of their coats.

Other prominent Irish Terriers at the beginning of the breed's history included:

- Mr C H Backhouse's Ch Blue Stocking, a big, racy bitch with the *real wicked varminty expression*, and Bumptious Blazer, Bumptious Biddy and Buster.
- Mr Sumner's Ch B A Pedlar and St George.
- Mr H Bennet's Derry Diamond, a *rare good one*.
- Mr Breakell's Bishop and his Ch Bonnet, thought *a little plain in head, but the best of bodies, legs, feet and coat*.
- Mr E A Weiner's Merle Grady, Bencher, Ballyhooley and Ch Norah Tatters.
- Mr T Ramsay's Ramsay's Ballyboley.
- Mr F M Jowett's Crow Gill Tartar and Crow Gill Sportsman (grandsire of Ch Bolton Woods Mixer).
- Mr Rufus Mitchell's Pugilist.
- Mr William Graham's Extreme Carelessness, the great bitch Breda Florence (dam of Breda Iris and Red Inez), and the lovely Breda Ida.
- Mr Barnett's Beautiful Star, *a rare made one, with a splendid jacket*, and Bosquet.
- Mr J W Taylor's Ch Breadenhill, a *grand headed dog, with perfect legs and feet and good body, but not the best of coats*.

Ch Breadenhill.

The Turn of the Century Dogs

Of the middle period in the early history of the breed, the most notable dog was Ch Breda Mixer, bred by Mr William Graham and purchased by Mr George Mayall, who campaigned him to champion. Ch Breda Mixer possessed great character in his head, good ears, the best of legs and feet and a sound coat, and made a significant contribution to the breed by siring Ch Breda Muddler, Ch Bolton Woods Mixer and a host of lesser lights.

Ch Treasurer was another high quality Irish Terrier by Ch Brickbat. F M Jowett argued that, like his father, Treasurer needed a little more *fire* and *go* to be ranked among the greatest; although said to have been *game at home*, he did not show well in the ring.

This period saw some other fine specimens:

- Mr Thomas Yarr's Poor Pat was a good, characteristic Irish Terrier, and was very prominent at the time.
- Mrs Smythe's Ch Sarah Kidd was a well-recognised winner.
- Mr Westlake's Ch John Ridd.
- Mr John Craig's Ch Blue Nettle.
- Mr F M Jowett's Ch Crow Gill Maureen and Ch Crow Gill Sally.

- Mr F Breakell's Blackbrook Bandmaster and Blackbrook Burgemaster.
- Mr G Mayall's Ch Charwoman and Ch Charmian, neither of whom bred particularly well. Also Ch Checkmate (a brother to Breda Muddler) who was considered by some to be *rather too much on red Fox Terrier lines.*
- Mr B Waugh's Ch Stackhouse Sportsman.
- Dr W W Fenton's Kineton Biddy, a wonderful bitch with *a rare coat and keen expression* who went to Mr William Graham's kennel.
- Mr R Everill's Erminie, exported to America, where she continued her successful winning career.
- Mr F Gregg's Ch Belfast Erin, considered one of the best in her day.
- Mr Butcher's Ch Bawn Beauty, a *truly Irish* golden red bitch.
- Mr Montgomery's Ch Celtic Bella and Celtic Badger, the latter having a phenomenally successful career in America after the turn of the century.
- Mr J Oates' Ch Straight Tip, sold for £400 to an American breeder.
- Mr Rigby's Ch Lady Peggy.
- Mr F Clifton's Ch Munster Grip, Ch Mile End Peggy, Ch Mile End Kitty, Ch Mile End Muddler, Ch Mile End Barrister, Mile End Rufus, Mile End Sportsman, Bunburb Star, Mile End Lustre, Crow Gill Aileen, Ch Mile End Vixen and Mile End Rattler.

Two dogs who stood out were Ch Breda Muddler (named this way by Mr Billy Graham because of an ensuing row and muddle after he bought the dog cheaply at the Crystal Palace Show) and Ch Bolton Woods Mixer (Crow Gill Sportsman ex Saskatchewan).

Although from the same sire, these two dogs were quite different in type. In appearance, Breda Muddler took after his dam's family, being a golden red with a sound coat and *a real Irishman in type and character.* In addition to beating every first-class show dog of his day, Breda Muddler did much for the breed by stamping on his progeny his excellent coat, body and Irish characteristics.

Ch Mile End Muddler.

Mrs S Wilson's Ch Bolton Woods Mixer, bred by Mr J Craig, had a phenomenal career in the ring and won more prizes in his day than any Irish Terrier that ever lived. He was at first a controversial dog, many of the old hands claiming that, being *bad-coated and linty-coloured*, he was not a *true* Irish Terrier. However, his length of head, small, dark eyes, keen expression, small ears and perfect shoulders, legs and feet did much for the breed.

Ch Paymaster.

Ch Crow Gill Ginger.

Ch Redeemer.

Ch Barlae Brickbat.

Up to the First World War

Although there were recurring criticisms of coat quality and terrier size during this period, there can be little doubt that the Edwardian era saw the golden age of the breed. The following were some of the key players:

- Miss Paull's Ch Paymaster, Postman and Postboy.
- Mr Watt's Ch Fulwood Ferenze.
- Mr J Edward's Ch Kate Kearney.
- Mr Porter's Paddington.
- Mr F M Jowett's Ch Crow Gill Patricia, Ch Crow Gill Phil, Ch Crow Gill Myra and Ch Crow Gill Ginger.
- Mr Ridley's Ch Redeemer.
- Dr Twamley's Ch Tipperary Tyke.
- Mr Baty's Ch Mourne Prince.
- Mr Darker's Botanic Sheila and Ch Botanic Venus.

- Mr Short's Ch Barlae Brickbat.
- Mr F Breakell's Ch Killarney Sport.
- Messrs Walters' Beauty's Boy.
- Mr Montagu Ballard's Ch Botanic Gael and Ch My Lady Montreal.
- Mr Stanworth's Ch Turf Commander.
- Mr Lowrance's Ch Double Shear.

Between the Wars

After the First World War, as the popularity of the breed fell away, those who played a key role in ensuring its survival included Mr A B Montgomery, Mr N Galway, Lady Hehir and Mr J C Hirst.

In 1926, Mr Tom Rorke bred Ch Rambling Sandy, by Mr Montgomery's Ch Celtic Timothy (whose sire was Ch Celtic Playboy) ex Ch Rambling Rose. Another important dog of that time, again by Ch Celtic Timothy, was Ch Galloper, bred by Mr W S Green. Like so many others, both these dogs could trace their ancestry back to Killiney Boy and Erin.

Details of the leading champions of the early 1930s can be found in Appendix A.

(Above) Ch Killarney Sport.
(Below) Ch My Lady Montreal.

(Above) Ch Botanic Demon.
(Below) Ch Turf Commander.

Chapter Three

World War II and Afterwards

Some of the Pre- and Post-World War II Lines

It seems a pity to have to 'measure' the dog scene in terms of World War II, but we do owe an enormous debt of gratitude to the dedicated handful of breeders who, despite food shortages and the terrible anxiety of a country at war, managed to keep their breeding lines intact. It amazes me how few there were; yet, as in other breeds, today's dogs are in direct line to the dogs bred by these stalwarts. Some of these were Mrs Howard Jones (Breezy); Mrs Hayes (Borstal); Mrs Moore (Russetone); Mr Howard Fairtlough (Ballymakenny); Miss Moylan (of the Mill); Mrs Shaw (Drumshaw); Miss Simpson (Merrey); Mrs Slater (Nadder) and, last but not least, Miss Woodifield (Pathfinder).

Mrs Howard Jones' Breezy The Volunteer.

Breezy – Mrs Edna Howard Jones

Foremost among these breeders was Edna Howard Jones, whose eminence in the dog world and devotion to Irish Terriers did an enormous amount to keep up interest in the breed. From her foundation bitch Culbahn Connie, purchased from Mr George Henry, she bred her first champion, Ch Breezy Molly O'Shea. Molly O'Shea was bought by Mrs Shaw, who bred Ch Drumshaw Shelagh from her. Mrs Hayes started her kennel with Breezy Pixie of Aira, who bred Ch Topsy of Aira.

Breezy Ballerina. Photo: B Thurse

Mrs Howard Jones' kennel was chosen as one important enough during World War II to be supplied with special food from Spratts – literally to keep her dogs alive.

Today the Breezy line pops up everywhere, both at home and abroad, and it has been hugely influential in the breeding of Irish Terriers in Germany, France, Italy, The Czech Republic, Russia, Australia and South Africa. The Breezys are famous for their wonderful temperament and depth of character, and must be some of our very best ambassadors.

Mrs Howard Jones always said, "It is not only a matter of breeding winners, but breeding better dogs." From her first champion after the war, Ch Breezy O'Sullivan, whom she bred and handled herself, she went on to breed many champions: Ch Breezy Cuchullin, Ch Breezy Red Sorrel and Ch Breezy Satisfaction, to name but a few. Breezy Herb Robert, though not a champion, sired some beautiful puppies.

The only line Edna ever mixed with her own was the Oudenarde. Ch Breezy Divine Emerald of Oudenarde, who produced four champions, was Breezy-bred, sire and dam.

Edna was a distinguished international judge. She held the post of Secretary of the Irish Terrier Association for 47 years and was then President. She was also President of the West of England Ladies Kennel Society (WELKS) and a prolific writer on breed affairs, one of her works being her charming and informative handbook *Irish Terriers* (a Foyles publication).

Ch Breezy Divine Emerald of Oudenarde.
Photo: Anne Roslin-Williams

Russetone – Mrs E M B Moore

The Russetones, bred by Mrs E M B Moore, were originally from the mating between Sherry of the Mill (bred by Miss Moylan) and Irish-bred Breezy Paddy (owned by Mrs Howard Jones) in 1936. This produced Russetone Whiskey (a pet) and Nadder Judy, the latter beginning the showing career of the Russetone family.

Mrs Moore produced some beautiful dogs, including Ch Russetone Nadder Brook, the famous Ch Russetone O'Shaunessy, Ch Russetone Simon, Ch Russetone Wag and Ch Russetone Whiskey, to name but a few.

Ballymakenny – Howard Fairtlough

The foundation of this kennel was Nadder Suzan. She was a lovely bitch and did much to establish the perfect ear set and brilliant piercing eye of the real Irish Terrier. She produced several champions, including the famous sisters Ch Ballymakenny Pippon and Ch Ballymakenny Dinkie.

Ch Ballymakenny Pippa.

Mr Fairtlough produced innumerable champions, and he outcrossed his line several times with Russetone, Brackenwood and Pathfinders, with great success.

Pathfinders – Miss Norah Woodifield

This kennel was founded in 1926, starting with Fox Terriers. The Irish connection began with a dog born in 1930 who later became Ch Eton Boy (made up at Crufts in 1945). Up to 70 champions were handled to their titles by Miss Woodifield, some 20 of them owned and bred by her.

Miss Woodifield worked on the buses during the war and struggled to keep the breeding lines intact. She was a colourful character on the show circuit, a brilliant handler who always showed her dogs on a loose lead. She inspired and trained many young people, not least the well-

Ch Pathfinders Seirios One Bell.
Photo: Anne Roslin-Williams

known judge Joan Simcock whose two champion bitches won well, Anne Wortel Waite (Holland) and Joan Flatman (Tyne) who bred Ch Pathfinders Gypsy. Her dogs were smart, beautifully presented and showy. The list of champions is endless (Appendix A) and her influence on other breed lines enormous. Her kennel was known as the Home of Champions. Ch Pathfinders Bandleader was one of her first, and Ch Pathfinders Drummer Boy, Hopscotch, Quickstep and many more followed in rapid succession. She is undoubtedly one of the breed's 'greats'.

Int Ch Roeside Pathfinders Stowaway.

Drumshaw – Mrs Shaw

Mrs Shaw bred some lovely dogs, the best known of whom probably was Drumshaw Shealagh, considered one of the best bitches of her day. Mrs Shaw was very active in the Irish Terrier Club of Scotland. One of her best breaks was the purchase of Breezy Mally O'Shea.

Aira – Mrs A G Hayes

This was a small but excellent kennel. The Breezy connection was strong and Breezy Pixie of Aira produced the outstanding Ch Topsy of Aira. The kennels were famously well run and goats were kept *for milk and each puppy is fed separately after weaning to ensure even development!*

Merrey – Miss F M Simpson

This was a small but very select kennel and produced a string of successful champions: Ch Merrey Melissa, Ch Merrey Maestro (her fourth home-bred champion) and Ch Merrey Mascot.

Ch Peg the Rake of Aira.

Ch Lynphen Bloom of Tara (see page 26).

Ch Red Dan. Photo: Hedges

Nadder – Mrs E P Slater

The name of the line is Red Dan, her first champion, written backwards! Her dogs were stylish and intelligent. She made up several champions including Ch Red Dan, Hoplite and Nadder Tracker. Her breeding was very influential in other lines, such as Ballymakenny and Lynphen.

Redlawn – Miss K Wilkinson

Although Miss Wilkinson did not produce champions she had some lovely dogs, mainly wheaten-coloured. She had a large kennel and did much to promote the breed in Essex and East Anglia. Red Racket,

Redlawn Victor and Redlawn Silver Kate were her best dogs. The Nadder and Solid lines were influential.

Drumcorrie Irish Terriers – Mrs M de Beaumont

Great credit must go to this kennel for producing one of the greatest sires of the breed, Ch Russetone O'Shaunessey. The kennels were at Shalbourne Mannon near Marlborough and were something of a show piece. Norah Woodifield kennelled and handled their innumerable champions who, on retirement, were returned home to Mrs de Beaumont. Ch Drumcorrie Blarney and Ch Drumcorrie Shamus were well-known dogs, and the line was crossed with Pathfinders many times.

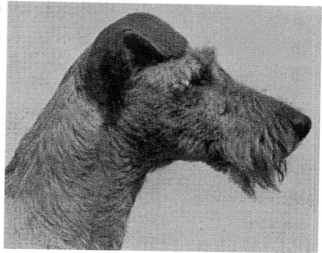

Redlawn Shandy.

Brackenwood – Miss Marjorie Abell

This line emerged in the 1950s and had strong links with the Pathfinders, especially Ch Pathfinders Drummer Boy. There were several matings, which produced Ch Brackenwood Ballerina, Ch Brackenwood Herb Tuppence, Ch Brackenwood Fiona and Ch Brackenwood Joyous Venture, who became a very well-known bitch with some spectacular wins in the late 1950s.

There was some Breezy influence, especially on the bitches Breezy Golden Coli and Breezy Penny Royal. They were stylish dogs, known for their lovely coats and smart presentation. They, too, were influential in establishing other breeding lines, notably Mr C Pollard's Lynphen.

Convoy – Mrs Connie Birch

Mrs Birch's beautiful bitch Safe Convoy became the first Irish Terrier champion after the war. Praised by many experts as 'near perfect', she produced some lovely puppies, not least Ch Happy Return.

Mrs Birch prepared and handled all her own dogs and was an expert on trimming. An artist and great breed enthusiast, she served on the Irish Terrier Association committee for many years. Her husband, Geoff, was the official photographer at breed shows.

Solid – Mr George Clayton

This was an example of a small but excellent kennel, of which there were many at the time. Only lack of space prevents mentioning them all. Solid Michael and Ch Solid Man (see over) showed well. The Nadder influence was clear.

Ch Solid Man. Photo: Thomas Fall

Of the Mill – Miss A Moylan

Our beloved bitch Mavoureen of the Mill (Ceilidh) was one of Miss Moylan's. There were several champions, and the Pathfinder connection was strong.

Newark – Mr F Dempster

Ir Ch Culbahn Commissar was an important stud dog. His early influence produced some excellent litters. Ch Newpark, Lovely Ann, Newpark Craad Girl and Newpark Note were excellent brood bitches. Mrs Dempster was influential in caring for the young stock.

Oudenarde – Misses Hamilton, Mrs Sheila Tarry and Mr and Mrs Somerfield

The affix originally appeared in 1927 when Helen and Margaret Hamilton began to show Cairn and Airedale Terriers, but they switched to Irish Terriers in the post-war period when Mrs Sheila Tarry joined the partnership. The foundation of the Oudenardes was Mr Davey's bitch, Farriers Home Girl (Solid Michael ex Golden Mannequin), purchased by Sheila Tarry in the 1940s and mated with Glenyafron Crusader. This produced Oudenarde Captivation, and the bitch Oudenarde Miss Nibbs, who produced Oudenarde Golden Wonder, sire of Ch Oudenarde Sellaand, O'Lady Caroline (Reserve CC Winner) and others. The first Irish Terriers to appear in the Stud Book under this partnership were

Oudenarde Farriers Comrade, by Ch Russetone Simon, and his son, Oudenarde Farriers Galloper, both bred by Mr Davy. Galloper ('Boy') became the first Oudenarde champion in 1951 and one of the all-time 'greats' of the kennel. Orangespark, by Pathfinders Bandleader, was the kennel's first champion bitch .

These were followed by a string of champions and many beautiful dogs, including Ch Thunderflash and Ch Irish Rose. Then came Ch Oudenarde Irish Mick and Ch Oudenarde Zelia, who some have said was the best Oudenarde ever. When Margaret Hamilton died her

Ch Oudenarde Farriers Galloper.

niece Ferelith Hamilton (now Somerfield), who is a very well-known international judge of many breeds and Patron of the Irish Terrier Association, promised to continue with the Irish.

Sadly Merrey Maid Marion, bought in from Miss F Simpson, had to be spayed but she did rekindle the Oudenarde interest in Irish Terriers. She became the devoted pet of Angela Davell (later Smith) who had joined the kennels as a girl of 14. From then on, Angela wanted to own and breed Irish Terriers, and this is how the Tubereasas came into the breed.

Mrs Howard Jones bred a lovely bitch who became Ch Divine Emerald of Oudenarde (Ch Conjola Iron Bank of Breezy ex Breezy Miss Muffet) and went on to produce Fred Bell's Ch Redneval Ballinruan Beau, four British champions and one German title holder. There have been more champions, including Ch Tubereasa Ben's Son and Ch Tubereasa My Demonara.

Stafford and Ferelith Somerfield decided at this point that the import of an American dog, Trackways Bodgen Red, would increase the gene pool. He has not only won well in competitions, but proved to be an excellent sire. They now have

Ch Oudenarde Thunderflash.

another 'American' – a lovely bitch, Gamekeeper Fergie, who has also become a champion. Her breeding is similar to Booger Red's but she has a Ben's Heir line, which is another valuable link up with the future.

Sadly, Stafford Somerfield died in 1996.

Gabledown – Mrs June Symonds

When Howard Faitlough died June Symonds with great generosity took over his Ballymakenny dogs. She subsequently 'rescued' the Pathfinders when Miss Woodifield died and must be seen as one of the breed's great benefactors. She shows under her affix Gabledown and has produced some lovely dogs. She has owned two champions, Ch Tanwell Lucky Chamrock of Merydais and Ch Chantalles Tanya of Gabledown, and is Hon Secretary of the Southern Irish Terrier Society.

Lynphen – Mr C Pollard

Lynphen Irish Terriers were founded by C Pollard on the purchase of the bitch Emerald Empress (Ch Brackenwood Midnight ex Denny's Girl) from Miss Abel's Brackenwood

Lynphen Judy.

kennel in 1958. The foundation dog was the three-year-old Deplead Kettledrum (Ch Pathfinders Drummer Boy ex Rosemorden Top Note). Both Kettledrum and Emerald Empress were of mainly Pathfinder breeding on their sire's side and Slemish on their dam's, and all Lynphens are directly descended from these two founding dogs on their dam's side. Kettledrum went on to win 16 CCs, including Best of Breed (BOB) at Crufts in 1960 and 1961, and BOB at the National Terrier in 1959, 1960 and 1961. He only gave way to his son, Ch Lynphen Brook of Tara, when he was nine.

Ch Lynphen Bloom of Tara (see page 22) was acquired by Mr and Mrs Brudenell, who founded their Lattenbury line, which was very successful for some time.

Torstan – Mr Whalley

This was a small kennel, but produced some valuable dogs. Ch Torshama Drumshaw Clover was a top winning bitch and several dogs were exported to the United States of America and Switzerland.

Keillor – Mr Alex Martin

Mr Martin was President of the Irish Terrier Club of Scotland and a great enthusiast. His foundation bitch was Culbahn Cynthia whom he mated to Int Ch Russetone O'Shaunessey. There were several champions, including Ch Keillon Eversure and Ch Keillon Effective, and some very good stock.

Penmore – Miss Eileen Batley

The foundation bitch was Caralmae Amber Rose and there was subsequently some cross breeding with Pathfinders. Miss Batley has a great knowledge of the breed and her dogs have wonderful temperaments and are full of character. She is on the Irish Terrier Association (ITA) Committee and can tell an Irish Terrier story better than most.

1960s and 1970s

The 1960s and 1970s brought on some good breeding lines.

Ch Redneval Ballinruan Beau – Messrs F W and P Bell

Mr F W Bell and his son, Peter Bell, owned and showed the beautiful dog Ch Redneval Ballinruan Beau during the 1970s. He was a very influential stud dog and is still talked of by some as the 'best ever'.

Carolmac – Mr Paddy Carroll

The Carolmac Irish Terriers came about in 1964 when Mr Paddy Carroll bought the nine-month-old bitch Swinpen Colleen for £8 and mated her to Lynphen Express. This produced his first CC winner, Carolmac Maureen, who, when mated to Pathfinders Hopscotch, produced his first champion, Ch Carolmac Fancy. Other champions followed. Mr Carroll now lives in Southern Ireland and continues to breed and judge.

Montelle – Anne Bradley

The Montelle Irish Terriers first appeared with Paddy's Girl, granddaughter of Ch Lynphen Blook of Tara and Ch Pathfinders Hopscotch, in 1969. All the Montelle Irish come down from her. In the first litter from Ch Pathfinders Leapfrog came Montelle Golden Daune, Montelle Golden Poppy and a brother who became Int Ch Montelle Splash of Gold (the latter two carrying on the breeding line). In a second litter by Ch Pathfinders Goldsmith was Montelle Golden Amber who produced the kennel's first United Kingdom champion and

Montelle Irish Terriers.

Montelle Amber Tweed. Photo: Anne Roslin-Williams

winner of BOB at Crufts in 1979, Montelle Amber Tweed.

An outcross, Ch Arran of Paddymac (who also won BOB at Crufts) produced some lovely puppies, not least Ch Gambling Miller and Ch M Star Return.

There has been a string of champions, all stylish, sound dogs, beautifully presented and shown by Anne herself. The saying goes, "Anne's dogs never forget her," and she is welcomed as 'mum' even by the oldies. She is Secretary of the ITA, editor of the Year Book and a very popular judge both here and abroad.

Anne Bradley with one of her Montelles. Photo: Tracy Morgan

Tanwell – Miss Jean Higginson

The foundation bitch, Tanwell Tamarisk, was part Pathfinder breeding and was mated to a Russetone. This produced the first Tanwell International Champion in Tanwell Mignonette.

Miss Higginson has used the Manelle and Breezy lines in her breeding with great success. One litter produced two champions, Ch Tanwell Treasure's Gift and Ch Tanwell Glint of Gold, both lovely dogs. The current dogs have Ch Tailways Booger Red in their pedigrees and produced Ch Tanwell Rainbow Quest.

The Tanwells have style and character and Miss Higginson has a great interest and success with them in obedience and agility training.

Harvestime – Mrs C S Jackson

Mrs Jackson has bred some lovely dogs, notably Ch Breezy Garland and Ch Harvestime No Shade, who was top winning Irish Terrier in 1977. Her foundation stock is mainly Breezy. Mrs Jackson has served the breed over many years both as a member of the Irish Terrier Association Committee (she is now Vice President) and as editor for many years of the Year Book.

Naranja – Dr A Noonan and Mrs L Williamson

The Naranja line was founded by Dr A Noonan in 1985 with the foundation bitch Ch Indian Spice of Montelle. Her second litter – the only litter sired by Ch Gatecrasher before he went to Germany – included Naranja Firedancer, who in turn produced Ch Dancer du Feu. Her outstanding dog, Ch Naranja Jumping Jack Flash, is a great favourite in the show ring and proving valuable at stud. Dr Noonan's sister, Lindsay Williamson, shares the partnership. She prepares the dogs, and none could possibly look smarter in the ring.

Dr Noonan is Chairman of the ITA and Mrs Williamson is a Committee Member and Show Secretary.

Josaka – Mr and Mrs Sam Price

The Prices' foundation bitch was Felicity of Breezy and all their dogs have a strong Breezy input. Ch Josakas Sorley Bay of Jackmo is one of my favourites: a really beautiful dog and excellent stud. He was followed by Ch Rory McRory. Sam Price is Vice Chairman of the ITA.

Alan Price (Jackmo) handles his own and the Josaka dogs and has a great knowledge of the breed.

Riogems – Mr and Mrs Paul Livesey

The Riogems Irish Terriers are bred mainly from Carolmac, Pathfinders (Carolmac Colleen) and Breezy. There have been two champions, Ch Riogem Thyme and Ch Riogem Paprika, both lovely dogs. We hope to see more in the future.

Newcomers To Watch

Inchicore – Lyn and Declan Fegan

Lyn and Declan were extremely lucky with their foundation bitch. Ch Ruffmar Flaithiulach of Inchicore (Huli) was bred by Mary Ruffles of true Pathfinder stock on her

Ch Riojem Thyme. Photo: Anne Roslin-Williams

mother's side by the then-newly-imported American stud dog, Ch Trackways Booger Red, owned by the late Major Somerfield. Huli received a great many compliments and has now become a champion. Lyn and Declan have bred four litters and have kept two further Irish bitches, Ishki (Inchicore Uisce Beatha) and Wysiwyg (Inchicore Caetarcosac). Despite considerable show success, the Inchicore dogs are above all pets, kept in the house and greatly loved. All Inchicore puppies are bred primarily for temperament, though several are shown and have proved successful. They are extremely well socialised, particularly by daughter Kate and her friends, before they go to their new homes, and they are in great demand.

Lyn Fegan (Inchicore) with foundation bitch Huli.

Newguild – Kiara Bentley

Kiara Bentley is breeding some lovely puppies from her bitch Breezy Star Turn. She has known Irish Terriers all her life and was given Star Turn by Edna Howard Jones to continue the line. She feels strongly and deeply about preserving the quality and temperament for which the Breezys are famous.

Biele – Mr Biele

These terriers are of mainly Carolmac breeding and Mr Biele has some excellent stock. Watch this space.

Brazan – Marion Lovelace

This is a kennel to watch, set in ideal surroundings, and the dogs have a wonderful lifestyle. Marion Lovelace has produced

Ch Brazan Villian.

some lovely dogs. Her foundation bitch was Mr Grant's Slemish Sweet Honey. Mated first to Riogen Thyme, she was then mated to a German dog, Santiago von der Emsmule. A different line, going back to Ben's Heir, produced Ch Brazan Villian (top puppy 1994 and top Irish Terrier since 1995).

Two superb champions, Ch Brazan Absolutely and Ch Brazan Caramel, are doing well, and some outstanding puppies are ready for showing. Mrs Lovelace believes in line-breeding. She is an expert at hand-stripping and presents her dogs in top show condition.

Irvonhill – Mr Tony Barker

A comparative newcomer to the breed, Tony Barker started his kennel with Ben's Heir Drogeeda. He has already had great success, breeding several champions, including Ch Ben's Heir Ed, who went to the von der Emsmühle kennel in Germany, and Ch Mickey Fynn, who also became a champion in Finland. He has imported an Australian bitch Coolay Contessa and expects some good puppies. He also owns Ebeneezer Ironbank, a young pup as yet unbeaten, and another outstanding youngster, Shamchilli Tweed. He has strong connections with the Finnish Irish Terrier group, especially the Jackpot kennel.

Northern Ireland
Ben's Heir – Harry Davis

The Ben's Heir line builds on a family tradition stretching back to the 1930s when Ben's Heir was shown at Crufts. It was started in the 1970s by Mr Harry Davis's father, who bought a pup from Mr Magill (Ida) that later became Ch Bonsire Major and the bitches Duncairn Marilyn and Ch Duncairn Mirabelle from Mr John Crawley,

Mr Harry Davis ran a very successful kennel with a line of champions: Ch Ben's Heir Ch Rambler, Ch Ben's Heir Ringo, Ch Ben's Heir Bean, and many more. Since his death, Mrs Davis has taken on the breeding line and we hope to see more of her in the ring in the future.

Ch Montelle Famous Star at the Belfast Dog Show Society Show.

Ardgabha – Mr W Semple
Mr Semple has owned some lovely dogs, notably Ch Enniskellen Dragoon (who had great presence in the ring) Ch Nic An–T-Saoir Ardgabha, Ch Ardgabha Mac An-T-Saoir and many more. He also made up Ch Tubereasa Beau Venture Ardgabha. He was a charming and popular judge.

Esperons – Mr Rommy Watterson
Mr Watterson bred Ch Esperon Robin Hood and other excellent dogs. He made up Ch Imperial Major in 1973 and there were several champions from this stud dog, including Ch Esperons Hillside Sandy.

Fairywells – Mr and Mrs P Dorrain
Their first champion was made up in 1980: Ch Danny Boy of Fairywells, son of Ch Golden Lass. There is a strong connection with the Esperons line.

Swinpen – Mr T Evans
There are strong links with Mr Sweeney's Telltown in Southern Ireland. Int Ch Swinpen Bright Boy and Ch Swinpen Dandy were outstanding dogs.

Eire
Very sadly there are few Irish Terriers in Southern Ireland, but some of the old lines are still strong and the dogs are stylish and authentic. Nowhere do you see more clearly the sparky terrier temperament.

Edbrios Murhart.

Slemish – Mr Aiden Boyle

Bobby Grant had a long line of Irish Terriers going back 60 years. He made up his first champion in 1920. Aiden Boyle has continued the line.

Telltown – Mr G and Mr J Sweeney

This is arguably the most famous line in Southern Ireland for over 60 years. Both brothers are legends in Irish Terrier circles. They are acknowledged international authorities and are very helpful to other breeders and also to newcomers to the breed. There have been a great number of champions and many of their dogs have contributed to the breed lines in Belgium and Denmark.

Toméilis – Mr and Mrs Deegan

Mr and Mrs Deegan have bred Irish Terriers for many years, their line being bred largely from Mr Sweeney's Telltown. They tend to show their dogs with a little more coat, and daughters Tracy and Mary handle them in the ring. Ch Limmerick Lad is very promising.

Edbrios – E and P O'Brien

The O'Briens have bred some lovely dogs. Ch Edbrios Dupluate was sold to an English breeder and has become an important stud dog. Phillip O'Brien prepares and handles his dogs with great style.

Chapter Four Irish Terriers Overseas

The Irish Terrier Association (ITA) has strong links and very cordial relationships with Irish Terrier clubs all over the world. The same enthusiasm and dedication towards breeding good dogs is very apparent throughout. There is constant exchange of ideas and dogs are exported frequently to improve the breeding stock.

Harpa:
a profound expression for a dog of great character.

France

Dr and Mrs Schwartz are old and valued friends and, although they no longer show their dogs, they are still very involved and interested in the breed. Dr Schwartz had a great hand in the production of the new book by Christian Limouzy *L'Irish Terrier*. It is a lovely book and will doubtless do much for the breed in France.

There are five main breeders in France today, and the British influence is strong.

- Golden Harp (J Pierre)
- Beddy Grelert (F Anderson)
- Killonglin (J Savigny)
- Mockcastel (A Marcillaud)
- Brookdene (J Mulholland-Mousset)

All work extremely hard to promote the breed, which has gained greatly in popularity. They had two group winners in 1996, Golden Harp Harpa and Wrakness Runner, which is very satisfying. There are classes for Irish Terriers at the two main shows, Longchamp and National Terriers.

It is interesting to note that Société Controle Canine (SCC), which is the

French equivalent of The Kennel Club, insists that every champion must pass a Natural Aptitude Test before achieving the title. The need would hardly apply to Irish Terriers, but it does ensure that breeders pay attention to a stimulating, varied life style and interesting environment for their dogs. If the dog fails once, it is disqualified for life.

Germany

There is a long tradition of Irish Terrier breeding in Germany. Countess Stauffenberg (see chapter 5) has kept her line and is still an international authority on the breed.

There are some beautiful dogs in Germany and some kennels with enough stock to line breed correctly, producing dogs of a real type. They are beginning to do very well in the groups in the important shows, which has put the breed in the spotlight recently. Ch Penny Stuard von der Emsmühle won Best in Show (BIS) at the Festival of Irish Breeds in Germany, and Ch Octavia von der Emsmühle has also had some spectacular wins.

von der Emsmühle – K Kirch and H E Grüttner

The Ben Heir's influence is strong in this kennel and the line is outstanding in type, temperament and soundness. I liked their remark that Ch Octavia is *proudly owned, loved and shown*, which conveys a great deal about their attitude to the dogs.

Attempto – Ulrick and Penate Eulitz

Ch Edbrios Boru is a true International Champion – Irish, French, German and Swiss.

A French puppy belonging to Mme Savigny.

Jamaica von den Emsmühle.
Photo: David Dalton

von der Wolfsquelle – J and U Reinhard

This kennel has some very good dogs and a bright future.

Others

Mona Lisa von der Emsmühle is a lovely bitch owned by H and R Lück and has done some serious winning.

Russia

Elena and Victor Girlo write about the breeding of Irish Terriers in Russia:

The first Irish Terriers appeared in Russia in the beginning of the 1950s, but active breeding started from the 1970s, when 10 dogs were supplied from Germany. Mainly they were bred from the von Marrienberg kennel.

At the end of the 1970s Irish Terriers from Chechoslovakia began to arrive in Russia. They were bred in the kennels de Galupo, Torisa and Miller. Some of these dogs had remote English roots. At that time three Irish Terriers were imported from England. They were two males, Aldjamyn Berry Rojal and Breezy Backet, and a female, Breezy About. Unfortunately, their performance as breeding and show stock was disappointing.

Up to 1993 the breeding of Irish Terriers in Russia was based on Czech and German lines. In the earlier days size, tail set and ear carriage were problems, and some dogs lacked their full sets of teeth. Coat and constitution needed to be addressed too. The Irish Terrier Club in Moscow has promoted the breeding of Irish Terriers for the past 10 years, and now there are about 100 dogs in the Club, many of which are Russian Champions.

Now we'd like to say something about three of our dogs. We have a female, Aida (English/Czech line) and two males. Our first and oldest dog, New Jerry Prismar, was Best In Breed six times. His great-grandfather is Camogy Crusader, an English Champion. Ida and Jerry are nine years old. They were great breeders and they both produced many excellent puppies. Many of their children won titles at different shows.

In 1993 we imported a puppy from Ireland: Rutlan Scrumpy Jack (born 7 September 1993, breeders Murphy, Dublin). Now Jack is two-and-a-half years old. He has won the titles Champion of Russia (twice) and Best in Breed (eight times). His father, Fintona It Had To Be You, was the winner at the World Show in Brussels in 1995.

We are very thankful to Mrs Rita Mason, well-known breeder of Irish Wolfhound in England, for her help in getting the English bitch Chantalle's Wanton (breeder: Diana Nicholls, owner: Margarita Usova). Wanton is also a Russian champion now and three times Best in Breed. Jack and Wanton had wonderful puppies, all of whom were awarded excellent marks at their first show.

In the spring of 1996 our club imported one more Irish Terrier from England. He was born in September 1995, his sire is Edbrios Duplicate, his dam is Chantalles Tanja of Gabledown, and he was bred by Mrs J Symonds. This puppy is very beautiful. He has a very long head, high set ears and tail, a very bright red coat, and he is balanced perfectly. His show career will start in the near future and we hope it will be successful.

Our club bases its activity on the best English lines. We hope for further cooperation with The Irish Terrier Association and are thankful for its help in getting puppies from England and Ireland. We read and translate the Association Year Book with great interest.

Czech Republic

I was in Prague several years ago and, in crossing one of the lovely bridges spanning the Danube, I saw at the far end two Irish Terriers. I ran across the bridge and met up with Josef Pavlica and two of his Irish Terriers. The ITA Year Book reports:

Ch Kilkerry's Harmony of Kalaney, owned by Judy La Bash, Lexington, USA.
Photo: DogAds

News from the Czech Republic comes from Josef Pavlica who reports that Irish Terriers are well known in his country with many exhibitions being well represented by the breed. Josef has four Irish Terriers who give much pleasure, exhibiting gives much enjoyment where he has achieved some excellent wins. In 1996 the bitch Funny Face Emisar featured in the 1995 Year Book produced a fine litter.

Netherlands

The affix Irish Red is owned by Ted and Yvonne v d Walle.

Another eminent Dutch breeder is Ann Wortel Waite. She was a kennel maid at the famous Pathfinders kennels. She married and left to live in the Netherlands, where she carried on the Gnomeshall line established by her friend and colleague Joan Simcock and founded on the

Redwatch Irish Terriers
owned by Connie Goff of Macomb, Michigan.

Pathfinders. She imports dogs regularly and is doing a great deal for the Irish Terrier in the Netherlands.

Australia

Irish Terriers were introduced into Australia in the 1880s and enjoyed enormous popularity until the mid-1930s. It is a familiar story and with this large demand came over breeding and a lowering of standards. The Second World War brought a complete halt to importing dogs and a few dedicated breeders struggled on to 'keep the torch alight'. They provided a base or foundation on which those who came after were able to build. Three names to remember are:

- Mr Noonan (Killarney)
- Mr G Tipping (Leinster)
- Mr G Bailey (Durrow)

Since that time more excellent dogs have been imported and home-bred and there is today a small dedicated group of breeders. To quote Mary Connolly, "Thousands of miles may separate us, but we are united in a common cause - the advancement of the Irish Terriers."

Present breeders include:

Victoria

Present Breeders:

Thomas . . . . .Belrua
Browne . . . . .Dunconor
Brenen . . . . .Kellington

Past Breeders, but owners:

Gerdsen . . . . .Laigin
Tipping . . . . .Leinster
Murray . . . . .Kinderscout
Hayward . . . . .Bellerin

New South Wales

Walmsley . . . . .Coolanry
Swelling . . . . .Bilstonwake

Tasmania

Stemislow . . . . .Firldgate

Western Australia

Collier . . . . .Anluan

Queensland

Davis . . . . .Roysmar

United States of America

Mrs Suzanne Griffiths writes:

Irish Terriers were first imported into the United States in about 1870, and James Watson claimed that his bitch, Kathleen, was the first to be shown here, the year being 1880. In 1881, the Westminster Kennel Club offered a class for Irish Terriers for the first time. Imports were frequent before World Word I, but decreased as the century progressed. Undoubtedly, Jack London's books *Jerry of the Islands* and *Michael, Brother of Jerry* contributed greatly to the popularity of the breed. *Jerry* was copyrighted in 1916 and published in 1917.

John R Thorndike's Thorncroft Marksman, bred by Jeremiah J O'Callahan, took the breed at the Westminster, and American-bred Irish Terriers began to come into their own.

Planning for the Irish Terrier Club of America began in 1896, and Samuel D Parker, O W Donner and H White called the first meeting, with 12 charter members, at Madison Square Garden on 23 February 1897. It was at this meeting that the first official publication, *Rules, Standards and Stakes*, was adopted by the Irish Terrier Club of America.

Show entries and interest were high in the 1920s and 1930s, and imports won a great percentage of the shows. The first third of the 20th century was a time of large kennels and numerous imports, and the breed enjoyed a relatively high level of popularity. By World War II, a decline had set in and numbers bred dropped, as did show entries. This condition held until the mid-1960s, when there was a steady rise in both interest and show entries.

Perhaps the greatest influence on the breed in this century was that of Jeremiah J O'Callahan, breeder, judge and exhibitor. His influence began early in the century and continues today through the bloodlines he established under his affix Kilvara and through his long association with Martha Hall, whose affix was Ahtram.

As the early part of the century was characterised by large kennels, wealthy owners and frequent imports, so today may be said to be the time of small kennels, few imports and many dedicated breeder/owner/exhibitors. Group wins and placings and BIS wins, once almost non-existent for the Irish Terrier, are becoming less of a novelty. This trend is nation-wide, whereas earlier almost all big wins were at shows in the eastern part of the country. In general, the quality and temperament of exhibits are good.

The Irish Terrier has never been a popular dog in obedience showing, but the breed has been present in this activity almost from the inception of the sport by the American Kennel Club in 1936. The first Irish Terrier to qualify for an obedience title was Ancon Avenger of Ardara Farm, in 1936. Since then there has been a small but steady interest in this activity, and recently the first Obedience Trial Championship was gained by Ch Begorra Katie Scarlet O'Henry, UDX. The first champion to attain all of the obedience titles then available was Ch Greenbriar Fiddler UDT. Several Irish have qualified over the years as tracking dogs and one, Ch Gloccomara Redrick O'Farin, completed the Utility Dog title (UD) in the United States and Canada.

Am Ch Greenbriar Fiddler UDT,
owned, trained and handled by Suzanne N Griffiths.

Chapter Five

The Breed Standard

There has been very little alteration in the scale of points and description of *The True Irish Terrier* (the words used by the Irish Terrier Club) since it was originally drawn up at the meeting in 1897. This is the present-day standard as laid down by The Kennel Club, and I have added comments after some sections:

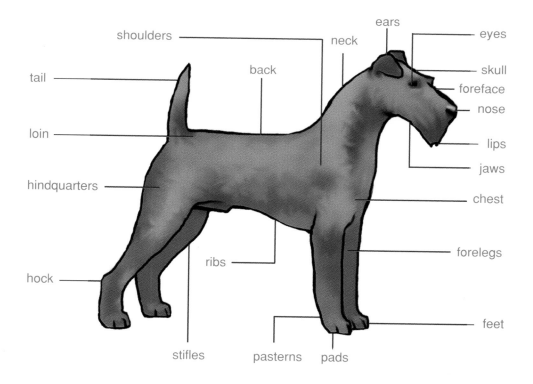

Fig 5.1: Points of the Irish Terrier.

Ch Montelle Sunarise demonstrates the typical Irish alert expression. Photo: Tracy Morgan.

The Kennel Club Breed Standard
(By kind permission of The Kennel Club)

General Appearance
Standard An active, lively and wiry appearance; plenty of substance but free of clumsiness. Neither cloddy nor cobby but showing a graceful racy outline.

Author's Note The Breed Standard calls for *an active, lively and wiry appearance; plenty of substance, but free of clumsiness.* Speed and endurance, as well as power, are essential requirements. They should be neither too *cloddy* (low, thick-set, comparatively heavy) nor *cobby* (short-bodied, compact), but should be formed on lines of speed, *showing a graceful racy outline.*

As a movement teacher, I have always admired the breed's seemingly perfect balance of mobility and strength and sheer manageability. *Lithe* and *plenty of substance* says it all, and the Irish Terrier's elegant line distinguishes it from any other terrier.

Characteristics
Standard There is a heedless, reckless pluck about the Irish Terrier which is characteristic, and, coupled with the headlong dash, blind to all consequences, with which he rushes at his adversary, has earned for the breed the proud epithet of 'the Daredevils'. When 'off duty' they are characterised by a quiet caress-inviting appearance, and when one sees them endearingly, timidly pushing their heads into their masters' hands, it is difficult to realise that on occasions, at the 'set on', they can prove that they have the courage of a lion, and will fight to the last breath in their bodies. They develop an extraordinary devotion for and have been known to track their masters almost incredible distances.

Temperament
Standard Good-tempered, notably with humans, it being admitted, however, that he is perhaps a little too ready to resent interference on the part of other dogs.

Author's Note Dogs that are very game are usually surly or snappish. The Irish Terrier as a breed is an exception, being remarkably good-tempered, notably so with humans, though less so with other dogs. They are essentially happy-natured dogs with a great sense of humour – their 'smile' is legendary. They are not troublemakers, but will enter a scrap with enthusiasm if picked upon.

Head and Skull
Standard Head long; skull flat, and rather narrow between ears, narrowing towards eye; free from wrinkles; stop hardly visible except in profile. Jaw strong and muscular, but not too full in cheek, and of good length. Foreface not dished or falling away quickly between eyes, delicately chiselled. Lips well fitting and externally almost black in colour. Nose black.

Author's Note As it says in the Standard, the foreface should not dish (fall away quickly) between or below the eyes, where it should be well made up, being relieved of 'wedginess' by delicate chiselling. The hair should be crisp and only sufficiently long to impart an appearance of additional strength to the foreface.

Ch Indian Spice of Montelle shows a good head with correct ear carriage.
Photo: Tracy Morgan.

Eyes

Standard Dark, small, not prominent. A light or yellow eye highly undesirable.

Author's Note The small, dark eyes should be full of fire and intelligence. A lighter yellow eye is a fault.

Ears

Standard Small and V-shaped, of moderate thickness, set well on head, and dropping forward closely to cheek. Top of folded ear well above level of skull. Ear must be free of fringe, and hair thereon shorter and darker in colour than body.

Early Irish Terriers had cropped ears, and for this purpose the ears had to be of a certain size, and wide at the base, to allow enough 'flap' after the procedure. When cropping was abolished, smaller ears were bred in, but occasionally a specimen does turn up with rather large ears. It is still a difficult subject for breeders; the ears must not be placed too high like a Wire Fox Terrier's nor must they be placed like an Airedale's, and to give the true Irish look they must drop closely to the cheek but not appear at all heavy.

Mouth

Standard Teeth even, strong and free from discolouration. Jaws strong, with perfect, regular scissor bit, ie upper teeth closely overlapping lower teeth and set square to the jaws.

Neck

Standard Fair length and gradually widening towards shoulders, well carried and free of throatiness. Generally a slight fringe at each side of neck, running nearly to corner of ear.

Forequarters

Standard Shoulders fine, long and well laid back. Legs moderately long, well set from shoulders, perfectly straight, with plenty of bone and muscle; elbows working freely clear of sides; pasterns short and straight, hardly noticeable, the forelegs moved straight forward when travelling.

Author's Note The hair on the legs should be dense and crisp.

Body

Standard Chest deep and muscular, neither full nor wide. Body moderately long; back strong and straight, with no appearance of slackness behind shoulders; loin muscular and slightly arched; ribs fairly sprung, rather deep than round, and well ribbed back.

a: Perfect conformation.

b: Too long in the leg.

c: Rib cage too short, loin too long. Not enough angulation of shoulder, pelvis and stifle. Shoulder placed too far forward.

d: Chest cavity too deep. Shoulders muscling up. Poor layback raises head carriage. Straight stifle, sagging topline.

Fig 5.1: Conformation.

Good conformation as demonstrated by Ch May Be Red of Breezy. Photo: Colin Wakenham.

Author's Note Note that the Standard calls for *loin muscular and slightly arched*. This is an interesting characteristic, and it has been known for judges who have not troubled to read the Standard to count this as a fault.

Hindquarters

Standard Strong and muscular, thighs powerful, hocks well let down, stifles moderately bent. Hindlegs move straight forward when travelling, hocks not turned outwards. Hair on legs dense and crisp.

Feet

Standard Strong, tolerably round, moderately small, toes arched, neither turned out nor in; black toe nails most desirable. Pads sound and free from cracks or horny excrescences.

Author's Note Feet have greatly improved and cracked pads with *horny excrescences* are exceptional today, but at one time they reached alarming proportions. In 1921, the Irish Terrier Association decreed that no Irish Terrier suffering from cracked or corny pads should be awarded an Association prize or trophy and that a certificate could be provided for unafflicted dogs to appear with their stud advertisements.

There is no certain cure for what appears to be a hereditary condition, and affected pads tend to get worse during hot, dry spells, but it does help to soften the pad by rubbing

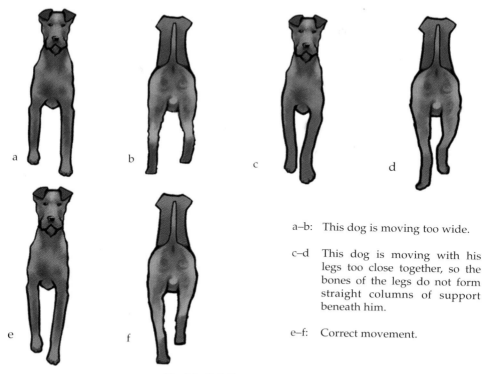

a–b: This dog is moving too wide.

c–d This dog is moving with his legs too close together, so the bones of the legs do not form straight columns of support beneath him.

e–f: Correct movement.

Fig 5.3: Gait/Movement

in vaseline, olive oil or Iodex and give small regular quantities of cod liver oil. Luckily, the decision taken by the Association in the early 1920s has largely safeguarded the breed from this one major fault.

Tail
Standard Customarily docked to about three quarters; free of fringe or feather, but well covered with rough hair, set on pretty high, carried gaily, but not over back or curled.

Gait/Movement
Standard Fore- and hindlegs carried straight forward and parallel. Elbows move perpendicular to body, working free of sides, stifles neither turning in nor out.

Coat
Standard Harsh and wiry, having broken appearance, free of softness or silkiness, not so long as to hide to outline of body particularly in hindquarters, straight and flat, no shagginess and free of lock or curl. At base of these still hairs is growth of finer and softer hair, usually termed the undercoat. Hair on foreface crisp and only sufficiently long to impart appearance of additional strength. Hair on legs dense and crisp.

Author's Note The basic variety of coat has remained essentially unchanged and is marvellously water-resistant; a couple of shakes and the dog is almost dry. Even the

Am Ch Mullaghboy Colin Murphy: a good American specimen with an excellent trim.
Photo: Missy Yuhl

muddiest outing can have all traces quickly removed by a wash-down with fresh water. This is one of the reasons why the breed is ideal as both a domestic pet and a farm dog.

Coats can vary a great deal, but a really pale, shaggy coat that curls on the legs and face is quite wrong. You will find that, with the very hard red coats, it takes a long time for 'furnishings' to grow on the face and legs, and it is quite common for a dog to reach the age of two years or more before the right amount of growth appears.

A type of coat not mentioned in the Breed Standard is a single or pick-out coat. These are usually hard on the back and nearly always red in colour, but there is no undercoat at all, and any attempt to trim or strip them leaves bare skin, which is always black in colour. These coats, easily detected in young dogs, do appear now and again, and it would probably not be at all wise to breed from dogs that have them.

Colour

Standard 'Whole-coloured', most preferable colours being red, red/wheaten, or yellow/red. Small amount of white on chest acceptable, white on feet highly undesirable. Black shading highly undesirable.

Author's Note As indicated by the Standard, white sometimes appears on the chest and feet. It is more objectionable on the feet, as a speck of white on the chest is frequently seen in all self-coloured breeds.

Size

Standard Ideal height: dogs: 48cm (19in); bitches: 46cm (18in).

Author's Note The most desirable weight in show condition is, for a dog, 11.8kg (26lb) and, for a bitch, 11.3kg (25lb). This has always provided a discussion point but it should be remembered that Irish Terriers were never meant to be big dogs. With an ideal height of 48cm for a dog, an Irish Terrier is only 9cm taller than the Wire Fox Terrier dog (39cm or 15½in) and some 15cm shorter than an Airedale dog (58–61cm or 23–24in). The word *ideal* in the Standard is used advisedly, as it would be absurd for a really outstanding dog to be penalised for a couple of centimetres, but there is no doubt that a great many of the dogs on the bench today are too big. Dogs and bitches that measure to the standard now appear rather small, and it would be a pity for the breed to become over-sized, as the correct size is ideal for today's average house.

It is not a new problem, for in 1922 the Irish Terrier Association passed a motion that no dog over 27lb or bitch over 25lb in weight should be eligible to compete for their trophies, and owners were asked to have the weight of the dog or bitch certified by a veterinary surgeon before wins could be accredited. A request was also made to The Kennel Club that scales should be provided at shows to check the weights in the ring. There might well be an advantage in using scales today.

Faults

Standard Any departure from the foregoing points should be considered a fault and the seriousness with which the fault should be regarded should be in exact proportion to its degree.

Author's Note The Irish Terrier Club lists the following as undesirable or negative points:

- White nails, toes and feet.
- Much white on chest.
- Dark shading on face. (Dark shading does sometimes crop up on the neck and shoulder, and this too is incorrect. Some of the best red-coated dogs will have some black hairs in the beard, but should not be confused with shading on the face.)
- Mouth undershot or cankered.
- Coat shaggy, curly or soft.
- Uneven in colour

Note

Standard Male animals should have two apparently normal testicles fully descended into the scrotum.

Amplification of the Breed Standard by Countess Stauffenberg

Translated by Eileen Batley

Countess Stauffenberg has bred Irish Terriers for many years in Germany, and is an international authority on the breed.

Proportions of the head

The head is the eye-catcher of the dog and must suit it in every respect. The proportion of the head must be in correct ratio to the dog's build. A head that is too long is just as disturbing as a head that is too short. The head itself must be balanced, like the body.

The proportions, length, breadth and depth of the head, the ear placement, size and

Int Ch Bravo v d Frankenlerche, owned and bred by Countess Stauffenberg.

the way they are held, the eyes, size, colour and how they are placed, the nose, teeth, beard, coat quality and colour, define the expression and thus the type of the complete dog.

Expression

The Irish Terrier expression is pure and simply the breed's characteristic. In the last analysis a beautifully-formed Irish Terrier lacking this typical and correct expression is just a good terrier, not an Irish Terrier. A terrier indeed, but one that could be ranged with many other terrier breeds. Therefore the greatest attention must be paid to the Irish Terrier expression, which dominates the integral character of the breed. The true Irish Terrier expression fully accentuates his arrogant, fearless, spirited, ever-happy, rollicking, enterprising nature. That must be seen in him at first glance.

Head

The head must be long and narrow in cheek. From the ears to the teeth an unbroken, scarcely visible, narrowing shape, well filled under the eye, where no visible deviation between cheeks and foreface shall appear. The stop is not visible from above and hardly visible in profile. The entire length of head of a standard-sized Irish Terrier amounts to 20–25cm (8–10in).

Skull

The skull must be flat, without bumps over the eyes or arch between the ears. The hair on the skull is short, hard and smooth. The powerful, muscular jaw fits him for use as a guard or hunting dog. It must not, however, appear coarse or inelegant because of heavy bone structure or muscular development. A weak jaw is a fault.

Foreface

The foreface (from the eye to the nose) shall correspond with the length of the skull (for eyes to the back of the head) and must not be more than 1cm shorter than the skull. Too short a foreface looks clumsy and inelegant; too long a foreface upsets the balance and expression. It looks too weighty. Both destroy the type.

The Irish Terrier 'smile'.

Beard

The beard must be thick and hard and only long enough to reinforce the lines of the head and to give the foreface added strength. Lack of beard destroys utterly the characteristic feature of an Irish Terrier. Often one finds with very hard-coated dogs very little or even no beard; it often goes together with sparse or no leg furnishings. Such a dog, especially if it is short-haired, appears as a smooth-coated terrier. It has lost the type and expression of the Irish Terrier. The same goes for the Irish with the soft, open, floating beard, that usually is light in colour and scanty, often combined with soft or silky body hair, and also soft, colourless hair on the upper body or legs. Too much black in the beard of an adult Irish Terrier is most undesirable.

Eyes

The eyes must have that certain something that characterises the impudent, challenging, intelligent expression of the Irish Terrier. The correct eye expression is defined by the size and the colour of the eye and how it is placed and shaped. Small and deep set, the eyes must not be too far apart and must be almond-shaped, almost triangular. They are full of fire and intelligence; I prefer the very dark brown eye, compared to dark hazel in the standard, to the black, as more expression is permitted through the various nuances of brown that are possible. Light, amber, fuller, protruding eyes are a bad fault. Strong, but not too long, eyebrows accentuate the desired 'Daredevil' expression. The skin around the eyes is dark brown; a strong black rim lends the eye a false, gloomy expression.

Ears

The ears of the Irish Terrier are also distinctly characteristic. Through their breed-type peculiarity in hanging, placement and carriage as much as by their usage they have an enormous significance for the expression. They are set high on the top of the head, held off the skull by the muscles, and fall forwards with the tips on the edge of the skull, above the outer corner of the eye. They stand rather close together, and by that emphasise the narrowness of the head. They are small, fine, V-shaped and come to a definite point.

The hair on the ears should be short and thick, like velvet, without fringes, and slightly darker than the rest of the coat. With very light-coloured dogs, this contrast is most attractive and striking.

The Irish Terrier conducts a lively conversation by the use of its ears. They vary in their carriage, from joy or sadness, boredom and embarrassment, to great anxiety, and therefore are very effective in expression. Ears that are dead, deeply set, folded, carried too high or motionless are not only a fault; they spoil type and expression.

Mouth

The teeth must be powerful, strong and white, complete in number (42) and meeting in a scissor bite. Over- or undershot teeth are a serious fault. The nose is black. Lack of pigment is a fault. The lips close tightly together and range from brown to black. Slack lips (flews) are a fault.

Neck

The elegant neck determines the proud carriage of the head and contributes the decisive factor to the complete nobility of the breed. It must be long and run in a lightly arched, fine, continuous line, blending into back and shoulders. In it strength and elegance are united. A short, thick, fleshy (with dewlap) neck, running into the back at an angle, is very detracting.

Front

The front (chest) seen from in front is narrow, powerful and perfectly straight. it must on no account be too narrow or too wide. The forehand stands in straight continuation to the shoulders. It must not be turned out at the elbows. The legs are moderately long, absolutely straight and strong-boned. They are absolutely straight from the top to the foot and are covered with thick, coarse hair (furnishings) that is thick enough to emphasise the pillar shape.

Shoulder

The shoulder is long, well muscled and yet flat. It runs sloping into the back at a good angulation. The elbows are tucked in. Also seen from the side, the legs are perfectly straight down to the feet. Weak ankles leading to a deviation from the straight line towards the front are a fault.

In movement, the legs move right from the shoulders straight forwards without turning the elbows out, without crossing (knitting) and without throwing them sideways. Slack or loaded shoulders or sticking out elbows are faults.

Feet

The feet are strong and round, toes well arched. The pads are likewise strong, elastic, healthy without fissures, cat-footed with black nails. Excrescence on or deep fissures in the pads are a serious, inherited fault. Equally, open, spreading or flat feet are a great fault.

Body

The body is of moderate length (racy). Whoever praises the short back of an Irish Terrier doesn't know the breed.

Chest

The chest is deep and muscular, with long, moderately-arched, flat ribs. The deepest point is around the height of the elbows. The underline runs in an elegant curve upwards towards the flanks.

Back

The back is strong, straight and firm. It runs into the tail without falling away. The contours run from the ears, over the neck, across the back, in elegant, continuous lines that flow into each other right into the root of the tail. Faults: too long or too short a back, an arched 'carp' back, a dipping back, a croup that falls away, back lines that fall away (like the German Shepherd Dog), too little or lack of chest depth, a barrel shape.

Structure

The structure must be substantial, muscular and firm, thus accentuating a noble outline. Obesity, cloddy appearance and weediness spoil this impression.

Hindquarters

The hindquarters are powerful. very muscular and well angulated, to ensure the greatest possible drive from behind. Powerful thighs with moderately bent knee joints, deep ankle joints with moderately proportioned short metatarsals, strong bones and muscles demonstrate his power and speed. Moreover, they enable the dog to cover a lot of ground when standing. The hindfeet are somewhat smaller than the front feet.

Movement

The movement of the hindquarters is always quite straight, free and far-reaching. It is the movement of a disciplined, active, vital dog. Mincing, weaving, hackneying or overstretching, as well as stilted and irregular movements, are faults.

Tail

Placing, carriage and length of the tail are powerful factors in the correctly-balanced appearance of the whole dog. The mood of the dog can be recognised from the tail carriage. About a quarter of the tail is docked. It must be placed high and carried vertical to the back. The desired tail is straight. A slight inclination to the front shows the fearless Irish Terrier spirit. A slight curve gives a pleasing appearance.

The tail is powerful and covered with moderately short, wiry hair. A crooked, sickle, as well as a low set tail is a fault. A tail that, when roused, is bent over is undesirable. It is still less of an evil than a drooping or whip-like tail.

Coat

The correct coat of an Irish Terrier is often not given its full value or assessed enough because this breed has many variations of coat and only a few experts know really what the ideal hair should be.

Normal terrier hair has pointed tips. If one passes the hand over such a coat, in spite of its being hard and wiry, it feels smooth, with no resistance. On the other hand, hair that is broken lacks pointed tips. It is as if it is broken off, with a smooth, cut surface. If one strokes a broken-haired dog, the ends of the hair can be felt distinctly. They convey to the stroking hand quite a different feel: one could say, the coat rustles. Other than in the Irish Terrier, the broken coat is only found in the Scottish Terrier and the Wire Fox Terrier.

The correct coat for an Irish Terrier is 'ripe', or fully grown, not to be confused with blown (moulting) – it is referred to as *in full bloom*. Because of its double growth, it appears uneven and gives the appearance of a wavy or broken surface. It is a strong, gleaming, water- and dirt-resistant coat that fits the dog for every kind of activity and protects him from external influences. It looks, in its ungroomed state, as cared for and shining as the coats of breeds that are groomed daily. The hair is smooth, straight or slightly waved, and very hard.

Soft, curly, bristly or woolly hair is incorrect. A hereditary fault is the so-called pick-out coat, whose hair roots are not firm. It falls into regular bunches, and the newly-grown, short hair is as easily picked out as blown hair. There is no undercoat at all. A dog with such a coat appears dishevelled and uncared for.

The condition of the coat is largely a question of trimming and feeding. In the hands of a specialist, a moderately-coated Irish Terrier can have a really good coat, while a better-coated dog, through irregular trimming and poor feeding, leaves much to be desired.

Colour

The most significant point of the colour in Irish Terriers is the evenness of it. Colour plays an important part for the devotee, according to his own particular taste, since the Irish Terrier ranges from light blond to dark red. For showing and breeding, however, the eye should be directed mainly to the evenness of colour. Colour varies from light, even wheaten gold to deepest mahogany red. The preferred colours are bright red (fox red), red wheaten (stag red) and red gold (hamster red). Each single hair is bi-coloured, the lower part being light while the tips are darker and determine the actual colour. Thus the Irish Terrier has the most shining and clearest colour when the coat is newly-grown to a suitable length, and becomes bi-coloured – colour on colour – when it has reached its full length.

A small white chest patch shouldn't worry anyone. Many of the most famous champions carried their little white stars from victory to victory. If the white spreads across the chest or appears on the feet, that is a fault; likewise black shading on the face, on the top of the head, on the cheeks or on other places on the body.

Size

The size has been debated and argued over from time past up to today. The Standard, nevertheless, has remained constant. Breeders of large dogs, like breeders of small dogs, have sought to draw the eye of the judge and of the admirer to the overall balance. Actually, this is really a very significant factor. A completely balanced oversized Irish Terrier, just like one that is too small, can be a fine and eye-catching animal.

But that is throwing the ideal of the Irish Terrier out of the window. Judges, as well as breeders, must be clear about this, about what damage is being inflicted on the breed because of frequently expressed views by left or right extremists (over- or undersized). This damage is very difficult to correct. Oversized dogs lead inevitably to the Airedale type or, worse still, to the Greyhound, while undersized dogs lead to the Fox, Lakeland or Welsh Terrier type. In the first extreme, the dogs become too large, cloddy, heavy and more massive than they should be, or else too long-legged, with light, fine, spindly limbs, weak bone and long backs. The other extreme leads to a miniature example, on the whole too light, fine-limbed, weedy, weak and often short-backed. Also, the typical Irish Terrier movement is lost and becomes that of other breeds.

The standard height of 46cm (18in) should be strived for. Every true, first-class Irish Terrier should come as close as possible to the height standard to be the best balanced. Males may be a little over, bitches a little under.

In Conclusion...

In the long run, we are dealing with living, bred creatures, not a mechanical conveyor-belt model from a stencil. The best dog is the one who most impresses, the one closest to the standard and the one who, by his actions and bearing, convinces us he is the best.

For the breeder, only the best is good enough. The admirer, however, should rejoice, untroubled, in his lovable, good and faithful Irish Terrier instead of bothering to look for points that have been described here as faults. There are as few dogs that have all the faults as there are dogs that have none.

One can always buy a good dog from a good breeder. Not often will a breeder part with a very promising puppy but it is in the hands of its owner that a dog is really formed or spoilt. Every breeder or lucky owner of an Irish Terrier should try therefore to make the best of his dog. That goes as much for appearance as for character.

Making Your Choice

Buying a Dog

Buying a puppy of any breed, especially for the first time, calls for careful thought and consideration. It is a big commitment as, hopefully, your dog will be part of your life for the next decade or more. Before you begin you must be absolutely sure you can provide a suitable lifestyle for your dog that fits in with your own and is a pleasure to you both.

If you live with a family or with a larger community, the acquisition of a dog must be a group decision. Everyone needs back-up help on occasions and no dog should be the responsibility of only one person. It is simply not practical. Illness, holidays, work and other commitments occur in everyone's life and should be part of your calculations. Taking on a puppy or an older dog is like having another child in the family, with all the potential for exasperation, joy and anxiety that brings. Your life will never be the same again and you need to be sure this is what you really want.

Children and Irish Terriers are a great combination and they soon learn mutual respect. Photo: Tracy Morgan

Finance

You need to consider your financial position. Dogs have to be fed daily, bathed and stripped or clipped regularly, and even the hardiest will sometimes require veterinary attention. This is not cheap.

More and more people are taking out pet insurance plans. If you do so, be sure you can keep up with the payments. Should your dog need kennelling at any time, or even the services of a dog-walker, these too can prove large expenses.

"This is my nest!" Photo: Tracy Morgan

Tea on the terrace.

You must be certain that, at all times, you can make provision for the comfort, happiness and safety of your dog. The tragic tales of dogs' lives in rescue centres up and down the country bear witness to irresponsible decisions, made very often through ignorance rather than intentional unkindness. The result, however, is the same – one more sad, neglected or unwanted dog.

Terrier People

I sometimes think that those of us who love dogs are divided into 'terrier people' and other ranks. Before buying any breed of terrier, you need to decide whether you are 'one of us'.

All terrier breeds show the same essential terrier characteristics – the Irish more than most. You need to understand that they have enormous natural energy and become restless if under-exercised. They are highly intelligent and have minds of their own. Though biddable enough if they love you, they are not naturally obedient and need careful training and a light touch – persuasion rather than stern disapproval. They will be friends and partners, but *never* submissive fashion accessories or appendages.

Terriers dig, chew and chase, but are clever enough to learn quickly where and what is considered suitable. They are plucky and loyal, with a sensitivity and depth of loving not to be wasted on the uncommitted. They are very sociable, love to be part of a family and to be talked to, and hate to be left out. They often show a particular devotion to 'their' children and themselves remain playful, often into old age. The older dogs (rarely bitches) can be feisty with other dogs, but they are never mean and are perfectly manageable in sensible hands. You will certainly know you have a dog in the house – are you sure you can cope?

All this and more needs to be considered carefully before you proceed further.

Princess Bega. Photo: Marc Henrie

Puppy Hot Line

When you have decided that an Irish Terrier is your choice of dog, you should contact The Kennel Club or one of the breed clubs. They will have a puppy register or 'hot line' with a list of breeders with puppies in hand or litters due. You should get your dog from a well-known breeder, who will give you much helpful advice. You will be asked a great many questions. These are routine and you must not be offended or put off by them.

Irish Terrier breeders are hugely responsible and extremely anxious to protect the breed, their own dogs in particular. They have an unsurpassed record of suitable placings of puppies and very few Irish Terriers are ever found in rescue centres. Provided that all is well and the hot line is satisfied, you will be given the names of breeders, and it would probably be sensible to find one as local to you as possible.

Faytime Dancing Deirdre taking a rest under a tree.
Photo: Christine Murray

Irish Terriers are natural athletes who can jump to great heights. Photo: Tracy Morgan

How Old?

Most people wanting a dog prefer to start with a puppy. We call it the 'Aahh!' factor, and undoubtedly puppies are enchanting. You probably feel a puppy would mould better to your character and lifestyle. However, puppies need careful rearing to establish a healthy pattern for life. They also need fairly constant company. No young creature likes to be alone, and 'bedding down' with the puppy requires a large part of your time, especially during the first few months.

You may be offered and decide to have an older puppy of perhaps 5–15 months that the breeder does not want to run on for show purposes. A puppy of this age may take a little longer to settle down and begin to be himself (or herself!). Being such a faithful and affectionate breed, by that age Irish Terriers have already learnt to depend on and love whoever tends them. It is a big break to go to strangers and different surroundings. We acquired a year-old puppy once, and I felt she was heartbroken to begin with. In time, a great bond did develop between us. Provided that you recognise this possibility and are prepared for it, the advantages are less feeding, less risk of infection and, after a possible period of adjustment, no house-training. Puppies do need to be house-trained and there will inevitably be a few puddles and worse (see chapter 7). They also tend to chew, especially when they are teething, and can be quite destructive. You need to be very patient and tolerant unless, like me, you positively relish the 'naughty little tyke' puppy phase. I always think that Irish Terriers have a much longer puppyhood than most dogs. They tend to go on being the proverbial 'handful' and anyway are always very playful by nature.

Nevertheless, for some people the choice of a mature dog or older puppy is a wiser decision. Although within the breed it has never been necessary to set up a separate rescue service because so few Irish Terriers ever need to be rescued, a mature dog is sometimes available. People's lives are more changeable today and circumstances alter, for example through deaths, family break-ups or moves abroad or into flats where animals are not allowed – there are so many reasons why a dog may need a new home.

Re-Housing

It is the breeders who take the responsibility for re-housing their dogs, should it be necessary. This requires very careful handling, as no dog should ever be put into this predicament more than once. Great care is taken to match up the dog and owner. For instance, it is not fair to place an old dog, unused to children, into a family with three toddlers.

Sometimes breeders like to find good homes for their retired show dogs. If these dogs have spent most of their time in kennels, they will probably take a little more time to settle in than a dog already used to living with a family. However, Irish Terriers are pretty quick to see the advantages of a new lifestyle and usually take to it like the proverbial duck to water.

The Show Puppy

If you are looking for a pedigree dog, male or female, with a view to showing and breeding, this is a very different situation. You will need long discussions with specialist breeders, who will give you very detailed advice about breeding lines and how to begin. One-off litters, unless supervised by an experienced breeder, are not recommended now, even by vets. There will be much talk about puppies with 'potential', but remember that even the most promising puppy can fail to reach show ring requirements or fail at stud or as a brood bitch. There may be many pitfalls and disappointments along the way and, on the whole, breeding today is highly specialised, requiring a great deal of knowledge and experience before you begin.

There is no guarantee whatsoever that the puppies of champions will automatically become champions in their turn. They may not fulfil their potential and, in any case, a great deal will depend on training, handling, care of the coat and how much time you can give to showing your dog. This can be very satisfying and interesting, but it is also very demanding and time-consuming.

Irish Terrier puppies look rather like little woolly teddy bears, often with touches of black down, but they are not small for long. By 12–14 weeks they can be very wilful and energetic and rather leggy and 'all over the place'. You may begin to despair that they will ever be sturdy and trim enough to look anything like proper Irish Terriers. Most don't look their best until they are over a year old. Some take even longer to mature and grow a respectable coat and proper leg and face furnishings.

Price

With most litters of Irish Terriers the price is the same for each puppy, but the overall breed price is not absolutely fixed and may vary with each litter. Different breeders may charge slightly more or less, according to how well-known and successful they are.

The Breeder

When you have decided on a breeder from whose stock you would like to buy a show puppy you will need to discuss it very fully, explaining exactly what you want. You will probably need to book your puppy, and this could involve waiting, as not all litters produce even one potential champion. If you are really serious, it is far better to wait until the breeder has a dog that he or she can thoroughly recommend, the best possible puppy – and even then nothing is certain. Showing is very costly, and you need at least to be in with a chance from the beginning. It is not courteous to commit yourself to several breeders, looking for their best puppy. Besides, Irish Terrier breeders tend to know each other, and word gets around. Take your time before you decide on a breeder, and then be patient.

Choosing an eight-week-old pup of any breed is something of a pig-in-a-poke. All breeders confess to having made the wrong choice of 'best' puppy at some time. Hours are spent watching, examining and discussing the latest litter before decisions are made.

When choosing an Irish Terrier, try to see the whole litter with the dam. Photo: Tracy Morgan

The puppy needs to look balanced, with the correct angulation in both the fore- and hindquarters. His basic construction will not change. However, the little, short nose must lengthen and the position of the ears, tail carriage, quality of coat, and position of teeth are all 'movable feasts' and far less predictable.

Remember too that show careers may not always be very long. As I have said, Irish Terriers can be slow to mature and, although some may go on showing as veterans, others have passed their best at seven years. Bitches have the additional problem of missing shows by coming on heat and by having puppies and then having to regain their top condition – coats often seem to suffer. Like females of all species, they can be more sensitive and temperamental, and will not show as well at these times.

Breeding Terms

Sometimes it is possible to make a private arrangement with a breeder whereby you can have a really good bitch for a reduced price on the understanding that the breeder has the choice of the stud dog you may use and the pick of the first litter. This is called a *breeding terms agreement* and does help you to start you off if you cannot afford a bitch. The problem is that, although you will bear the expense of the stud fee, care of the bitch, vet fees and the cost of rearing the puppies, you will not be able to keep your best puppy.

There should always be a formal written statement signed by both parties to avoid misunderstandings. It can be held by The Kennel Club. These arrangements require a good deal of trust and are best undertaken between friends.

Please note: you will not make a living from breeding Irish Terrier puppies. An alternative source of income will always be necessary. Many breeders strip and trim, run boarding kennels or follow other professions.

Pet Dogs

For most people, buying an Irish Terrier puppy is about choosing a pet, a loving companion, friend, guard and playmate. You will probably be invited by the breeder to see the litter and meet the mother. There may or may not be a choice, as some breeders assign their puppies very early on, but often it will be left to you. Mostly it is love at first sight – the one who played hardest, came to meet you or sat quietly by itself. Perhaps a variation in colour (Irish Terriers range from wheaten to red) might influence your choice. You may well feel rather emotional, especially if you have just lost a beloved old dog or have longed for a dog for some time. My hands have always trembled as I pick up *my* puppy for the first time, so be prepared for the odd tear!

Dog or Bitch?

One big decision is whether to have a dog or a bitch, although people often change their minds on the day, and it does depend on what is available. Temperaments will vary within the same litter but, on the whole, dogs are more pushy and up-front characters, more independent and naturally assertive. But they are great fun! My brother's dog, Jock, remains, 50 years on, one of the great characters of my life. Many hotly contend that bitches are better, more charming, easier to train, more intelligent, and so on. I have always had bitches, so my preference must be in their favour. Irish Terrier bitches can be very gentle and sensitive but most of them, though deeply loving and affectionate, can still 'stand on their toes' like the dogs.

Unless bitches are spayed, you do have the recurrent problem of coping with their coming on heat (see chapter 9) with all the difficulty of safely exercising them without attracting the entire male canine population for miles around. I'm sorry to say that sprays and Amplex are not foolproof. On the other hand, dogs can wander for this very reason and need much tighter control and a tactful approach towards your neighbours.

One Dog or Two?

I have always had puppies in pairs as they have such fun together. Litter-mates are particularly devoted, but even two unrelated puppies of the same age growing up together will almost certainly be good friends, and company for one another when left alone. Some dog experts think this makes them less devoted to their human family. This cannot be so with Irish Terriers. They are not 'one man dogs', and tend to love the whole family anyway, especially the children. They are probably harder to train if they are working dogs, but ordinary household good manners and discipline are not problematic.

The additional cost of keeping two dogs is not inconsiderable, as everything is doubled, from veterinary fees to food costs.

A lovely litter of quality Irish Terriers. Photo: Tracy Morgan

Should you decide to have two dogs, it is essential to consider their sex. A combination of two bitches works well, or a dog and a spayed bitch. If the bitch is unspayed, the dog may become aggressive towards other dogs approaching the bitch. You may also have the anxiety of unplanned puppies, or at least a very agitated dog to deal

Terriers love to play tug-of war. This one is attacking Nylabone Dental Floss, which will help to keep tartar at bay.
Photo: Tracy Morgan

with while the bitch is on heat. Two males, especially if they are both entire, are not an easy combination. They may well not get on and never quite decide who is top dog. It is far easier to settle a male puppy with an older dog, especially if there is three or four years' difference. The hierarchy is then already clear, and the pup will learn from the older dog and often idolise him. This also applies to bitches who have not grown up together. There is the added advantage that you are less likely to lose them at more or less the same time. This can be distressing and heartbreaking for everybody.

If you are aiming at founding a line of your own, it is not good practice to buy a dog and a bitch at the same time. As mentioned before, you need to acquire the best possible bitch – your foundation bitch – and breed her to the best and most suitable stud dog and then keep her best puppies. You can breed charming pet dogs from the start, but you need to establish a good reputation within the breed and found a successful kennel in order to sell your puppies. After all, it costs the same to breed and raise a pet puppy as to breed and raise a successful winner.

Other Pets
Many Irish Terriers live happily with cats, especially if they have been puppy and kitten together. However, all terriers love to chase cats, and I would certainly never trust a terrier with rabbits, mice, guinea pigs or gerbils. The ancient urge to hunt could easily prove too strong. Nevertheless, they are very quick to learn and, with correct training, can be trusted with sheep, goats, cattle and horses. Mine are perfectly safe with our flock of canaries, after one mishap when they were puppies.

Official Paperwork
Kennel Club registration
There is a certain amount of official paperwork concerning your puppy which you will need to sort out immediately. Most pedigree puppies are registered with The Kennel Club by their breeder, but this is not always the case, and you will need to clarify the situation when you buy the puppy.

Transfer of ownership

If the registration has been made, it will need to be transferred to your name to keep records straight. This means completing the back of the Registration Certificate and sending it to The Kennel Club. If you show your puppy before this procedure is complete, you need to write TAF (Tranfer Applied For) on the show entry forms. This has to be done until you have received a new Registration Certificate.

Vaccination certificate

Some breeders, though not all, start the vaccination procedure before the puppies go to their new homes, in which case the puppy will come with a Vaccination Certificate. This will indicate to your own vet exactly

"I don't mind sharing a chair with cats as long as they're warm!"

what has already been given and when the next shots are due. Don't count on this, however, as several of the best-known Irish Terrier breeders are strictly homeopathic, so you need to understand precisely what is involved in this alternative approach. If the puppy has received no inoculations at all you need to visit your vet and arrange immediately to begin the programme.

Worming information

The puppy will have been wormed, and your vet will need to know when and what was used.

Diet sheet

You will also need a diet sheet with precise details of how your puppy has been fed and how to proceed as he or she grows.

Breed information leaflet

Most Irish Terrier puppies come with a leaflet about the breed, including advice about stripping and caring for the coat.

Warranty and disclaimer

It is perhaps a sign of the times that some breeders now consider it necessary to protect themselves by issuing a Warranty and Disclaimer along the following lines (see overleaf):

In consideration of the sale of the dog (details of which are set out below) by

me . . . .(the Vendor)

to . . . .(the Purchaser)

it is agreed as follows:

1 The purchaser shall have fourteen days after the date of purchase in which to have the dog examined by any professional veterinary surgeon that may be desired and shall have the right to return the dog without question during the said period of fourteen days.

2 Should the purchaser choose to return the dog as provided above, then he/she shall be entitled to the return by the vendor of the purchase price and no more. If the purchaser does not exercise the option of returning the dog as so provided, the vendor shall be under no further obligation in respect of the sale of the dog whatsoever.

3 It is a condition of this sale and purchase that no warranty can be given as to the ultimate show potential of the animal on reaching maturity.

Breed and description of dog . . . .

. . . .

Date of purchase . . . . .Purchase Price: £   :

Name of purchaser . . . .

Address . . . .

. . . .

Signature of Purchaser . . . .

Name of vendor . . . .

Address . . . .

. . . .

Signature of vendor . . . .

Insurance policy (if any)
See below.

Insurance
Veterinary fees can assume astronomical proportions, and it is wise these days to take out a veterinary insurance policy. Sometimes the breeder may have arranged this but, more usually, you will need to do this yourself. You need immediate cover, as puppies can be accident-prone and have health problems that are less common in grown dogs. These policies are not by any means blanket covers for all health problems and you should examine the small print carefully. Routine inoculations, worming and check-ups are never covered.

General Condition of your Puppy

Breeders are usually extremely busy people, and it is not always easy to contact them during the day. I know several who get to the telephone only after 10.00 pm. You will need to make an appointment to see the litter, which could be any time after the puppies are five weeks old. As I have said, personal fancy is often the reason for choosing a certain puppy but, if you are looking for a particular temperament, do be guided by the breeder. Breeders spend hours with their puppies, getting them used to being handled and properly socialised, even when these are 'kennel' rather than 'house' puppies. They will have a far better idea of the different characters within the litter than you can perceive on a flying visit. Young puppies sleep a great deal, and can seem very quiet, with only short bursts of activity. It is really very difficult to read temperament in a short space of time.

It is most unlikely that a puppy from a reputable breeder will not be in excellent health. It is also safe to say that you will not find an Irish Terrier from one of those iniquitous puppy farms. Rarely, if ever, will you find an Irish Terrier – or, indeed, any other pedigree breed – in a responsible pet shop. This is not so in the United States of America, where it is not uncommon to find a whole range of pedigree dogs for sale. Buying a puppy under such circumstances requires a much more cautious approach to ensure that it is healthy. Check that:

- When the puppy is awake, the general appearance is lively and friendly.
- There is no restriction in movement.
- There are no signs of runny eyes and nose. The eyes should be bright and the nose cool and moist.
- It is not too thin with prominent ribcage and spine. Puppies are often fairly rotund, but should not be pot-bellied. This can indicate worms and/or malnutrition.
- There should be no sign of lice or fleas, which would be the result of very poor living conditions.

Breed-specific problems

We are most blessed to have a breed with virtually no major structural breed problems. We don't produce a table for hip dysplasia or eye problems, as do some other breeds. Cracked paws, which were troublesome among terriers in the 1930s, are very rare today, except in the odd throw-back. No dog with cracked paws should be used for breeding.

Irish Terriers tend to be hardy, with few things to go wrong and, in any case, it is impossible to tell whether a small puppy has genetic faults such as congenital blindness or a poor heart. It is also difficult to assess bad temperament. Some people think that, if a puppy panics, struggles or becomes aggressive when you playfully turn him on to his back and hold him there for a few seconds, you probably have a nervous, highly-strung dog on your hands. This is not an 'official' test, and in any case a normal, playful reaction should not be mistaken for aggression.

Umbilical cord

Holding the puppy by placing one hand under the forelegs and supporting the hindquarters with the other, check the umbilical cord. This should show as only a slight lump, not a large swelling, which could indicate a hernia that would eventually require surgery to correct.

Dew claws

Check also that the dew claws have been removed. These vestigial 'thumbs' are found on the insides of the front legs. Most breeders remove them, as they can be very troublesome and painful if they get caught and torn when the dog is playing or being exercised. They would then have to be removed surgically, which is a more serious operation for an older dog. The nails in the dew claws tend to go on growing, as they are not worn down by being placed on the ground.

Nails require regular attention for comfort and the development of good feet, and I have always found it best to ask the vet or the person who strips the coat to do it. Irish Terriers are extremely fussy about their feet, and a nail guillotine requires some skill to use without twisting the nail or taking off too much, which is extremely painful. A terrier *never* forgets, so one painful experience for a wriggling puppy can leave a lasting dislike of having nails cut.

Tail docking

Check the puppy's tail. By long tradition, all terriers had docked tails. It was considered safer and less likely to cause trouble through injury to a working dog. It seemed to suit the jaunty terrier character and give a better balance to the outline of the dog. It causes very little more than a few moments' discomfort to the puppy.

The controversial 1996 law banning tail docking by breeders has caused much anger and heartache and left a very confused situation. Some vets will dock, and some will not. Up until now, I have not seen an undocked Irish Terrier in the show ring. You may ask a breeder to leave your puppy undocked but it will be up to the breeder to consent or refuse. See also chapter 9 (page 126).

The finished product: a beautiful Brazan bitch. Photo: Carol Ann Johnson

Your New Irish Terrier

Chapter Seven

Irish Terriers are devoted to 'their' people.

Your Puppy's Main Need

May I say right from the start that Irish Terrier puppies need, more than anything, loving and affectionate homes. From the beginning of their history they have always lived as an integral part of the family. It is where they belong and are at their happiest and best. All dogs have a primitive need to be part of a group or pack. You and your family or household group will be part of your Irish Terrier's pack. Irish Terriers need a great deal of socialising and company, especially between two and six months of age. An Irish Terrier isolated in an outside kennel will be utterly miserable. Irish Terriers are not lap-dogs and will not like or insist on being petted continuously, but they are deeply affectionate, loving and absolutely committed and loyal to those they love. They need people – especially when they are puppies.

Equipment for Your Puppy

Even if you inspect the litter earlier, you will not be allowed to take your puppy home until it is properly weaned. This will not be until the puppy is at least eight weeks old. If you book a puppy, you may be asked to put down a deposit, and you will certainly need to make some sensible preparations for your new arrival.

Food and water bowls

You will need two suitably-sized bowls for your puppy, one for food and one for water. There is a wide range of choice, from brightly-coloured

Your new puppy will need food and water bowls of suitable sizes. Photo: Tracy Morgan

plastic to stainless steel. You need something that is difficult to tip up and impossible to chew. That rules out plastic, which can be too light and is very dangerous indeed if chewed and swallowed in large, sharp pieces. It is difficult to keep clean, too. Some people favour the old-fashioned ceramic bowls. These can be scoured out easily and do not tip up, but they are heavy, may need two hands to lift them up and break if dropped. They come in various sizes and make excellent bird feeders when the puppy has outgrown them.

Toothbrushes and toothpaste

Vets nowadays encourage owners to have toothbrushes and toothpaste for their dogs. You need to open a puppy's mouth gently, with one hand over and one hand under the jaw. Choose a word – 'Teeth', 'Brush teeth' or whatever – so that Puppy knows what's coming. I laugh when I remember how we used to clean our terrier's teeth, unbeknown to our parents, with our own toothbrushes – *not* to be recommended, however. A show dog would need to have its teeth examined in the ring, so should be well accustomed to having its mouth opened. Regular cleaning helps to prevent plaque, which can lead to infected gums and tooth decay. Dogs seem to like the taste of the toothpaste, and it does freshen the mouth.

Grooming equipment

Details of grooming for shows are given in chapter 12.

For day-to-day grooming, you will need

- a wire brush
- a comb
- a stripping knife

Use these very carefully and make it a 'love-in'. Be careful not to scratch the puppy's sensitive skin.

Disinfectant and cleaning materials

It is a sensible precaution to have a disinfectant or deodouriser handy. Some are manufactured with dogs in mind, but almost any household disinfectant will do to help deal with puppy 'slip-ups'.

Since more and more dogs (like people) are showing allergic reactions to biological washing powders, it would be sensible to have soap-based washing powders for your puppy's towels and blankets.

Beds

Where your puppy sleeps is entirely up to you but, from the start, puppies should have comfortable beds of their own where they can settle down and sleep or rest. It is important that everyone, including small children, understands this and that no puppy should be disturbed or heaved out of its bed, even in play.

Irish Terriers love to climb on to beds and chairs, and you need to get the rules straight about this. Some people have one chair with a rug on it where the dog is allowed to sit. There is a wide choice of beds and bedding for dogs, in every shape, size, colour and material. None is perfect, but there are pros and cons for each. For years we had baskets, with large blankets for warmth and comfort. These always look nice, but can be chewed.

"I'm making my bed!"

One of our bitches went through several and when, in exasperation, we gave up replacing them she was left on a sort of wicker tray. However, baskets are cool in the summer and always seem very clean and well aired.

Shaped nest beds are popular and the dogs love them, especially in winter. You can top up or lighten the bedding according to the season. They can be machine washed and dried relatively quickly. You can line the base with newspaper covered with Vet Bed, rather than a blanket, in case of 'accidents'. They can, of course, be ripped by an enterprising puppy, as can any padded dog beds or mattresses. Padded mattresses have the advantage of easy-change covers.

I do not recommend bean bags as beds for dogs, especially puppies. They are very difficult to keep clean and, should the puppy tear the bag, hundreds of little polystyrene balls littering the room are a great nuisance.

You may feel tiny puppies need smaller beds for the first six months – they certainly look very lost in big beds. Dogs generally seem to like beds that fit them sufficiently snugly for them to push their backs against the sides.

Of course, you are free to improvise, and a laundry basket or large, wooden box makes an excellent bed for a dog and is cheaper, too.

Vet Bed

Vet Bed is a great invention. It is a safe, man-made, washable fabric, woolly on one side and backed with stiff webbing on the other. You can buy it cut to a specific length or in pre-cut sizes. It tucks well into a chair, car boot, or any shaped plastic dog bed. Moisture goes through it, so the woolly surface remains dry and comfortable. It cannot be shredded like a woollen blanket, and puppies tend not to try to chew it as they might a blanket.

Where to sleep

Many dogs sleep in the kitchen or utility room, but probably just as many sleep in

Dream ticket.

bedrooms – it is entirely up to you. No young dog, and certainly no puppy, should be cold at night, which can happen in utility rooms. Their great advantage is that, should there be any mishaps, an uncarpeted floor is much easier to clean.

Wire cages

Some breeders strongly recommend a wire cage as part of every puppy's equipment. It gives the puppy a safe place and keeps him or her out of harm's way when the household is in a whirl. It can also be used as a travelling cage and, provided that you buy one large enough to fit your puppy when it is fully grown, it makes a useful kennel in many circumstances throughout the dogs life, such as at shows or when you are staying with friends. At the puppy stage it does save wear and tear on the house, when you have to be out, and some people think it facilitates house-training. Make sure the cage has a dog-proof door and handles for carrying. Most are collapsible for easy storage.

A puppy under your feet, especially in the kitchen, is a hazard to both of you. Like small children, puppies should be kept away from the stove. Here again, a cage would solve the immediate problem, but a puppy kept in a cage will never learn as quickly as one able to make mistakes and learn from them. It's rather like a toddler being kept in a playpen and never learning about stairs or hot kettles. Be quite sure, too, that the cage does not become a prison of convenience, stuffed with toys. Puppies should not be left for long periods in cages; they need to be around you, learning as they go, even if it is much harder work for you to begin with.

I must confess that I have never used a cage. Cages are (in my opinion) fairly unsightly and awkward to carry, and they take up a lot of room. However, they are a great help in managing a puppy. They are quite expensive, but an investment, as they are fairly indestructible and will last for at least your lifetime. Most pet shops stock them, or you can order straight from the manufacturer. Advertisements are often placed in the dog papers, and you can sometimes pick them up second-hand.

Baby-gates can be recommissioned or acquired to keep a puppy either in or out of a room. However, they are not very high, and Irish Terriers can jump like steeplechasers very early on.

Collars

To begin with, your puppy will need a very small collar, which has to be adjusted and replaced as the puppy grows. Make quite sure you check frequently, as a collar that is too small can cause great discomfort.

It is a good idea to measure the neck with a piece of string. Tie it in a knot at the right length *before* you arrive at the pet shop and start debating what size you need. It is curiously difficult, even with an adult dog, to decide the size of a new collar.

As with all pet accessories, today there is a huge choice. Terriers, by tradition, do not wear the jewelled 'poodle' look. I think Irish Terriers look best in plain or studded beige or brown leather collars, but a few flights of fancy into pale yellow, blue or green may be forgiven. Some have fluorescent reflective material or discs that are easily spotted at night. Webbing collars are also available, in a variety of colours. These are hardwearing and washable.

You will need to introduce the collar gently and show your dog exactly what you are doing (see chapter 8).

Leads

You will need a suitable lead to go with the collar, although perhaps not initially. It will prove an aid to introducing your puppy to the beginning of obedience training. Don't expect too much at first, as the lead could be seen as a tug-of-war rope and an excellent chew. Be very patient. Do not even attempt to use a choke collar or restraining device on your dog unless you have been shown exactly how to use it (see chapter 8).

Normal leather collar and lead.

Do not use a choke collar like this on your dog unless you have been taught how to put it on.
Photo: Pete's Photographics.

Leads vary in length and width and can be made of nylon or leather. Nylon is more durable and less tacky in the wet. However, it is hard on the hands and never quite feels like a dog lead to me. There are also extendible leads, but these need to be used properly and require some practice. A puppy dashing out on an extendible lead could have tragic consequences. These leads are also less easy to hold and carry as they will not hook over the wrist. I have seen many pulled and sent flying out of the owners' hands, and more than one is difficult, if not impossible, to manage in one hand.

Remember to remove the lead if the puppy is playing. The puppy can easily get tangled and hurt itself.

Identification

Discs and capsules By law, you have to attach your name, address and telephone number to the collar. Some people put their vet's number as well. An engraved metal disc firmly attached is more practical than a capsule and less likely to become detached. It is also easier to read quickly. I remember catching a stray dog in the park, and it was terribly difficult to unscrew the capsule with freezing fingers, only to find the paper too smudged to read until I arrived home. Check regularly that the disc is in order. Should your puppy stray, you can then be contacted immediately.

Some people remove collars at night to avoid marking the coat. A collar can produce a slight dent in the coat if worn continuously, and collars do need airing overnight so that they don't become smelly.

More recently, webbing collars with dogs' names and addresses stamped or woven into the fabric are being sold by specialists who manufacture them with matching leads. As I have already said, they are washable, but they may not be to your taste.

A word of warning: it is possible for puppies to get caught in each other's collars if they are playing rather roughly together. This can cause serious injury, and no puppies should play together unsupervised with their collars on.

Tattooing Tattooing is another option, and every police dog is identified in this way. This tattoo can be put on the inner side of the ear and is a relatively painless procedure. It provides permanent identification and can be done at any age. A special code is used for registration within the scheme, and this can be added to Kennel Club documents. You would need to contact The Kennel Club to find an approved tattooist in your area. This method is becoming quite popular, but to me it always seems rather drastic. In any case, a lost dog is often frightened, and I would be nervous about examining its ears too carefully. There would also be the nuisance of contacting the authorities to decode the message. A secure disc on the collar and an escape-proof garden seem a better option.

Toys

Puppies love to play, and there is a huge range of specially designed toys. Nylabone products, which help to keep the teeth free from tartar as the dogs play with them, are ideal. Be very sure that any toy you give your puppy is too big for it to swallow. A blockage in the trachea (windpipe) or gut can be fatal. Puppies swallowing dangerous objects are a nightmare. One of ours swallowed a riding glove, and stories of pebbles, lumps of coal and socks are legion. You have to be very vigilant and tidy up carefully.

Make sure the puppy has plenty of toys. We had a toy box and the puppies, when asked, would select something. Some Irish Terriers are obsessive ball chasers and seem to chase them, catch them in mid-air, throw them high and return them without being taught at all. Old shoes or slippers make good chewing toys, but do be careful to pull off string or anything that can unravel.

"Me and my teddy-bear!"

Terriers love to tug and will hang on to a stick, towel or special toy, growling in mock anger. If the game gets too rough, stop at once and make the puppy sit and be calm.

Irish Terriers are zippy and up-beat, and at no time is this more apparent than when a puppy hurtles around playing enthusiastically.

If you have a puppy with show potential, be very careful not to let it damage or displace teeth by playing with sticks or tugging too hard. Sprains and damages to joints, for example through falling down stairs, must be avoided. Irish Terriers are compact and good at looking after themselves, but injuries are not unknown.

You will probably find your puppy has a habit of trying to hide toys or, worse still, bury them. Puppies look so comic, with heads and tails held high, carrying some precious object and looking everywhere for somewhere to put it – under your pillow or down the back of the sofa are routine places.

Taking Your Puppy Home

For obvious reasons, it is easiest to collect your new dog or puppy by car. You should have someone with you to hold the puppy safely on the journey. No puppy travelling, possibly for the first time, by car should ever be unrestrained. It would be a comfort for a small puppy to be nursed on a lap, and easier too, as otherwise the puppy could easily be pitched forward off a seat. Come well prepared for mishaps – apart from wetting, puppies can be car sick. You need a roll of kitchen paper, bottle of water, sponge and at least two old towels to fold under the puppy. If you have or can borrow a wire cage, it does make things easier, but you will miss the bliss of the puppy near you for the first time.

It is utterly unsuitable to use a boot or the back of a hatch-back to transport a dog at any time. Heat can be a real problem in the summer. Do not leave the puppy alone in the car. Dogs become overheated very quickly, sometimes with fatal consequences. Have a bowl and drinking water to hand. A damp towel wrapped around a dog to keep the temperature down is an excellent idea. It is often a great relief to our older dogs, who do not like to be hot.

If you need to use public transport, it is far easier and safer to have a small puppy in some sort of portable cage – even a cat basket will do. People cannot resist talking to a puppy on your lap or tucked under your arm. It is hard for the puppy, confused, separated from its mother for the first time and recognising nothing that it knows, to be patted constantly. You will arrive home with a very exhausted and possibly slightly traumatised pup.

Immunity

A young puppy that has not finished its course of inoculations (perhaps not even started them) does not have full immunity against the major canine diseases. It should not come into contact with other dogs, and never on any account whatever should it be walked in a public park or street.

If you are collecting an older dog, it will probably be adequately protected and safe to walk in the street, provided that you can manage it on a lead. Even retired 'showmen' tend to know all about the outside world, and Irish Terriers are quick to learn the ropes. Be careful that the collar cannot be slipped and that the lead is secure.

Time of collection

Try to collect your puppy in the morning if possible to allow it time to settle into the new surroundings before bedtime. I remember Edna Howard Jones telephoning rather late to hear how one of her puppies had fared on her first journey. We were still playing with her. Edna's rather sharp "Haven't you put her to bed yet?" had me wishing we had fetched her earlier.

Settling Into Your Home
The first night

Puppies usually cry and even howl at night when first parted from mother and litter-mates. They can be cold and frightened, which is very understandable. If this happens, put a warm hot-water-bottle into the basket, well wrapped and not too full. A ticking clock (hard to come by nowadays) is thought to help, and even leaving a light on seems to comfort them. Give the puppy something soft to snuggle into (an old scarf, sweater or baby blanket would do). There will not be a chewing problem at this stage.

A great deal has been said about *starting out the way you mean to go on* and insisting on the puppy sleeping where it will always be expected to sleep. This seems to me ridiculous and over harsh. Irish Terriers are clever and adaptable, and all the puppies I've ever had have spent the first few nights beside my bed, where a comforting hand quietens them at once. A slightly disturbed night seems a small price to pay for an unstressed puppy. Some puppies settle, and do not cry at all. After settling in, puppies will sleep wherever you choose, understanding perfectly well, especially if they spend some time during the day asleep in their own beds.

Have some newspaper handy as a floor cover in case the puppy gets up during the night. This is not very likely, but puppies are very tiny, after all, and the 'damage' is minimal.

Basic hygiene

For everyone's sake, including the puppy's, rules of hygiene need to be strict. There has been a fair amount of anxiety about puppies with worms affecting children but, with sound hygiene and basic common sense, there should be no danger whatsoever. Your puppy will already have been wormed by the breeder, and you will need to follow up the programme with your vet's advice. Washing hands after playing with the puppy, especially before eating, should be standard practice.

Separate bowls are needed for the puppy, and even washing-up brushes and drying cloths used for these should be used for nothing else. The utensils should be kept scrupulously clean: always use hot water, soap or detergent and a scrubbing brush and make sure the bowls and brush are properly rinsed under a running tap. Keep the bowls in the same place, preferably stacked with the food so that everything is handy when needed.

Introductions to other pets

Dogs Be very tactful about introducing the puppy to older family dogs. Dogs, as descendants of the wolf (*canis lupis*), are pack animals by nature, with a distinct tribal structure; each one has a precise social position and role within the group. Your resident dogs will insist on their positions in the hierarchy being respected by the newcomer.

Leave the puppy in the car until you have greeted the other dogs. There will be huge interest in the new smells and probably some excitement at your return, anyway. It is

Be very tactful when introducing the new arrival to family dogs.

better for the introduction to take place in the garden, or even in the street, provided that someone holds the older dog on a lead and you do not put the puppy down. Dogs are very territorial, and a new puppy thrust into the house without a proper first meeting could provoke some aggression.

You could stage a little walk down the lane or round the block, carrying the puppy. Irish Terriers love to go out and about, and it is surprising how quickly the puppy is accepted if a walk seems part of the new deal. When you go indoors, hold the puppy on your lap and tell the other dogs about it. Make it clear, with a sharp reprimand, that snapping is not acceptable behaviour.

The puppy usually makes things difficult by being overjoyed to see another dog, especially if it looks like Mother. Puppies can often be very provoking and will not leave the older dogs alone at first. They will have to learn the pack hierarchy eventually, but you do not want a frightened or, worse still, damaged puppy while your resident dog(s) is defending his position as top dog. It is difficult not to defend the puppy constantly and scold or punish the older dog, but that would be seen as a challenge to the older dog's supremacy, so is not advisable. Far better to remove the pup. I have never allowed snapping or squabbling, and the older dogs understand this perfectly well. They are far more concerned about keeping my approval than quarrelling with each other. The word mine dread is "Outside!" (pointing to the door). They hate it, and for them nothing is worth this amount of disapproval and embarrassment. You should try to avoid situations that could make this flare up.

"A moving stone? Now I've seen it all!"

One last plea – for the older dogs. Try not to make them feel rejected by fussing over the puppy too much, especially in front of them. Find a time when they can all be patted and fussed together. Once they have accepted it, some older dogs take on the proverbial new lease of life with a puppy in the house. In all probability, the puppy will become devoted to them and even cry when, at walk time, it has to be left behind.

"Cats do have their uses!"

Try to take time off to settle the whole family. The arrival of a new member is not an everyday occurrence, and concentration and tact at the start bring joy and rewards for everyone in the long run.

Other pets As I have said before, I would never rely on a terrier not to chase small pets such as rabbits, mice and hamsters – it would be foolhardy to do so. However, Irish Terriers are often fond of, or at least on very good terms with, family cats, especially if they have grown up together.

Resident cats are often offended by the arrival of a new puppy and may sulk and keep out of the way for a time. If there is an encounter, the cat will almost certainly come off better and send the puppy away squealing after a sharp clout or scratch on the nose. This is usually enough to make the puppy careful at home, but probably not enough to stop neighbours' cats from being chased.

Picking up your puppy

It is a good idea to pick up your puppy frequently. There are always occasions when it has to be done – on to the vet's table, into the car, or when crossing the road – and the puppy should be used to it. A show dog especially would need to be used to this sort of handling.

There is a special technique in lifting and holding a puppy and, if

"Funny puppies!"

Dogs and cats in the same family usually settle down happily together.

there are children in the house, they should be taught immediately and carefully. Puppies can be injured through being pulled around, and they can wriggle and have a bad or even fatal fall.

The correct method is to put your arm under the puppy, resting the chest on the palm of your hand. Tuck the back legs up under your elbow and hold the body lightly against your chest, side-on. Should the puppy wriggle, you have it in a firm hold, and a free hand to restrain it if necessary. You can also put it back on to its feet more easily without a sideways tumble. If you bend your knees as you lean forward, it will be easier for your own back.

House-training

Irish Terriers are not usually a problem to house-train. You must understand that a small puppy, rather like a baby, has neither the muscular control nor a large enough bladder to be completely clean, so be patient. Our puppies have always arrived with the idea of 'outside' learnt already, presumably from their dams. If you have older dogs, the puppy will copy them almost at once, but that may not be quite enough for a small pup. The garden can be wet and muddy, too, or very cold, and that is the last thing you want for either of you, as no pup should be shut out alone to begin with.

I have always used the old-fashioned method of training them on to a piece of newspaper. It is so simple. Put down newspaper, sprinkled if you like with a special product from the pet shop that is supposed to encourage the pup. Choose some words – "Good Girl/Boy" or "Clean Dog" will do – and, whenever the pup begins to squat and is about to puddle, lift it on to the paper, repeatedly saying the chosen phrase. If there has already been a mishap, don't panic. Put the puppy immediately on to the paper and deal with the puddle like this:

Mop the floor, using a drop of disinfectant. Carpets suffer no permanent marking if you pour some lightly-disinfectanted water on to the spot at once. Fold up a wodge of kitchen paper and press it on to the place. This lifts the stain and, hey presto – no puddle, no mark. You can then dry it with a hair-dryer if necessary. Do not rub or scrub the carpet – you'll rub the stain in.

If the puppy fouls the carpet, put on your rubber gloves and remove the stool with kitchen paper. Again, it is wiser to soak and lift the soiling rather than scrub the carpet, which may leave a permanent mark. Disinfectant will remove any trace of smell, which might otherwise encourage the puppy to re-offend.

Be careful about your choice of disinfectant. Most pet shops sell them with a built-in deterrent to discourage the pup. Some household bleaches, even when dilute, can damage carpets and fabrics, although they may be useful on tiles or stone floors.

Newspaper training works very well, especially if you do not have easy access to a garden. In that case, you can put the paper at the door or even out on the terrace or balcony, but be aware that small puppies can squeeze through railings and may fall.

Sleeping partners. Photo: Tracy Morgan

If you do have a garden, stay with the puppy and praise it when it performs. If you want the dogs to use a particular part of the garden, carry the puppy there each time. This will save the lawn from burn marks caused by urine. You will need to keep this area very clean; dogs hate dirty places. I remember trying to get my dogs through the gate of one of those 'dog loos' in a park. They were horrified and tip-toed and jumped, and nothing would get them to perform.

You will always be required to clean up after your dog in any public place. A scoop and plastic bags are the answer, and very often special bins are provided by the local council. Failing to clean up is not only anti-social and an irritant to the non-pet-owning public, but also a real health hazard. The spreading of Toxocara infections, which can cause blindness in children (see chapter 11), is quite unacceptable. In some places, fines are becoming quite punitive, £500 being the current maximum in some London boroughs.

You need to realise that few puppies are completely house-trained before they are six or seven months old, and some take longer. If they get excited or are playing hard they tend to forget, and mishaps occur. Even the newspaper training is not fool-proof. Many a time have I found the puppy looking angelic, with front legs on the paper and a large puddle appearing on the floor behind it. Should you catch your pup in the act, speak severely, but not harshly, and remove the puppy outside or on to its newspaper at once.

Never get angry with the puppy, and certainly never smack or follow the barbarous old wives' remedy of rubbing the puppy's nose in it. This has no value whatever; the puppy cannot possibly understand, and it is very confusing and unkind. If you discover a puddle or mess, it is already too late, as puppies have no long-term memory and will not understand why you are cross. There are key times when a puppy should go out, such as after meals and playtimes, first thing in the morning and last thing at night.

If you are plainly getting nowhere by the time your puppy is six months old, it is wise to check with your vet. Sometimes, though fairly rarely, there is a defect that involves urine by-passing the bladder and causing incontinence. This requires correction by surgery.

Dogs are naturally clean, and Irish Terriers are particularly fussy and, even as puppies, can get very embarrassed and ashamed after a puddle has appeared. Praise enthusiastically whenever they manage to 'score' in the right place. When you hear yourself saying, "But you've only just come in!", you can be quite sure we've all said that before.

The garden

If you are a proud gardener you will need to make a few compromises with your puppy. Irish Terriers love to dig and bury things, and a nicely dug flower bed would appear an ideal spot. Having said that, my dogs have never liked being alone in the garden and will remain there only if I am gardening or relaxing. They are interested in everything, and you will need to watch that the shed, with its string, slug pellets and weedkiller, is kept locked, or that the dangerous things are well out of reach.

Everything is fair game for a puppy, and flying flowerpots tossed into the air or disappearing gardening gloves are considered good sport. There are so many things *not* to do that it's almost easier to relax and give up the garden for a summer.

You will need to be very careful about fencing, as a hole is an open invitation to squeeze through or under, and older puppies have been known to dig their way out. Grown dogs can jump extraordinarily high, and a low wicket gate is no problem to clear. A two-metre fence is recommended.

You will need a spring on the gate to close it and a very secure catch. A clever terrier has no trouble learning to open a gate. A *Please Close The Gate* sign is a good idea, as it is a reminder at least to your visitors.

If your puppy escapes and runs off, it is in mortal danger, mainly from traffic, but also from thieves. Remember too that it will not have full protection from the inoculation programme at first. Sadly, puppies are not infrequently stolen from gardens, so it is necessary to be vigilant at all times. Never go out and leave a puppy in the garden – it is inviting disaster.

Other serious hazards in a garden are ponds, ornamental pools and swimming pools. Dogs are good swimmers, but a puppy unable to scramble out would become exhausted and terrified and drown very quickly. A frozen pond is lethal too, as the puppy may venture out across the ice and fall through, with fatal consequences. Small children are in danger as well, and every garden pond or swimming pool should have a mesh netting cover or be securely fenced off.

Irish Terriers are active dogs who need outside exercise.

Feeding time

Feed the puppy separately at first. The older dogs will certainly realise that the puppy is being fed (they're not fools) but don't let them see the more frequent meal times. It will appear to them as unfair favouring with titbits. If they do see, you could hand out a biscuit to everybody first for decency's sake.

When they are eventually fed together, stick to a routine so that each knows the correct order, starting with the oldest dog. Keep the bowls well apart and never allow one

"But I thought you *wanted* me to help with the gardening!"

83

Make sure your boundaries are secure.

dog to approach another during feeding. A sharp reprimand is required immediately. A puppy approaching an older dog's bowl would almost certainly be in trouble, and this should never be allowed to happen. Meal times should be peaceful, without any need to bolt the food before another gets it.

My dogs have always had to sit and give a paw before the bowl is set down. I dislike hectic feeding times with dogs barking and leaping up. It always seems very bad manners and can lead to squabbles and upsets. On the whole, bitches and neutered dogs are more tolerant, but much depends on the individual temperament.

In the car

The car can provide another flash point. Once an older dog has leapt in and is sitting tight, he will very likely challenge a younger dog who leaps in afterwards.

Keep the dogs separate to begin with. Put the puppy in its cage or restrain it on a seat. Well designed harnesses are a help. As the puppy grows, and you want the dogs to travel together, lift the puppy in first and hold its head away as the older dog leaps in. This avoids a mistaken challenge by the pup. Soon the joy of an outing will far outweigh the need to bicker.

Sleep

Puppies sleep deeply and can be startled and frightened if woken up suddenly. This is especially so if they have tucked themselves away under a chair or bed and have to be pulled out. It is best to get down to their level and call them first as a warning.

Generally, when a dog has put itself to bed and is properly bedded down it is best not to disturb it. Dogs can be very territorial about their beds, and another dog or small child should be warned off.

Children

Most children are thrilled to have a puppy, but they do need to be supervised at first. The big lesson for some is that puppies are not animated teddy bears, but living creatures like themselves. Puppies need to be treated with care and respect and not mauled about, squeezed or sat upon. It is essential that you are around at first to prevent puppy and child from coming to harm.

Irish Terriers are born to the role of family dog. They usually dote on the children and I have always been very touched to see the awestruck pleasure with which the new family baby is received by the dogs. This too is a situation that needs sensitive handling, with a proper introduction and care not to leave the baby alone with the dogs at first. Bitches especially may try to lick, but Irish Terriers, with their deep, instinctive love of children, will rarely be far away from the young of the household.

Playtime

Time and space for playing is for puppies, as for all young growing creatures, a vital part of their development. They become stronger and more in control of their limbs and practise all the movement skills of the mature dog; walking, running, jumping, pouncing, escaping, climbing, getting up and down – it's all there. They learn about their environment and become properly socialised, knowing their own strength and when to stop. Irish Terriers are inveterate players, and even the old dogs will often chase and gambol about.

The trouble with puppies is that playtime can get rather rough. Small children can be knocked over and furniture sent flying unless a little care is taken. For the most part, children understand rough and tumble (after all, they do it themselves) and it seems to be part of the intense bonding between child and puppy.

Puppies, especially when teething, can nip, or even hang on to small garments. A light tap on the nose or a firm 'Leave!' or 'No!' is usually enough to persuade them to let go. Giving up a toy is one of the first lessons. It does not come easily to terriers, as they do love a good tug-of-war. Kneel down facing the pup and hold the precious shoe or any other unsuitable 'toy'. Try to ease it away – you may be lucky! – and don't forget to praise the pup's generosity. The puppy must not be allowed to bounce back at a toy, as you could have your fingers caught by mistake in the process. Again, use a sharp "No!" to deter the puppy.

Sometimes, instead of making a grand gesture of principle, it is easier to divert the pup by offering another toy. One that squeaks is a good bet.

Do not allow a pup to hop or dance on its hind legs – it could hurt itself. Irish Terriers hate having their feet squeezed or tugged, and may be provoked into snapping if this is done.

Some Irish Terriers will retrieve, but more as an invitation to continue the game than with any idea of parting with the toy. But they can learn almost anything.

It is safer to leave an exhausted pup who has had a long playtime and is therefore far less likely to embark on a project (such as chewing up the carpet) and more likely to be ready for a rest or sleep.

Chewing and digging

However many toys puppies may have, they do tend to chew anything to hand. If left alone for long, a puppy, or worse, two puppies can be very destructive – rugs, cushions, chair legs. It's done in fun, but is infuriating, expensive, and to be avoided if possible. When the teething stage is over, the need to chew eases off slightly, but that is no guarantee that they won't do so.

Digging with sharp little claws is another destructive habit. I've mentioned holes in the garden, but

All children together. Photo: Tracy Morgan

Recipe for delight: children and puppies.
Photo: Tracy Morgan

holes in the carpet are not unknown. Say "Who did that?" in a stern voice and take them to the scene of the crime. The message gets through eventually. Always try to leave the puppy where there are no soft furnishings and make sure there are no live electric wires, which could be chewed and cause death by electrocution. Put away shoes, gloves, hats, and tennis racquets.

Routine

Young puppies, at least at first, are best kept within a daily routine. They should be fed at the same times and not have to wait, fretting and hungry. They will soon recognise the household routines: walks, playtimes, children coming home from school and other family members coming home from work, and even Sundays when the extended family arrives. Even as puppies, Irish Terriers are sociable and soon recognise, love and welcome enthusiastically anyone who comes to the house regularly: the daily help, the gardener, and the window cleaner.

Barking

Irish Terriers love to be into everything, meet everyone and know what is going on. Shut away, they will grow restless and unhappy and probably bark and make a thorough nuisance of themselves. They have a wonderful, deep bark, and are not yappers for the sake of yapping. You will soon be able to recognise the different barks and their meanings, from the tiresome "I'm bored!" to the urgent "Someone we don't know is about!". They have acute hearing and grow up to be instinctive and fearless guard dogs.

Walks

As mentioned before, until your puppy has completed the immunisation course there must be absolutely no walks outside the gardens and no meetings with dogs other than your own house dogs. The hazards you will be likely to meet when you first venture out with your puppy are dealt with in detail in chapter 8 under **Out and About.**

Do not over-walk your puppy. It is not good for the joints, and puppies are far better playing and resting in their own time. It is unnecessarily unkind and potentially harmful to drag an exhausted puppy along a pavement. You may well find yourself having to carry your puppy home amidst a throng of outraged on-lookers.

Two lovely puppies.

In Conclusion…

You may now be wondering why on earth anyone ever has a puppy in the house, but take heart – the unruly phase does pass and the moments of anxiety or exasperation are far outweighed by the sheer joy of having a lively, wicked and endearing puppy who will love and entertain the whole family for a lifetime. This is described in my poem below, which I have simply called

Love Song

How do I love you
My little brown dog
So sweetly asleep in my hand
I love you like springtime and dew on the grass
And honey and bluebells and angels that pass
My dear little, soft little lamb

How do I love you
My wild brown pup
So wicked and wayward and bold
I love you with laughter and fury and fear
I've called till I'm hoarse, but still you don't hear
Why will you not do as you're told?

How do I love you
My clever brown dog
So much in charge of my day
I love you with wonder and awe and respect
You watch every move and you never forget
You know every step of the way.

How do I love you
My wise old dog
So courageously facing the end
I love you with sadness and joy and regret
But the gleam in your eye says there's life for us yet
My beloved, my funny old friend

How do I love you
My brown spirit dog
I still hear your foot on the stair
I'll love you forever, you're part of my soul
Till the sun melts the sky and the moon turns to gold
I know you will always be there.

Lucy Jackson
July 1998

Chapter Eight

Care and Basic Training

Irish Terriers love to live in close contact with their families and absorb a great deal of household behaviour without being taught directly. Rather in the way that some working breeds have an instinct for herding or retrieving, Irish Terriers seem instinctively to fit in with their families and know exactly what each member is about. They have a great facility for understanding words and will recognise their own and everyone else's names very quickly. Most owners confess to resorting to spelling words or even speaking French if they don't want the dogs to understand.

A family party.

Irish Terriers, however, are not naturally obedient; they are not programmed to take instructions. After all, you need to be a free thinker to catch a rat or a rabbit, not wait to be told what to do. They get bored easily, but they love to please you and, with lots of praise and time, will learn almost anything. Individuals vary considerably in their aptitude, but no terrier should be expected to behave instantly like a guard or police dog.

Irish Terriers often come up with tricks of their own. One of ours always selected a toy from her box when friends came. She would walk stiffly up and down, head held high, parading it for all to see and making a soft, growling sound. It was not for giving up, but only to show and, after much clapping and praise, she would walk out on tip-toes, deposit it somewhere and rush back, wagging her tail and delighted with herself.

"Is it time to go out yet?"

Irish Terriers love to live in close contact with their families.

Name

To begin with, repeat the puppy's name clearly whenever you are talking to him: "Come here, Jack" – "Sit, Blarney." If you decide on an older dog, it is best to keep the original name, but Irish Terriers have no problem in learning a new one, especially if you say both names together: Jack Rufus or Blarney Rose.

Voice

Tone of voice is important when training puppies. Don't be too stern over little misdemeanours, which are probably just due to high spirits, or you will have nothing left for the real crimes. Keep your strict voice for the chewed carpet or hole in the lawn.

Basic Commands

Practising the following simple commands should be a part of the pup's everyday routine. Let it be part of his playtime and make sure that everyone in the family can manage him. It should always be fun for him, and can help to build the great bond of trust and affection. Praise is the key, so say "Clever boy" effusively whenever he gets it right.

Keep it up, with short learning sessions three or four times a day. Do not become over-enthusiastic and set goals and targets to compete with the pup next door. Just like children, puppies need time to develop and understand things at their own individual paces.

Sit

Irish Terriers need to learn the important command, Sit. It is the first lesson in obedience and is essential in controlling an excitable puppy.

My experience with Irish Terriers is that they like best to stand or lie down and will never sit for hours like gundogs. However, they *will* learn to sit, especially if their bowl of food is used as encouragement.

Call your puppy at dinner time and, placing your hands on his hindquarters, push down gently, saying "Sit". When he sits, praise him and give him his dinner. You can train him with special titbits following the same idea.

Lie down

You can go from Sit to Lie Down. It requires great patience, so keep the lessons short and never get cross. Make him sit and gently pull his legs forwards so that his body goes down. Say "Lie down." He'll probably roll over and play at first, but will eventually get the idea.

Stand

If you are considering showing your pup, it is a good idea to teach him to stand 'correctly' right from the start. Stand astride him and, lifting him up under his chest, place his front legs straight and in line with his shoulders. Ease them forward so that his hind legs are stretched out slightly and try to keep his head facing front. He will not stand for long, but encourage him, saying "Steady", "Stand", or any word you choose.

No

As your puppy grows he (or she) will probably become rather more rough and exuberant. She will almost certainly jump up to greet anyone and everyone, standing on her hind legs and trying to get her nose up to their faces. This can be a hazard to older people, and children too can be knocked over. Quite apart from muddy feet and scratching claws, cups can be sent flying and drinks spilled.

This behaviour has to be discouraged, kindly but firmly. Hold shoulders in both hands and push her down, saying "No!" very sternly. Try to make her sit quietly for a few moments, and praise her at once when she does. It is not easy, especially as she is expressing her joy, exuberance and affection for you, so you must not react too harshly.

"We're sitting!"

Come

Some people like to train their dogs to a whistle, which you can buy in a pet or gun shop. The dog is usually intrigued by the sound and comes running to you. Praise her for coming, pat her and make a fuss – "Good dog!" You can use the whistle to play a game, pretending to run away. The puppy will be frantic to follow you. I have never used a whistle, but I have a high-pitched call and can whistle pretty loudly through my teeth.

Playing hide-and-seek is an excellent way to make a pup come to your call. Ask someone to hold her, and run away and hide. Call loudly from your hiding place and she will be most anxious to seek you out. Make it fun, and tell her how good and clever she is to have found you.

If you intend to show your dog, it is a good idea to teach him to 'stand' from the start, as demonstrated here by Breezy Mr Blarney.

Give

You need a word that means 'give up or release something from your mouth instantly'. Hold the pup's cheeks just below her ears and, facing her, say "Give" firmly and open her mouth, removing the object. It is important, as it could be anything from your best shoe to a duckling. Praise her as soon as she complies.

All terriers chew, but make sure your puppy knows what *not* to chew and will give it up to you.

Dogs can be very possessive about their toys, and older dogs especially need to be approached with care. Children need to understand this, and it should be one of the strict rules of the household.

Hand Signals (With Voice)

Hand signals can be introduced as the puppy gets older. Start by using the word and hand signal together.

The gesture my dogs understand best is a wide sweep of the hand, which means, "Come round to the side, I'm not unlocking the back door again yet."

Sit

Sit should be reinforced with a downward gesture, with the flat hand pointing towards him.

Lie down

Lie Down is the same gesture, but with the dog in a sitting position.

Come

Come should be accompanied by a beckoning gesture towards your chest.

Stay

Stay is a difficult one. When your dog has learned to sit on command, take a step backwards, facing her. Hold up your index finger and say "Stay" firmly. If she sits still, take another step back and repeat the command. If she follows you at once, gently take her back to the same spot and try again. She may simply amble off, in which case it is probably sensible to try again later.

Hand Signals (Without Voice)

Terriers can become bored very quickly with the same routine every day, so it is a help to introduce variations. You can begin to train your Irish Terrier to hand signals only, having first removed her lead. Do not attempt this outside your garden until she is properly trained. You will probably have to reinforce hand commands with the appropriate vocal commands at first but, once she has mastered Sit, you can proceed to Stay, and then to Come, using the hand signals described in the previous section.

Never forget to praise your dog when she comes towards you and sits in front of you. Your praise is entirely what motivates her to obey you.

Lead Training

The early lessons should be kept short and frequent. Be gentle and full of praise and remember that the aim is to walk your dog, even in the show ring, on a loose, not a tight, lead. Titbits as rewards are not a good idea as they can prove distracting. A clever terrier will want to empty your pockets before she will begin to concentrate on anything you are trying to teach her. Try not to over-excite the puppy with too much praise. A pat or stoke on the head or back and a quiet, encouraging voice are all that she needs or should expect.

If you have more than one dog, hold both or all the leads in your left hand, leaving your right hand free. A lead held in each hand makes for tangles and will probably trip you up. You can have a single lead with two ends, but these are probably more suitable for small dogs. Roll the lead's slack around your hand to shorten it, and always keep the loop around your wrist.

Collar

As I said in the last chapter, it is a good idea to get your puppy accustomed to wearing a very small collar when she is small enough not to notice it. I made a great mistake with one of my puppies. It was at the time of the parvovirus epidemic, and she was kept playing only in the garden until she was four months old. When we eventually set out for a proper walk in the park, for which she needed to wear a collar and lead, she protested for days. She hated her collar and rolled and scratched. I was exasperated, but I had left it too late. We had to start at the beginning, with her wearing it for only short periods, and she gradually became accustomed to the idea and stopped trying to remove it.

Leads

Attaching the lead to the collar can, for some pups, be a signal to leap about and play. They often hold the leads in their mouths, shaking and chewing hard. You have to give a firm "No!" and try to extricate the lead. Use another toy to attract the puppy if you are desperate.

Walking sensibly on a lead is important. It is most annoying, and potentially

"What's that? Is it worth chasing?"

dangerous, to have a puppy lunging about. You may be tripped up or pulled over, especially on ice or slippery pavements.

When you first try to walk your pup on a lead he will almost certainly tug forwards or drag behind you, or even rear up. Try to steady him, placing him firmly on his four feet and always on your left-hand side. Hold the lead firmly, and wind it around your hand so that you have what is called a 'short lead'. This gives an immediate check on him, and you are less likely to lose the lead should he suddenly tug away. It sometimes helps to walk him along a wall or fence, or even along a path. This seems to focus him better.

Start walking with a steady stride and, if the pup pulls ahead, give him a sharp tug backwards and say, "Heel, Stop", steady him, and start again. If he lags behind, a sharp forward tug is required. Try to keep walking, but you may well have to stop and start, bending over to straighten him up firmly and kindly.

When he does manage a few good paces, try to urge him on,

Well trained Irish Terriers out for a walk.

saying quietly, "Good dog", "Clever boy", or any other words you have chosen. It is better not to praise him too much by stopping and fussing, as the intention is to move on without interrupting his rather fleeting concentration. Should he start to pull away, keep a firm hold on the lead; he will get the idea eventually.

Check or choke chain Never use a check or choke chain on a puppy. Incorrect fit and unskilled use can lead to serious injuries. It can also be frightening and painful, especially when a young puppy is still being obstreperous.

In unskilled hands, these curbs can be very cruel. Use one badly on a highly intelligent terrier and you will receive nothing but outrage and opposition – *never* submission.

A check used with care on an older dog can, however, be useful. You need someone experienced to show you exactly how to use it. The loop of the chain that you attach to the lead should be uppermost, so that it grips and tightens around the dog's neck when he pulls away and is released immediately when he stops tugging. There is only a momentary check and brief discomfort. If it is incorrectly fitted (and you need to remove his own collar first) it will not release and could choke and panic the dog.

Check chains come in various sizes and lengths. The rule of thumb is to measure the dog's head under the chin and round the ears and add 5cm (2in) for the correct length of chain.

Check chains make a horrible, clanking sound and I would never use one on a terrier. Remember, too, that terriers do not carry much padding around their necks, so quickly choke, cough and become distressed if tugged and pulled. Once you fret and worry your dog it can take a very long time to sort him out again. Tell him exactly what you want and, as always, the light approach works best.

Unfortunately, check chains and choke collars were made popular as a training aid for problem dogs by a certain television personality. No lively young terrier should be considered a problem simply for being lively. You are far more likely to create rather than solve a problem by the harsh and clumsy use of these chains and leads.

Slip collars Slip collars are kinder than check chains, but work on the same principle. They are made of strong fabric (usually nylon) with a metal ring at each end, one of which attaches to the lead. They grip the neck firmly like the check chain but at least do not make a clanking noise and 'bite' less fiercely.

'Halter-type' curbs Another curb lead that is becoming increasingly popular goes over the dog's head and around his mouth. The pressure, should he pull away, is on the head, not the neck. At least it will not choke the dog, but again, with perseverance and kindness, should not be necessary in training a willing and clever terrier.

Kerb Drill

Once your puppy is walking well on the lead, start to introduce the idea of kerb drill. Encourage him to sit on command and "Wait" as if you were waiting to cross the road. Say "Walk" as you move forward and then "Heel" if he moves too far ahead. Introduce the idea of "Stand," meaning 'stand still,' at this stage, too. It will prove useful if you intend to show him later on.

Classes

There are professional trainers around, but these are much more costly than joining a local dog training class. It is sometimes thought that, while your puppy may behave like an

Irish Terriers are not 'naturals' at obedience competition, but some do well.

angel with his trainer, he will still be unruly when out with you. In any case, training him yourself will foster the deep bonding between you.

It is sensible to find out about local training classes before you are ready to join. They are very helpful and popular, and there may well be a waiting list. It is also a good idea to look in first without your puppy to see exactly how they are organised. That way, at least one of you would be less astonished to begin with. You can obtain a list of classes, with necessary telephone numbers, from The Kennel Club, your vet, your local library or the pet shop.

It is fun for your pup to meet other dogs at the classes and learn to socialise without becoming over-excited every time he sees a friend. You will probably enjoy meeting the other dog owners, too. All my dogs have had lasting puppyhood friends. My own dog-walking chums have always been a very special part of my life and there is a huge mutual support through the inevitable adventures and eventual sadness of losing your dog.

At a dog training class you will work with your dog within the group of owners and dogs. It can be noisy, and you will probably go home exhausted after the first few classes. Try to persevere, unless your pup is rather shy (not usual in Irish Terriers) and finds it all rather unnerving. In this case, you would probably be better training him – or, more probably, *her* – at home.

Agility

When you have both mastered the basic training, you could well go on to other areas of training. Agility work is often on offer as part of the local dog training programme, but you may have to go on to a specialist club for this. I often think that Irish Terriers have more natural ability for this sort of activity. There is usually a simple course with a tunnel, jumps, hurdles, balance and a slide. There are other variations and more difficult obstacles. You have to be fairly energetic and fit to keep up with a dog, but it can be great fun for you both.

Dill demonstrates that Irish Terriers have a natural ability for agility work.

There are also competitions that you can enter, at a local or even county level, and this could be an on-going interest and enormous bond between you. However, you do *both* have to enjoy the excitement and competitive side of it. Always be sure not to spoil the fun by being too desperate to win. Keep a sense of humour, especially with Irish Terriers, who often manage to come up with a few surprises.

Learning to cope with the see-saw.

At Home

What you decide is suitable behaviour for your dog in your own home is entirely up to you. Do try, however, to be consistent and, once the rules are set, to keep to them, as you would for children; it is very confusing if you keep changing them. It is tempting to allow puppies on beds and chairs only to change your mind as they grow older. This is unfair. Begging for titbits from the table may seem rather cute from a small pup but is totally unacceptable from a grown dog who keeps trying to sit on your lap or put his paws up on the table.

I have to say, however, that with Irish Terriers, even the best-disciplined puppy will try every trick in the book for the rest of his life to do what he finds comfortable or amusing – always in the nicest possible way. We had one who would tear the newspaper as it came through the door. It was not good household behaviour, but it made us laugh, as she would hide behind the sofa, wide-eyed and innocent, giving her "Who, me? Never!" look. She knew perfectly well it was

Good friends.

naughty, but the fun was worth it. As a breed, they're so funny and charming that is is difficult to be cross. Another of ours would push her nose up under my elbow in mock contrition as I was filling in holes she had dug in the garden: "It's me nature to dig," she would be saying.

It is quite unnecessary to become angry with a puppy. It is rather like having a lively, buoyant child whose energy and adventures you may as well enjoy, even if sometimes you have to pick up the pieces. If you are a control freak, an Irish Terrier is not for you.

Discipline

It should not be necessary to hit or even to smack your Irish Terrier, and certainly not as

Be very clear, right from the beginning, whether
your puppy is allowed on the bed.

Penmire Trixie demonstrates the importance of
creature comforts.

"Is it worth stealing?"

"You called?"

Digging for rabbits.

part of his everyday training. Irish Terriers are extremely intelligent and sensitive to your disapproval. However, rather like children, they need to know the limits and where and when your patience is likely to snap.

There are elaborate theories about never using your hand to smack. It seems the dog may become confused and unable to distinguish between a pat and a punishment. Irish Terriers, however, are not complete fools and, provided that the dog is confident in your affection, he will understand exactly what you are cross about and decide next time whether it is worth another try!

A tap with a rolled-up newspaper is another idea for showing extreme disapproval. I trained one of mine to walk through a field full of sheep by brandishing one at her every time she turned to look at a sheep. I daresay she would have learned just as quickly with a firm "No!" and a tug on the lead.

The most effective punishment for real misconduct, such as unpacking a box of groceries for the second time in a week and strewing cornflakes, sugar, butter and biscuits everywhere, is to exclude them – "Bad dogs, out!" This is what they hate most and it makes them contrite at once.

House Training

The house-training of puppies has been discussed at length in chapter 7, so I will not go over it again here.

Always make sure the boundaries to your property are secure.

Older dogs on reaching maturity do occasionally start lifting a leg around the house. It is, no doubt, some primitive urge to mark out territory, but it is quite intolerable and needs severe correction. A harsh voice and loud reprimand are quite in order, and an immediate and undignified exit through the back door. It is most unusual in Irish Terriers, but sometimes the arrival of a puppy or even a baby can set it off. Seek advice from your vet, who may suggest that neutering the dog could be the easy solution. It often works when training has failed.

In much older dogs, especially elderly, spayed bitches, you may have a problem of overnight incontinence. She is always acutely embarrassed, and it is very unfair to make a fuss about a wet bed she couldn't help. Deal with it by placing a layer of clean newspaper under an old towel or, better still, Vet Bed, and change it every morning. Be very tactful, as your elderly bitch will be far more contrite and put out than you can imagine. We had one who, at 16, had to be comforted and reassured to take away the look of absolute misery on her face whenever she awoke to find she had wet her bed.

Third Party Insurance and Medical Plan

We looked at the subject of insurance for when you first take your puppy home, but it is sensible to have something in place before you start to walk her out of the garden. Should the unthinkable happen and your dog cause an accident or injury, you may well be held legally responsible for any injury or loss sustained. Check with your insurance company that your household insurance policy provides you with third-party liability in this event.

It is sensible today to have a pet medical insurance plan. Veterinary fees can be catastrophically high and, although routine inoculations and check-ups are not covered, it is an enormous help in the case of sudden illness or an accident. Your vet will provide you with details, or you may make the arrangement directly with the company (see also chapters 7 and 11).

Walks

At about three months, when his immunisation programme has taken effect, you need to take your puppy out into the big, wide world. Some puppies are a little shy and need to be reassured at first, and possibly picked up and comforted. Most Irish Terrier pups, however, are bursting to get out, and you need to keep a sensible control on the excitement.

You will have taught him already to walk on the lead. Make sure he understands, keeping him on your left side. Do not let him off the lead to begin with. This would invite disaster. Take things in easy stages, as he needs to learn about traffic and how to approach other dogs. You can graduate to using a retractable lead, which gives more scope for him to play, but keeps him safe and close to you.

You will probably find that all the careful training in the garden has suddenly been forgotten. Every blade of grass will be sniffed, and every lamppost inspected. You need to be very firm, and to establish that walking on the lead means *actually moving forward*. Urge him on, saying "Leave" if he stops to sniff for too long.

You have to reach a compromise. It is amazingly new and exciting for him, and walking should only happen in short burst. Try not to tug and get at odds with each other. You do not want your pup sitting on his haunches, throwing his head about and pulling in the opposite direction. It is better to pick him up and calm him before trying again.

You will have plenty of advice from passers-by; we all love to stop and talk to a puppy. This is not good for discipline, but excellent for fostering the Irish Terrier's instinctive love of human beings. It is sensible to begin somewhere quiet, where there may be fewer distractions and less traffic about. It would be foolhardy to go shopping at this stage and, in any case, many shops do not admit dogs. No puppy should ever be left tied outside a shop. It is unsafe, possibly terrifying, for the puppy, and puppies are not infrequently stolen.

"You'd think somebody could take me for a walk!" says Sorley Boy.

Be absolutely sure that your puppy will return to you before you allow him off the lead. He needs to be clear about traffic and crossing roads (see **Kerb Drill**). To begin with, you can arrive home a nervous wreck, having watched your puppy streak away with

Irish Terriers in a landscape.

A group of Irish Terriers doing what come naturally.

another dog, disrupt a game of football or invade a picnic. Most people are kind about puppies, but by no means all. You need to be watchful and apologetic when things go wrong. Recent adverse publicity about dangerous dogs has not helped. Try to keep a cool head if you can. I have caught many a puppy on the loose and discovered the owner in tears, searching dementedly. It can be a very frightening experience, and we know that pups can get lost. Be careful, and be prepared.

Your pup will have to learn not to dash up to other dogs and expect an instant welcome. There is a code of behaviour among dogs, as among people, and sometimes an exuberant pup has to learn a few painful lessons.

If your puppy is frightened or, worse still, nipped by another dog, he may run off shrieking and in panic. Try to catch him at once and close his muzzle with your hand to stop the noise. Puppies can be prone to hysteria if badly frightened, and the noise they make alarms them even more. Comfort him by holding him close and speaking in a reassuring voice. If the aggression towards your pup is anything more than a nip, it needs to be reported at once to the police. They will give suitable warnings, and procedures such as muzzling may be put in place. This is a most unusual occurrence, but you need to be wary.

Having said all this, there is no doubt that every dog loves to be exercised off the lead. It is the ultimate joy to run about, trail behind, meet other dogs, 'talk' to friends, explore, and sniff every corner of the landscape. Even more than dinner, it is the long-awaited high spot of the day. Irish Terriers, with their streak of independence and intense curiosity about everyone and everything, need this valuable time to decide things for themselves and perform as free agents, which is how they function best. But do not rush it. You need to be confident that your pup will respond to the basic commands, "Sit", "Stay" and, above all, "Come". This is where being trained to a whistle is useful, as dogs can hear it from a considerable distance. Try to find a quiet place where there is not much traffic and there are not too many other dogs. It is wise to remove the lead towards the end of the walk rather than the beginning. Quietly undo the hook or pull the slip lead over his head. The same applies whether you have a pup or a newly-acquired older dog. Call him back to you frequently, especially if he disappears, reminding him to sit at your left side or simply patting and praising him for returning.

Irish Terriers very quickly give you the feeling that they are in charge and taking you for a walk. Any small interruption is immediately supervised. If you sit down or stop to greet a friend or watch a bird, an anxious face appears immediately with the "What's up with you?" look. I once tripped over a stile and even now, after 10 years, the dogs still rush back to stand by while I make a safe descent. They will persuade you to choose the route of their choice and put off the moment to return home with every delaying tactic. However, all that lies ahead – you will need some time of very careful training to make sure your puppy is safely in hand.

Keep a large towel handy or, if it is cold and wet, one of those zip-up dog bags is useful. My dogs have never liked them, probably because their legs feel tied but, when the mud is dry, you can shake out the mud and launder

Waiting at the style.

them easily. They are also useful in the car as they stop the dirt from flying about when the dogs shake themselves. By the way, when your dog shakes instinctively, say the word "Shake" and praise him immediately. He will soon learn to shake on command, so the worst mud will be removed before he gets into the car.

Hazards of the countryside

Livestock If you are in the country, keep well away from sheep or any livestock and game birds. Farmers have every right to shoot a dog for pestering sheep or other animals and, in any case, you could be prosecuted and fined. Quite apart from the financial loss you may incur, it is extremely cruel and irresponsible to cause alarm and pain to domesticated animals that can neither escape nor defend themselves.

Water Some terriers dislike water, and most hate the rain and even tiptoe gingerly across grass wet with a heavy dew. Nevertheless, many are excellent swimmers and will sea bathe or paddle into rivers or ponds. Be absolutely certain that the water is safe and unpolluted. Some lakes contain algae that are dangerously

Irish Terriers like water sports, but make sure the water is not polluted.

Your dogs will enjoy the family holiday.

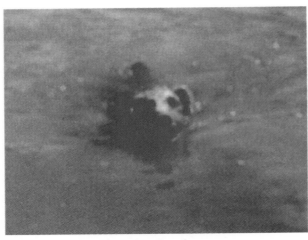

The swimming champ.

poisonous to dogs. The sea has tides and currents, and canals have steep sides that are real hazards. Check carefully before you allow your dog into any water at all; you will not be popular if the area is for fishermen who may be disturbed.

In winter, a fall through ice into freezing water can very quickly prove fatal. Avoid any possibility of accidents on ice. No terrier has the fat on its body to withstand the cold for long.

Rolling All dogs occasionally indulge in the maddening trick of rolling in the foulest smelling things they can find. It seems to happen most often when they have been bathed and stripped and are looking particularly clean and smart. Horse dung, cow pats and dead rabbits all provide delightful possibilities for rolling. It is a very primitive urge that has never been fully explained. You need to be watchful and severe in your disapproval. If there is no suitable water to hand, wrap your dog up and hose him down or wash him in a bucket when you get home. He will hate that and, with many muttered curses from you and a little luck, you may avoid repetitions.

Bitches on heat

To walk your bitch in a public place when she is on heat is a serious nuisance to other dog owners. Sprays and deodorants provide only the mildest protection and you are quite likely to attract a whole battalion of admirers This may frighten or, worse still, attract your bitch, who may well be looking for a mate. You can get into a dreadful muddle with other dog owners, who will be furious, fights between dogs can occur, and you may even have an embarrassing and unwanted mating. If you must take her out, always take a stout stick to wave off the admirers and try to go out when there will be few dogs about – early morning is ideal. You may have dogs hanging around the gate and being thorough nuisances. The proverbial bucket of cold water is a good deterrent.

Male dogs may take off in pursuit if they scent a bitch on heat. You may have a few seconds to catch them when you see them sniffing excitedly on the ground and scenting the air. Trying to catch them is infuriating and exhausting and can be very dangerous if there are busy roads to cross. A neutered dog is a much safer pet, and many vets recommend neutering as standard practice for dogs who are not to be used at stud.

Aggression and socialising

There should be no problem at all when your dog meets other dogs, especially if he has been to a dog training class. It is good for all dogs to have friends they know, but there is always the odd dog that can be aggressive.

Generally, when dogs meet, they tend to walk around each other, rather stiff legged. There is usually a fair amount of sniffing at rear ends. Most encounters end there but, if the dog should challenge yours, his hackles (hair on the back) will rise and he will snarl and show his teeth. Unfortunately, Irish Terriers will seldom back down, so you are probably in for a scuffle.

It is essential to avoid these confrontations as far as possible. Irish Terriers will never forget or forgive. The same dog seen again, or sometimes even the same breed, will draw a feisty response. You have to be clever and spot the 'enemy' first. Put your dog back on the lead, call to the other dog's owner and wave your stick. Insist on walking on and have no nonsense. Avoidance is the better part of valour, and it is extremely tiresome to find yourself with a dog who thinks that fighting is an acceptable sport. You need to be absolutely adamant that you will not tolerate quarrels. They are an absolute nuisance and can get you into real trouble with other dog owners.

Entire dogs are more likely to be aggressive towards each other, but the odd assertive bitch is not unknown. Dogs and bitches rarely fight one another.

Should a fight occur, you will have to intervene and be very careful not to get bitten. Use the lead as a noose over your dog's head and pull him away. If the other dog should attack again, use your stick, your boot and and a very loud voice. Most dog owners understand the form and will rush up to deal with their own dogs.

It is extremely rare to have a fight, but it can be unnerving if you have never had one before. Keep a cool head and be thoroughly assertive in your disapproval to all parties. I would not walk any dog without carrying a stick. Even if it is never used, it can have the desired effect of enforcing general tolerance and good manners.

Should you sit down on a bench for long, have a picnic or spread out a rug or towel, most terriers will immediately establish a 'camp' that needs to be defended. Ours have always had to be tethered to prevent them from dashing out to chase away 'intruders', which does not make for a peaceful picnic.

Chasing

Young dogs sometimes chase after joggers and cyclists out of pure playfulness. This must be discouraged before it becomes a habit. You may have to resort to walking your dog on the lead again, pointing out each time he tugs that this is not in order. Make him sit and say "No, no!" as the jogger passes you.

Games of football or cricket, other people's picnics, school parties or outdoor karate classes are all of great interest to the sociable Irish Terrier. Mine have always loved small children and stop to inspect every pram and buggy. You have to steer your way through these encounters. Most people, especially the elderly, are pleased to stop and talk and your dog will be doing a great social favour. However, you will find the odd person who dislikes dogs. Remove your dog quickly and try to be apologetic. Your dog being friendly and sociable is not direct disobedience, but can try your patience sometimes.

Cars

Even before her immunisation programme is complete, it is safe to take your puppy out for short rides in the car. This gets her used to going out of the house and garden, and also to the motion of the car. We have already discussed the need for a towel, water and kitchen paper to cope with emergencies.

Most dogs get used to the car and love to ride or sit and wait in it. It is an excellent place from which to watch the world go by.

Travel sickness

Some puppies are very travel sick, especially if they have just been fed, but a short car ride each day helps to accustom them to the motion. Take a friend with you to hold your puppy, or put her in her cage. Should the sickness persist, your vet may prescribe a travel sickness remedy. You may find that giving it to her earlier than the prescription suggests makes the cure more effective. Do not scold her for being sick; it is not something she can control, and you will then end up with an adult who hates cars. This can be a great nuisance. Try to combine a short car ride with a long walk, so that she begins to associate the car with pleasure and fun. This will encourage her to get over her sickness.

It is never sensible to leave young dogs, especially puppies, alone in the car. They may become anxious and set about tearing or soiling the uphostery.

Barking in the car

Barking in the car can be a nuisance with Irish Terriers. They have a strong guarding instinct and are great protectors of property. Anyone approaching the car will prompt noisy barking. It can be distracting when they bark at every dog, horse, bicycle, or anything else in the street they choose as a token enemy. It is difficult to stop them, as they know very well that, when you are driving, you are too occupied to check them. It helps if they are in their wire cages, but for short trips not everyone uses these.

Severe disapproval is necessary. You have to stop the car – at which point they realise at once that they are in trouble, and silence reigns. It is not an easy problem to solve. If someone else is driving you can keep your dog under better control and, should she bark, use your harshest voice of disapproval. I have even resorted to saying the dreaded "Outside!" – the word of dismissal they hate most. While the threat is hardly likely to be carried out, it does silence them.

Barking is more a problem with two dogs than with one. Dogs, like children, pick up each other's worst habits and, once introduced to the idea, they keep it up for fun.

Heat

Summer heat, or direct sunshine at any time of the year, can lead to an overheated car, with fatal and tragic results. We all have our own horror stories of distressed dogs left in cars. Every year there are prosecutions, but this does not help the pitiful animal collapsed and panting inside a locked car. It can happen very quickly, and a few centimetres of open window is little if any help. Conversely, young puppies left in cars in winter may become ill with a severe chill when the temperature drops.

Note that estate cars are cooler than hatchbacks, as the sloping hatchback window attracts the heat and the car can become a deadly furnace. Take some old blankets or bedspreads, or even large, old towels, and throw them right over the car, especially where the dog or dogs are sitting. This helps to keep the car cooler.

Another excellent tip is to wrap your dog in a wet towel if he is becoming overheated. This is a life-saver for old dogs, stopping the panting and distress almost immediately. You can top up the moisture with more water, and cover up his head and ears for maximum benefit. This is probably not advisable if you are about to show him, but for me the dog's comfort and well-being should always be the first concern.

Keep a bowl and a bottle of fresh water in the car (a plastic two-litre screw-top milk bottle is ideal) and always give your dog a drink after a long, hot walk. It is wise, especially with older dogs, not to venture out during the hottest times of the day; early mornings and evenings are best.

Restraint

Experiments have shown that we are all safer when travelling with fastened seat belts. It is now considered necessary and safer to restrain dogs with a seat belt, harness or wire cage. The use of a harness may soon become law. Dogs should never be allowed to move or leap about, as they may then distract you and cause an accident. Should an accident happen, any unrestrained dog would be catapulted through the windscreen or thrown about inside the car, which would almost certainly be fatal. If you have a hatchback or estate car, you can have bars or a mesh fitted to keep your dog off the front seats. Some people like to have a matching mesh guard at the back, preventing the dog from jumping out as you lift and open up the door.

Seat covers

Seat covers made of a strong, waterproof fabric are available, and you can buy them at shows and large pet shops. These covers fit over and tuck into the car seats, preventing hair and mud from getting everywhere. They can be removed, shaken out and washed very easily.

Buses and Trains

You may need to use public transport at some stage. Do not attempt any long journey until your dog is safely house-trained. Make sure, before you set out, that the chosen transport will carry dogs. Most buses allow dogs, but you may well have to lift your dog on to the step and make sure she is not a nuisance to anyone. She is probably safer on your lap.

Be very careful indeed on the underground or anywhere that has escalators. You will have to carry her on escalators, as dogs can get their feet caught, which can cause dreadful injuries.

Steps up into trains can be steep and dangerous, and often there is a yawing gap between the platform and first step. Take great care to lift or guide her upwards.

Air Travel

Should your dog need to travel by air, very specific procedures have to be followed. No pup under 12 weeks is accepted, and there is a mass of paperwork to put in order first. Your vet will advise you about immunisation certificates and the airline of your choice will provide export details, which need careful attention. Travel cages are made to specific measurements and purpose-built for air travel.

Sending your puppy abroad to a new home can be a heart-breaking experience and you need to prepare yourself carefully. It is of vital importance that you have direct contact with the person to whom you are sending your puppy. Make sure that the time of arrival is clearly understood and insist on a telephone call as soon as the pup has been collected.

I am still haunted by the pitiful sight of a very young Labrador bitch going around and around on the luggage carousel in Bogota airport. She had been sick all over the newspaper in the cage and had neither food nor water. I was very distressed and insisted they at least remove her from the carousel. We filled up her water bottle, but she was so unhappy, and had apparently been there for hours. I found out later that she was not collected until the next day. This should not happen to any dog – you must make watertight arrangements with the new owner.

Home Alone

There may be occasions when you have to leave your puppy alone. It should not be for more than an hour or two when she is very young, as any young creature hates to be left. Train her from the start to spend a little time on her own, even if you are only in the next room. Make sure she is well exercised before you leave, as she is far more likely to settle down and sleep if she is tired. Leave some toys and chews to amuse her. Her water bowl should always be full. Some people think that leaving a radio on makes a dog think someone is still around.

Confine her to one room – the kitchen or utility room is best as linoleum or tiled floors can be mopped if necessary and there is less to damage through chewing. Puppies can be very destructive, especially when teething. Leave some newspaper down and never scold her for mishaps. Put her outside as soon as you return and spend some time playing and being with her. She will need your attention and reassurance.

It is not wise to leave a young pup alone with an older dog or dogs until she is an established member of the household. Keep her in a separate room or put her in her wire cage, if you have one, where she will be quite safe.

Barking mad.

Barking When Left

Irish Terriers are born guard dogs who bark loudly to announce the approach of strangers. It is a wonderful, deep-throated bark and is not usually excessive or continuous. Sometimes dogs will bark if left alone, which can be very annoying to neighbours. This is where early training helps; you will have to teach your dog to behave quietly for short periods when he is left alone as a young pup. If the barking proves troublesome, you can leave him in a room alone and pretend to go out. Should he begin to bark, return quickly and scold him severely. It is difficult, as pups are so pathetically pleased to see you come back, and it does seem rather mean.

Irish Terriers have a wonderful, deep-throated bark.

Holidays

If you are taking your dog...

Some hotels and guest houses do welcome dogs, but you need to check carefully when booking. They are never allowed in the public rooms, but can sleep overnight in your bedroom. I need hardly say that the utmost care is necessary. You will be liable for any damage caused by your dog, and this sort of behaviour would make it very difficult for other dogs owners, who may then be penalised.

Beaches are increasingly out of bounds for dogs in the summer months, and we have already noted the dangers of leaving a dog in an overheated car.

If you are a townsperson, be very aware of and abide by the countryside code. We have always taken our dogs, and have had some lovely walking holidays all over the country, but it does need to be planned carefully with the dog's enjoyment as part of the package.

If you are not taking your dog...

If you are going abroad, you will need to make careful arrangements for the care of your dog. Unlike with cats, who do not mind, it is absolutely out of the question to leave a dog alone in a house, even with people popping in and out to feed him. It is cruel and, if reported, you may be prosecuted. Your dog may also dig, chew and bark if left for long, which would hardly be surprising.

It is increasingly popular to have a house-sitter for your dog. This is someone who moves into your house while you are away. You may persuade a member of the family or a friend who knows your dog. Failing that, there are reputable agencies that provide an excellent service. You may need to take up references first. The added advantage is that your house will be safe and other pets and plants cared for as well. If you have several dogs, it is probably less costly than boarding kennels. Check with your insurance that the cover is sufficient for this sort of arrangement. It is not cheap, but it does make for peace of mind. Make the arrangements well ahead of time and make sure you can meet the added expense.

The alternative arrangement is a good local boarding kennel. A word-of-mouth recommendation from your vet or a friend is helpful. Do telephone, however, and arrange a visit to be quite certain of the level of care your dog is likely to receive. Check that he will have his own, individual kennel and run, which should provide adequate space. If you have two dogs, they are usually happier kennelled together, but make sure there is sufficient room for two.

Be quite clear about your dog's diet and exercise, especially if there is anything unusual. On the whole, kennels supply very adequate feeding, but you may have to provide cans of food for any special diet. Medication can be another problem and needs to be discussed and clearly understood. Always leave your own contact number and that of your vet in case of an emergency.

If your bitch is due to come on heat, inform the kennels when you book her in. Most kennels can manage perfectly well, but will need to plan where to place her without causing upset to other dogs.

Although your dog is unlikely to suffer any ill effects from being kennelled, there is a slight risk of kennel cough (see chapter 9). Your vet may recommend immunising him. Be sure to leave the necessary time for it to take effect. No reputable kennel will accept a dog without up-to-date immunisation certificates for the major canine diseases (distemper, canine hepatitis, parvovirus and leptospirosis). These are usually required with the booking form. Popular kennels are often full to bursting over Christmas, Easter and the summer holidays, so you need to book as early as possible.

Leaving your dog can be rather an emotional parting, especially if children are involved. Take his blanket and favoured toys, which will help him to settle. Explain to him that he must be good and that you will come back for him. Keep it brisk and brief, for your own sake and your dog's. It is probably more sensible to take him alone, or you may drive away with a car full of weeping children – not a good start to a holiday! Keep reminding them – and yourself – of the joyful homecoming.

Parties, Christmas and Bonfire Night

Although Irish Terriers are famous for their pluck and courage, some find Bonfire Night a dreadful ordeal. Make sure your dog has been out before dark, and then put him safely indoors, draw the curtains and turn on the television or radio. If he is still very shaky and distressed, you should stay with him, giving constant reassurance. It should not be necessary to resort to sedatives. Some dogs are a great nuisance, barking loudly with each bang. They should be made to calm down, and again you would need to stay with them if possible. They might be unwilling to go out afterwards and need to be coaxed. Thunderstorms also sometimes alarm dogs, and the drill is the same as for noisy fireworks.

Unless you are having a very quiet Christmas, this is not the time to get a new puppy. Households can become noisy and disorganised. Puppies can get out, eat the wrong things and be sick, chew up Christmas presents, make puddles and generally increase the chaos. It is most unwise and unfair to expect a puppy, or indeed an older dog, to settle properly at this time. Wait until after Christmas. Better still, if you can, wait until the spring, when the weather should be much better for house training and exercise.

Parties and weddings can also prove hazardous to your dog's welfare. Many new people around, and much going on can prove disastrous if everyone is too busy to check

Christmas dinner.

the puppy. He may become nervous of the music and escape out of the house, with all the dire consequences that may involve. A few hours in a freezing garden can be enough to kill a puppy, quite apart from the accidents that may occur. Always remember, when arranging family celebrations, to consider your dog's safety and welfare as part of the preparations.

Chapter Nine

Breeding
Irish Terriers

At one time, anyone with a bitch was told that it was a good thing for her to have puppies at least once in her life, and the litter might well have given enormous pleasure to both bitch and owner. Today, however, when far too many puppies are born, it is not considered sensible to breed from your bitch unless you are a recognised breeder or can be absolutely certain of finding good homes for the entire litter. You may have to run on puppies that are not spoken for, which entails a great deal of time and expense and requires suitable accommodation.

Vets today tend to be more in favour of spaying bitches even before their first season. It is a much simpler operation and recent research seems to suggest that bitches treated in this way are less prone to mammary tumours later in life.

Warning: breeding puppies entirely for financial gain or as the main means of livelihood is considered disgraceful and thoroughly reprehensible. It is called *puppy farming*, and has nothing to do with good breeding practice. Fortunately, it is unheard of amongst Irish Terrier breeders.

Dr Alex Noonan with (right to left) Ch Indian Spice of Montelle (grandmother), Ch Naranja Firedancer (daughter) and Ch Naranja Danse du Feu (granddaughter).

Your Bitch

It is sensible to remember that not every pedigree dog is worth considering as breeding material. Most breeders want to improve their stock by using only the best specimens. Even if you do have a lovely bitch who is winning prizes, it is very important to find a suitable stud dog. If she is an adored pet you need to consider very carefully whether you really do want her to have a litter.

Any bitch used for breeding should be in peak condition like this Montelle beauty.
Photo: David Dalton

It is sensible to ask the advice of your bitch's breeder, as most breeders have an intimate knowledge of the breed lines and the best stud dogs around. Between you, you can assess your bitch, noting her good and not-so-good points. No dog or bitch is absolutely perfect and in choosing the stud you should aim to consolidate the good and eradicate, or at least dilute, the bad. If your bitch is a little short in the leg, be sure to find a stud dog with a good length of leg. Try to discover too whether he sires puppies with the correct leg length. Never reinforce a fault by breeding from a stud dog with similar imperfections.

Before being mated, your bitch needs to be in top physical condition, and in no way should she be overweight. If she is she will be more difficult to get in whelp and more prone to whelping difficulties. Neither should you breed from a nervous or highly-strung bitch, who will be difficult to manage during mating and whelping. In any case, this is not a characteristic you would wish to pass on.

You need to consider the temperament of your bitch carefully. Read the description in the Breed Standard and see whether she matches up. After all, you are not breeding just a 'brown dog', but a terrier with a long history, famous for its particular traits. Most bitches are more sensitive than dogs, but she should be able to stand her ground. She should not just be 'sweet', but should have a certain larkiness and feeling of confidence and fun about her. There should be absolutely no sign of viciousness or over-excitability. Irish Terriers are very outgoing and love people; if your bitch is shy and backs away, she should never be used for breeding as she does not have the typical Irish Terrier temperament.

The Stud Dog

Find out as much as you can about the stud dog of your choice; like sons-in-law, they are rarely quite splendid enough. It is an excellent idea to see him in the show ring or at home. His temperament too must match up to the Breed Standard: friendly, steady and outgoing, but also bold, alert and confident. A quarrelsome dog is a complete nuisance in today's crowded world and should never be used at stud. The old-fashioned terrier man's idea of 'a good fighting terrier' is now considered intolerable in a public place, and you would be setting up troubles for yourself, the dogs and their future owners by choosing such a stud.

Ch Major General of Montelle: a top quality stud dog.

Breeding Methods

In Irish Terriers we are most fortunate to have no serious breed faults. You will not have to check with The Kennel Club and your vet or have signed affidavits about hip dysplasia, slipping kneecaps, heart disease, congenital blindness or the many other genetic faults. Cracked pads, once a problem in the breed, are now very rarely seen. Work is being carried out in Switzerland's Zurich University on finding a way to isolate the rogue gene, but it has been virtually bred out. I can only reiterate how fortunate and grateful we are to have such a sound breed.

A healthy litter of quality pups.

Nevertheless, breeding your own line of Irish Terriers is extremely complex, requiring a great deal of knowledge and skill, expert advice, patience, instinct and luck. I sometimes think successful breeders are born, not made. They seem to have a feel for it that transcends reading pedigrees and studying dogs in the ring. Setting up a successful breeding plan involves studying the pedigrees of successful dogs and relying on the wisdom and generosity of established breeders to point out the pitfalls and lead the way. They will have a close understanding of their own and other breeding strains.

We need to remind ourselves that we are considering show dogs specifically. They are the standard setters of the breed: the ambassadors who carry the name and keep up the quality. While in no way underestimating or under-valuing the role played by the hundreds of adored pet dogs, we should not breed from them only to produce more, and possibly unwanted, puppies.

Never mate an unproved sire with a maiden bitch. If there are no puppies, you will be unable to tell whether the fault lies with the dog or the bitch; if there are puppies, it is difficult to know just how they will turn out. Experienced breeders do sometimes break this rule within their own stock because they know the quality of the forebears.

Irish Terriers are difficult to breed to a set pattern. They rarely, if ever, come up as the proverbial 'peas in a pod'. Everything about them is hugely individualistic, and this seems to apply as much to their physical make-up as to their characters – or is that the universal cry of all breeders?

When you begin, you will hear a great deal about the three methods used in establishing a line or strain: line-breeding, inbreeding and outcrossing. The great skill is to combine these three elements of breeding into a successful plan.

Line-breeding

Line-breeding is the main means of establishing a strain: the mating of dogs of the same family or clan who are all related to a greater or lesser extent and are usually descended from one outstanding dog or bitch. The idea is to keep the relationship as close as possible to preserve the greatness of the original dog or bitch. Examples of line-breeding could be cousin to cousin or niece to uncle. Sometimes the same 'great' dog appears on the pedigrees in a different relationship on each side.

This method works well if only the best dogs are used. The whole idea is to preserve the best characteristics without diluting or losing them through the use of mediocre specimens. It requires great knowledge and skill. Sometimes, even when you have worked it all out on paper, the right specimens simply do not appear and you have to wait for the next season.

You need to be very honest and able to recognise the faults as well as the best characteristics of your stock. It is extremely difficult, because dogs you know, love and see every day always seem as near perfection as you can possibly get. This is why it is a good idea to see them with others in the show ring, and it can also be helpful to hear the opinions of other experienced breeders.

Inbreeding

Inbreeding involves the mating of close relatives, such as father to daughter or mother to son. It has become something of a disreputable word in some breeds, and is thought to be the cause of some of the dreadful breed faults from which Irish Terriers are so happily free.

Inbreeding can be the quickest way to establish type, but there are inherent dangers. In mating close relatives, you may well establish or reinforce faults as well as virtues, and even produce serious health problems. Only the very best stock in both type and temperament should ever be used.

To be realistic, there are few, if any, kennels with the breeding stock to support this sort of programme.

Outcrossing

Outcrossing involves the use of a dog of the same breed who is unrelated to your breed line. This can be useful as a means of introducing new characteristics that may be desirable, such as a much-improved coat, but you will need to line-breed their offspring back to your original stock to establish the traits firmly and make sure they will run true to form.

Artificial Insemination (AI)

This procedure is becoming a fact of life, and semen from stud dogs of various breeds is being shipped around the world. It is expensive and highly regulated, and there are a great many legal safeguards to negotiate. The Kennel Club does not encourage it, and you would need a very good excuse and its written permission before using AI on your bitch. However, I am sure that, sensibly and responsibly applied, it could prove a valuable means of improving the breed in the future.

If you are considering exporting your stud dog's semen, you will have to consider very carefully the welfare of the puppies produced. You will have little control over how the semen is to be used.

Updated information is coming through all the time, and you must check carefully with both The Kennel Club and your vet before you begin.

The Breeding Cycle

Bitches

The ideal time to mate a bitch is during her third or fourth heat, and not before. Irish Terriers remain puppies for some time, and a bitch under two will still be very playful and not sensible enough.

It is best to mate her in the first half of the year so that the puppies arrive in the spring. The worst weather is over by then and they can be out of doors sooner and spend more time with people around them in the longer hours of daylight.

First comes the *pro-oestrus* stage. The bitch's vulva becomes swollen and there may be spots of blood when she sits down. Some young bitches find this embarrassing and get rather fussed and worried about the mess they seem to be making. They lick themselves constantly and become restless and unsettled. Your bitch may ask to go out and urinate more than usual. She will not permit mating yet, but will attract male dogs and, from this time and all through her season, needs to be kept under close supervision.

After 10–14 days comes the true *oestrus*, when the bitch is fertile and ready to be mated. The discharge from the vulva will become paler pink and clearer. The start of this must be marked exactly, as breeders consider it to be the best time for a successful mating. The bitch herself will probably be anxious to find a mate and will often present her rear, with the tail turned sideways, to almost anyone who is around to look.

You will need to be absolutely sure that garden fences are secure and that doors and gates are kept shut. Her scent will undoubtedly attract dogs from all around and, with a spirited bitch, you need to be very watchful that she does not slip out and choose her own mate. Should this happen, an injection can be administered to end the pregnancy, but no-one will be very pleased, so avoidance is the better path.

Sprays and deodorants can be used to make the bitch less attractive. They are essential if you are exercising your bitch, but by no means fool-proof. You need to keep your sense of humour and not become too exasperated with the hangers-on in the park or around your gate. During one hot summer I remember taking out bowls of water for three panting fellows who had waited all day!

If mating has not occurred, the oestrus cycle passes gradually. The bitch's vulva returns to normal and she soon settles down. This is the *anoestrus* phase.

If you have decided to mate your bitch, make sure that she is wormed just before the season is due. Some breeders worm during pregnancy as well, but be very careful to consult your vet about the brand, as not all are suitable.

Dogs

Dogs reach puberty at about the same age as bitches, but are not used at stud until they are a year old. It is considered wise to use an experienced older bitch for a young dog's first mating, as she is less likely to be difficult or aggressive towards him. Similarly, a maiden bitch is probably better mated first to an experienced dog. However, the experience of the stud dog's owner is of much greater importance, and no mating should take place unsupervised.

It is neither wise nor necessary to use every dog at stud simply because he is a nice

These pups show the characteristic Irish alert expression.
Photo: Tracy Morgan

Irish Terrier. In fact, it is absolutely unnecessary for dogs, other than stud dogs, to be mated at all. The notion that it is good for their general health is total nonsense. Celibacy for pet dogs is the sensible option, as the occasional mating can prove very unsettling for him, and you may then have a wanderer on your hands, with all the implicit dangers.

Only a dog of high quality should be used at stud. He should be healthy, sound and as near perfection in looks as possible. His temperament should be steady and sensible, but with that special charm and fire that is the hallmark of Irish Terriers. He should also have been seen in public and shown successfully.

It is advisable for your stud dog to be mated before his second year. It is essential to mate him to good quality bitches only, as his quality as a stud dog will be judged by his offspring, and this should never be compromised. No stud fee should be charged until he has sired puppies and is therefore proven. A good stud dog can do an enormous amount for the breed. His influence in numbers of puppies alone can be far greater than that of even the best known bitch.

Stud dogs should not be treated any differently from other dogs. They need to be part of the family and have all the fun and contact with people that is so vital to an Irish Terrier's happiness. Being at stud will only be a very small part of their lives, after all.

Mating

At the time of mating, your bitch must be in good health and condition. Make sure that her immunisations are up-to-date and that she has been wormed. Once she is pregnant, she may not be given live vaccines, as it could affect the puppies adversely. Make sure she has emptied her bladder before the mating.

The stud dog needs to be in prime condition: neither too thin nor overweight. He should be well fed and properly exercised and the proverbial picture of health.

The bitch is usually taken to the stud dog, so all the arrangements to travel with your bitch to the stud kennel need to be thought out carefully. Give due warning of the probable dates, as you might need to stay over night or even longer. In Great Britain, distances are relatively small, so it is usually possible to take your bitch by car. However, distances are much greater in countries such as the United States of America or Australia, where it may be necessary to fly her to the kennels well in advance.

Both should be kept on the lead and allowed to meet and spend time together. Some bitches will play and become quite flirtatious. Others can be snappy and occasionally even become quite aggressive towards the stud dog. A maiden bitch may not be ready, but she could be refusing just through nervousness. There is now a progesterone test which can be carried out by your vet, but it is expensive and some vets will not do it anyway. It is usually accurate enough to judge from her behaviour and the change in colour of the discharge from her vulva.

The bitch's owner should hold her head to steady her. She may need to be lightly muzzled with a small bandage, but placing your thumbs under her collar and holding her firmly but gently is normally sufficient to restrain her if she is fussing. Speaking to her reassuringly helps. When she is ready, she will indicate her willingness to mate by standing still with her tail to one side. The dog then mounts her and grasps her with his front legs, and penetration occurs. The muscles in the bitch's vagina tighten around the penis, and they are in what is called the 'tie'. The stud owner supports the dog during the tie, when they are unable to separate. The bitch must be kept steady at this stage, or the dog may be injured if she tries to pull away.

The couple will still be effectively locked together after the dog's thrusting movements have resulted in the ejaculation of sperm. The dog will usually turn at this point by dropping down and lifting a leg across the bitch's back. They are still tied. but back-to-back, facing in opposite directions. If the dog does not turn, it will be vital to support him, or this weight may be too much for the bitch.

The tie can last anything from 5–45 minutes, and on no account should the dogs be left. The bitch may salivate and seem uncomfortable but she is usually quiet. It can be very exhausting for the owners, and it helps if they have a stool or low chair handy – even a bucket will do! When the bitch's muscles relax spontaneously, the dogs part quite naturally.

It is difficult to understand how this tie should be such a significant part of the reproductive act. The sperm are ejaculated early in the mating and for successful fertilisation there need be no tie at all. However, fluids that may aid the passage of sperm to the uterus, where fertilisation of the ova takes place, are passed across during the tie. Some breeders think the tie prevents spillage and try to keep the bitch from urinating for an hour or so afterwards for the same reason.

Sometimes a second mating a day or two later is considered necessary. This is not always convenient if long journeys are involved but, if the dog and bitch are on hand, it can make doubly sure.

After Mating

After the mating, both bitch and stud dog should be rested and given water to drink.

If your bitch lives with other bitches, it may be necessary to keep her apart from them for a day or so after the mating. She may be unsettled and, rather curiously, other bitches sometimes show aggression towards a bitch who has just been mated. Similarly, if you have more than one stud dog you need to be tactful about putting them together again, as dogs too can be assertive and quarrelsome in such circumstances. You have to make it clear that you will not tolerate aggressive behaviour. They will be far more worried about offending you than scoring points against each other. However, you may have to separate them if they will not settle down.

You need to be very watchful of your bitch with other dogs even after she has mated. She is still attractive to them and, until her season is completely over, she may mate happily and conceive again. This would make a nonsense of your breeding programme. Although it is now possible through DNA to determine which puppy was sired by which stud dog, it is an extremely costly procedure. You would have to obtain genetic profiles from the dogs with whom she mated and match them up with the puppies.

Fees and Paperwork
Stud fee
The arrangements with regard to the stud fee – whether it is to be paid immediately, after the bitch is in whelp, or anything else – should be worked out, understood, put in writing and signed by both parties before the mating takes place.

In fact, it is best to settle the stud fee immediately if you can. You are paying for the service, not the litter itself. Should your bitch fail to conceive, most stud dog owners allow a free visit the next time your bitch is on heat.

Some stud owners prefer to have the option of the first ('pick of the litter') and possibly also third choice from the litter instead of a fee. Such arrangements should be clearly written down, signed, understood and honoured to the letter. While they can help immediate finances, such arrangements may mean you consistently lose your best puppy.

The owner of the stud dog should always be invited to see the puppies when they are born. An experienced eye and informed opinion can be a great help to you in deciding which puppy or puppies you should keep – or 'run on', as some breeders say.

Infections
Some stud kennels are extremely anxious about any possible infection passing from the bitch to the stud dog. They may ask for a note of health from your vet or even insist on an injection of antibiotics. This is highly controversial, as some breeders feel the antibiotics may adversely affect the puppies.

Certificate of mating
This form is signed by the owners of the bitch and the stud dog, acknowledging that a mating has taken place. Care should be taken that the pedigrees are correct. The stud owner should not sign until the stud fee has been paid or any alternative arrangements regarding puppies have been recorded in writing.

Stud book
A stud dog owner should record all matings, with details of dog and bitch, in a stud book, and the counterfoil from this could be signed and used as a receipt for the stud fee.

Is She Pregnant?
It is not easy to tell whether your bitch is pregnant for about the first five weeks. There may be great activity inside the uterus, but nothing much that you can see, and no indications from her behaviour that she is in whelp.

The fertilised eggs will form a placental attachment to the lining of the uterus after the third week. The bitch's abdomen will become gradually more swollen as the puppies increase in size towards the end of the pregnancy. The teats become firm at first and soften later on, nearer the time of whelping.

False pregnancy

Some bitches show all the signs of pregnancy despite the fact that they have not conceived and in some cases have not even been mated. Their abdomens swell and they may produce milk and behave exactly as if they were in whelp.

It is very difficult to tell whether it is a false pregnancy, as the urine and blood tests show the same hormonal changes as in a real one. By the seventh week, when the bone structures of the puppies would show up on an X-ray, it is possible to find out for sure, but it is not advisable to use this method in case she is pregnant, as the X-ray may not be good for the puppies. Scanning is becoming more commonplace now, and gives a more accurate reading of dates and numbers of puppies. Vets often have the facility to scan, and some people operate mobile scanners and will come to the bitch and scan her at home. Some breeders still disapprove, but it is a technological advance that is widely available.

You will need to be very patient with your bitch if her pregnancy is false. She may become agitated and collect her toys, seeming to think they are her puppies. We had one who collected rolled-up socks and brooded them like a hen for weeks. It is rather sad, and you need to warn everyone, especially the children, not to disturb and upset her. She may protect her 'babies' fiercely if you try to take them away.

Unfortunately, once the pattern of false pregnancy is established it may happen after each oestrus, irrespective of any mating. Having a litter is no cure – a false pregnancy is then probably even more likely to occur after the next heat. You can simply wait for it to pass and let nature take its course. However, if your bitch becomes distressed and unsettled, your vet may prescribe hormone treatment or at least tranquillisers to calm her. If it persists, spaying is the only way to avoid the problem in the long term.

Reabsorption

Curiously, the scanning machine has proved the possibility of reabsorption of puppies. For years, breeders who were convinced that their bitches were pregnant had to accept, when no litter appeared, that the pregnancy must have been false. Now, puppies seen on scans are known very occasionally to disappear. It is interesting, and research is in progress to find out why it happens.

Pregnancy

Care in pregnancy

The pregnancy lasts usually from 58–63 days, although puppies can arrive a few days early or late. For the most part, the bitch should be very well, and there is no need to change her lifestyle at all. Keep up her exercise so that she remains fit and does not put on any extra weight.

Halfway through her pregnancy, at about 30 days, she should be wormed, to prevent the foetuses from being infected with roundworm. This should be highly unlikely, but it is a vital precaution.

Not until about 40 days after the mating will you see any real changes in your bitch. The foetuses will be growing fast, and you will doubtless debate endlessly about how many puppies she is having.

At this stage you should increase her food by up to 50%. Small meals several times a day are best, and you need to encourage her to eat. She should have a high-protein diet and, if she is not on a complete food, make certain that her supplement of vitamins and minerals is correct. Make sure you introduce her special diet tactfully and start by mixing it in gradually with her usual food. She may not like the change and may refuse to eat until she is used to it. If she is having complete dry food for bitches in whelp, be sure she has plenty of cool, fresh water at all times. She is likely to be very thirsty anyway, and the dry food will increase this thirst.

Towards the end of her pregnancy, your bitch may well become restless and uncomfortable. This is quite understandable, especially if she is carrying a big litter. Watch her carefully, and make sure that she is not constipated. You could add a little cooking oil or liquid paraffin (medicinal) to her food. You may even consider changing, or partly changing, from a dry diet to a wet food. There are excellent canned diets that are considered easier to digest than the dry. It would provide a little variety and may tempt her to eat well. Limit her exercise to short outings, with no long walks.

Your bitch may become a little clingy and not like to be left as whelping day approaches. Like all mothers-to-be, bitches vary greatly. Some bounce through pregnancy with few signs of stress, while others fuss, sulk and demand attention, especially if they are rather spoilt pets. You need to go along with it without getting agitated yourself. Make sure that you will be at home when she is due to whelp.

Preparations for the Whelping
Whelping box
You will need to beg, borrow or buy a whelping box. These are now available with hygienic, easy-clean surfaces and in different sizes to suit each breed. You can make your own, and some breeders still favour wooden boxes.

The whelping box needs to be big enough for the bitch to lie comfortably on her side and stretch out her legs. The front should be lower, so that the bitch can get in and out easily, while the puppies are safely restrained inside. As a precaution, most boxes have poles along the inside, about 10cm (4in) up the sides. These create a gap around the edges, providing an escape route for the puppies should the mother lie on top of them. Generally, this is not such a problem with Irish Terriers as with larger breeds.

Where to locate the whelping box
The whelping box, lined with newspaper, should be put in a quiet place where the bitch will not be disturbed. A garden room is ideal, provided that you can maintain a temperature of at least 20°C (70°F). Anywhere warm and quiet, away from the other dogs (if any) and with easy access to the yard or garden, is good. It is best to have a washable floor surface – carpets are too difficult to clean and liable to stain.

There should be enough room for you to sit comfortably on the floor or on a low chair beside her. Once you have lined the base of the box with layers of newspaper, the bitch may, when close to whelping, start to tear it up. She is trying to make a nest, and it is very good occupational therapy, keeping her active and preoccupied.

If for some inexplicable reason she decides to abandon the box and choose her own place, you will have to decamp with her until the puppies are born and can be moved to the whelping box. Take plenty of newspaper to spread on the floor and a pile of old towels. These should be clean and warm and can be slipped under her to keep her dry and comfortable.

Whelping
The early signs

As whelping time approaches, your bitch will almost certainly eat very little, if anything, but she may be thirsty. Keep her water bowl close at hand. Usually there is also a slight drop in her body temperature, from 38.3–38.9°C (101–101°F) to 36.6–37.2°C (98–99°F) or even less. Make sure that you know her normal temperature so that you can gauge this.

She should, of course, be safely in the whelping box, and most Irish Terrier bitches will want you to be with them even if you are up all night. Keep things quiet and speak to her in a low, reassuring voice, especially if it is her first litter. On the other hand, if she is happy and settled and prefers to be on her own, keep away from the box, but remain where you can see that she is managing.

She may produce milk from her teats, and there is often a discharge from the vulva just before she begins to whelp. Contact your vet at this stage; you may need professional help later on.

The birth

Most Irish Terrier bitches cope very well with whelping, and there is no need to interfere. Thankfully, they and their puppies are the right shape and size for natural birth.

Your bitch may need to drink at times during the whelping. You could give her some warm milk in her water and add a little glucose. If she can tolerate milk, you could keep this up for the first week after the birth.

The first contractions may cause her some pain, or at least discomfort. She may pant and shiver. This could go on for hours, or for very little time at all. Keep her quiet and reassured, even if she wants to get out of her box to drink or relieve herself.

There is a change of gear when stronger contractions begin. These are very obvious, and the bitch may seem to be straining and pushing downwards. The first puppy should appear fairly soon – if it is not born within the hour, you should call your vet without delay.

Each puppy develops within the uterus inside an amniotic sac, which looks like a little water bag. Sometimes the sac remains intact at birth, and the bitch will then bite and tear it open to release the puppy, or it may have broken before birth. In either case, she will lick the newborn puppy vigorously, cleaning it up and stimulating breathing.

The bitch may cry and whimper as the first puppy is born, particularly if it is her first litter. Try not to be alarmed, and reassure her quietly. An injury to the bitch is very rare. If she is too upset or already feeling the next one on the way, she may fail to deal with the puppy properly. In this case, you will have to 'act mum' yourself, as follows:

- Break open the amniotic sac so that the head is free. This is essential, as the puppy could otherwise breathe in the fluid and drown.
- Dry the puppy with kitchen paper or a towel, making sure you mop up the mucous around its nose and mouth.
- Open the mouth gently with your little finger. This will encourage it to breathe.

There are occasions when one of the puppies seems limp and lifeless. Do not panic, but try the following procedures:

- Gently hold the puppy upside-down in your hands. You can even swing it gently. This will drain the fluids out through the mouth and nose.

- Hold the tiny puppy on its side and rub your fingers up and down firmly. You can also rub it with a towel.
- If there is still no sign of life, try blowing gently up its nose. You have to establish the breathing rhythm, but you must neither blow nor press too hard, as you could injure the puppy.
- As a last resort, you can place it in a bowl of cold water, and then into warm water. Dry the puppy careful afterwards and make sure that it is warm.

As soon as it is breathing and showing real signs of life, place the puppy with its mother and the rest of the litter in the whelping box. If there is a puppy you cannot save, wrap it up carefully and take it away from the bitch.

Each puppy was attached in the uterus to its own placenta. It is of vital importance to account for each placenta because, if one remains inside, it can cause a serious infection. The placenta looks rather like a piece of raw liver and is usually delivered within minutes of the puppy to which it is attached. There are often signs of a greenish fluid, which is perfectly normal. Bitches will often eat the placentas, which contain valuable nutrients.

The bitch should sever the umbilical cord by which the placenta is attached to the puppy, but you may have to help. It is better to pinch the cord between your finger and thumb rather than cutting it. This staunches the wound and helps to stop the bleeding. However, you can cut it with sterilised scissors if you are happier doing this, but the cut must be pinched afterwards to stop the bleeding. Leave at least 3cm attached to the puppy to avoid the possibility of an umbilical hernia developing.

Do not tug the cord at any time. The puppy is very small and could be injured.

Change the towels frequently throughout the whelping; they are sure to become wet and messy.

Breech birth

The usual way for a puppy to be born is head first and the same way up as the bitch. This is the easiest way through the birth canal. However, many puppies are born in a breech position, which means that their bottoms come first and then their hind legs. The bitch still may be able to manage, and the puppy may be born safely.

If the puppy does not come out quickly (within five minutes) you will have to help. The puppy may be blocked and, as a consequence, suffocate. Remember that it is tiny and fragile and you must not squeeze or tug.

- Wrap the puppy's legs in a cloth, or even kitchen paper, so that you can get a light, firm grip.
- Try to ease the puppy downwards, working with the bitch's contractions. This should remove it, but you may well have to resuscitate the puppy as recommended above.

Warning: Do not leave your bitch in the last stage of labour for long if no puppies are appearing. One hour is the absolute maximum before you contact your vet. There could be a problem in the uterus, and a caesarean section may be necessary.

Aftercare

Puppies are usually born fairly soon after one another. You can normally tell when the last puppy has arrived, as the bitch settles down with her litter, although you do get some surprises.

Suckling

She will lick and groom her puppies, and they will suckle instinctively. Some breeders like to attach each puppy to a teat as soon as it is born. In this way, you have checked that the puppy can suckle properly. Suckling could increase the strength of the bitch's contractions.

The first milk (colostrum) produced in the first two days contains vital antibodies that boost the puppies' immune systems and help to protect them from infection.

Keep a wary eye on the litter and make sure that they all get a fair share of milk. Sometimes weaker or smaller pups are pushed out to the side. You need to attach each to a teat and wait for it to feed.

During the first weeks puppies will suckle frequently, probably waking every two hours. They will sleep and feed, moving over each other to reach the favoured teats.

It is a good idea to have a low light on all night. If you hear any crying, you can be sure the puppy is cold or hungry or needs to be sorted out. Most breeders like to sleep close enough to hear any distress.

Most Irish Terrier bitches – in fact, most bitches of any breed – prove excellent mothers. Some adore their puppies, and it is charming

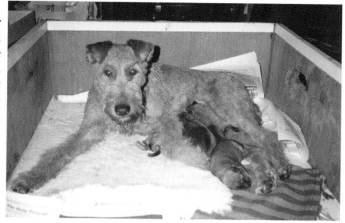

(Top and centre) A contented bitch with her newborn litter. (Bottom) A group of 'toddlers' showing an interest in their environment.

to watch them peacefully feeding them, cleaning them and later playing with them. A very indulged house-bitch may be less enchanted and long to get back with the family. You may have to coax her to be patient, and you would not be the first or the last breeder to sit beside the whelping box encouraging her to stay put!

Room temperature

As regards room temperature, there something of a clash of interest: the vital need to keep the puppies warm and the need to keep your bitch from becoming uncomfortably hot. You will need a means of raising the room temperature to at least 21°C (70°F), even higher to begin with. Make sure that the air is kept moist with humidifiers attached to the heaters, or even an extra pan of water in the room.

Some breeders use a 'pig lamp' (an infra-red lamp with a reflector which emits a steady heat), and this needs to be suspended over the whelping box. Pig lamps are obtainable through agricultural suppliers or the dog press. You can adjust the height of the lamp to control the temperature. Keep one thermometer in the whelping box and one in the room to check that the temperature is correct. Your bitch will pant and become restless if she is overheated, which is why some breeders no longer use lamps but rely entirely on the correct room temperature.

Cold puppies do not flourish. Newborn pups are blind and helpless and, although covered in fur (which is more than can be said for many other small creatures), they have no means of warming themselves. However, they do snuggle up together, and the bitch's body heat helps.

The new, non-allergenic veterinary bedding (Vet Bed) is excellent, allowing the moisture to drain away and thus keeping the puppies warm and dry. You should wash your Vet Bed in non-allergenic washing powder to avoid upsetting the puppies.

Puppy Check

When all is quiet, probably within the first 24 hours, have a careful look at all the puppies. They may vary in size, the dogs generally weighing slightly more than the bitches. Experienced breeders say they can feel whether puppies are strong and healthy when they hold them in their hands. Healthy puppies have a special elasticity in their muscles – plump, but not 'puddingy'.

Make sure that there are no 'orphans'. Occasionally a bitch will reject a puppy for no apparent reason. It used to be said that it was because she *knew* it was unsound in some way. In my opinion, this is not so. Encourage her to accept the puppy, placing it back with the others. It deserves a chance, even if you have to hand rear it.

Tail docking

You will need to decide about tail docking and consult your vet about this. It is usually done at home at about three days old and, in my opinion, is not the trauma recent legislation would have us believe. It takes only a second, and the pup settles quickly, although it is wise to remove the bitch to the garden so that she is not upset by the short cry. If you have difficulty in finding a vet to carry out this minor operation, you can contact the Council of Docked Breeds (see **Useful Addresses**), which keeps a list of vets who will dock.

Checking the New Mother

It is important that the bitch should feel relaxed and in charge of her puppies. Discourage visitors for the first week – even family members should keep a discreet distance. Do not let other dogs anywhere near her, as she may become upset and even aggressive towards them.

Keep a careful check on your bitch – occasionally problems do arise in the days after the birth.

Placenta retained

If a placenta, or part of one, is left inside the uterus, your bitch will become unwell. She may run a temperature and go off both her food and her puppies. Your vet should make a home visit at once, and would probably prescribe antibiotics. This condition is potentially dangerous.

Teats

You should check the bitch's teats every day, or even twice a day, to make sure that she is not developing mastitis (see below). Check also the puppies' nails, as they could be scratching as they suckle.

Mastitis

This is an inflammation of the milk glands in a lactating bitch. If the infection is severe an abscess may form, but even the milder condition when the glands become red and hard is extremely painful.

The bitch may run a temperature and feel generally low. She may be unwilling to feed her puppies, but most breeders encourage her to continue, as it relieves the pressure of milk and helps drain off the infections.

Your vet will probably prescribe antibiotics and some vets suggest applying a hot poultice or fomentation to draw out the infection. Some breeders apply cloths wrung out in hot water. It must not be too hot, for fear of burning her. Try it first on the inside of your arm.

Feeding

You will need to increase the bitch's food, both in quantity and frequency. She will be extremely hungry and thirsty and should be having twice her normal amount of food by the second week. Puppies grow fast and make great demands on the bitch's physical strength. Make sure that she does not lose weight or condition. Between the third and fifth week, you can increase her food intake again. Spread over four meals during the day, she could have three times her normal diet.

Eclampsia

Eclampsia, or milk fever, sometimes affects bitches, especially if they have very large litters. It is caused by loss of calcium through feeding the puppies, and is potentially fatal.

The bitch will appear uneasy and try to stand. The puppies may also become distressed. She will then almost certainly collapse and may even have convulsions and die.

Your vet will probably give your bitch a calcium injection and, provided that it is early enough, the bitch will make a spectacular recovery. You will then need to adjust her feeding carefully, making sure that her calcium intake is correct and balanced with the amount of phosphorus in the diet. In very severe cases it may be necessary to hand rear the litter.

Exercising your bitch

Make sure from day one that your bitch makes regular visits to the yard or garden to relieve herself. Most bitches will hurry back anxiously at first, but very soon she will want to take short walks, especially if she can hear the other dogs setting out. It will do her good to stretch and have a change of scene, and she will return to her puppies refreshed. It is sensible to wash her teats and dry them thoroughly before she feeds the pups. It is also good management to make sure they are well fed and sleeping peacefully before you set out.

Fostering

In the case of a large litter, or if the mother is not coping well, it may be wise to remove some of the pups, making a less demanding litter. In kennels where there are two or more lactating bitches, it may be possible to foster puppies. You have to be careful to rub your hands over the fostering bitch's litter and then over the puppies to be fostered. This will transfer the scent – she will not accept them unless they smell familiar. At first, keep a wary eye on her. Once the newcomers are suckling, they should be fine, and you will be spared a great deal of effort and time spent in hand rearing them.

Hand Rearing

If for any reason your bitch fails to feed her puppies or does not provide enough milk for them, and no foster mother is available, you will have to take over the feeding immediately. This is not easy: if they are very tiny, they need to be fed every two hours, day and night.

It is safest and best to use a special puppy-milk substitute diet available from pet shops. Cow's milk is not ideal, being less rich in fat and protein. The calcium and phosphorus ratio may be correct for calves, but not for puppies. Follow the instructions for preparing the substitute to the letter. This is extremely important, as puppies are prone to tummy upsets triggered by over-rich diets. An inadequate feed will leave them hungry, restless and crying.

Some breeders have their own special methods of substitute feeding, but for the novice it is easier to buy a special puppy feeder. Premature baby bottles with adapted teats work perfectly well, too.

Never rush a feed. Each puppy needs to drink at its own pace, or it will choke or even breathe in the fluid. This could cause inhalation pneumonia. Seek advice from anyone who is skilled and has reared puppies before. They seem very tiny and can make you feel clumsy and inept, but there is a knack of holding them securely, cleaning up their faces and rubbing their tummies with a piece of damp cotton wool to 'empty' them – playing 'mum', in fact – which needs to be mastered. Try to set up a rota so that each pup is ready to be fed at the right moment, or you could have them all squeaking together. A probiotic can be added to the feed to help boost the immune system.

It is necessary to confine the puppies within the house.

Equipment

Organise a special tray with everything you need to hand. The feeding equipment should be scrubbed, rinsed and then immersed in a sterilisation solution, as you would for a baby's bottle. Rinse the equipment carefully in boiled water before you feed. Have some paper tissues and cotton wool balls and a bowl of boiled water ready for mop ups.

"Isn't life exciting?"

Everything has to be kept scrupulously clean, and the tray must be covered when not in use.

If you have orphan puppies who cannot be fostered you may need a special incubator unit. Your vet may be able to lend you one. In this, the temperature can be controlled more easily than with an infra-red lamp. If you use a lamp, make sure that part of the box is sheltered so that the pups can escape if they become too hot.

Weaning

Puppies grow fast and, at three or four weeks, they are beginning to move about, if a little unsteadily. At this stage you can introduce the idea of solid food.

Many excellent prepared foods are available, and these can be mixed into a fairly thick porridge. The puppies will probably sniff and sneeze, fall into and even wade in it.

A lively Tanwell litter.

They will then need to be tidied up and cleaned! You can put some food on your little finger and put it into the puppies' mouths. Once they get the taste, they learn to eat quite quickly. Some breeders still insist that the old methods are best in the long term, and feed a mix of chicken, tripe and biscuit, but this involves much more trouble and care.

The bitch will still be feeding them and it is not unknown for her to vomit up some of her own food for the pups. If you feed the puppies when she is about, she may well join in too. Her milk supply will decline gradually, and she will become more unwilling to feed the pups. This can cause a considerable amount of squealing, especially if she keeps getting up and walking away. You will have to increase the puppy supplement food. Follow the instructions carefully and set up a feeding tray as suggested.

By about eight weeks, the pups are usually feeding themselves completely. It is essential not to overfeed puppies, and they should be ready and eager when the next feed is due. Feed them according to their weight chart and the instructions on the container.

Puppy Development

Like all pups, Irish Terriers are enchanting. They look like little teddy bears, with woolly coats, rather flat faces and eyes as bright as buttons. They are born with quite a lot of black hair, particularly on their faces. This is usually long hair, unlike the rest of the coat, and either falls out or can be stripped out as they get older. The puppy coat changes gradually into the two-layered, tough, waterproof adult coat.

Try to spend as much time as possible with the pups. You will begin to notice their different characters emerging and no doubt be looking to spot the champions.

From about four weeks on they will be very aware of the people around them and love to play and be petted. This is an important stage of their development. They need to see people around them and slowly become part of the household.

By eight weeks, the puppies will be moving about, playing and tumbling together. They will tease and pester their poor mother, who may or may not always happy to comply. Some toys are a help in diverting them – try rubber rings, balls and squeakers.

You have to be careful not to lose the puppies in the house or garden. It is a good idea to put them into a collapsible pen, rather like a baby's playpen, and use baby gates to keep them in one place (see chapter 7). In this way they can see what is going on without straying under your feet. They also need plenty of fresh air or walks in the garden, or you could have a puppy run in the garden.

Worming and General Puppy Welfare

Your puppies will need to be wormed, and your vet will prescribe a suitable brand and tell you when it needs to be done.

You may need to trim their claws again. Do this carefully, as even the smallest squeak from a distressed puppy can upset the bitch and make her fuss.

You need to check for mites and fleas and spray if necessary (see chapter 11).

Make sure that the puppies will not be harmed by anything you use on or near them. Change their blankets, towels and Vet Bed regularly, washing them in a non-allergenic washing powder, and keep the floor area around the puppies as spotless as you can.

Registering the Litter

You will need to register your puppies at The Kennel Club. The owner of the stud dog should have filled in and signed the relevant part of the Application for Registration certificate after you paid your stud fee. You will need to complete the form and send it, with the correct fee, to The Kennel Club for registration.

Affixes

If this is your first litter, you may decide to have your own individual kennel name or *affix*. This takes time to arrange, so you would have to ask The Kennel Club for a Registration of Affix form and allow up to three months for the processing. There is an initial fee of about £50 and a small annual maintenance fee thereafter.

The affix for which you have applied will appear as an application in the monthly *Kennel Gazette*, to give people a chance to object to it if they feel it is too much like their own affixes.

Once the affix is granted, no one can use it except you, provided that you have paid the fee. For an additional small fee, you can add it to the end of the name of your bitch. For instance, if your new affix is *Robinswood*, and your bitch is called *Breezy May Morn*, she could become *Breezy May Morn of Robinswood*. Her puppies, however, and all subsequent generations bred by you would bear the affix before the name; for instance, *Robinswood Roving Jack*.

Endorsements

The registration form has a section headed 'Endorsements'. It is most important that you sign this part, as it forbids the registration of your puppies' future progeny and forbids an export licence. It does not usually happen with Irish Terriers, but it has been known for puppies of other breeds to be bought by puppy farmers or dog dealers who send them abroad to an uncertain fate. The endorsement gives you more control over your pups' lives. After all, you owe it to them and, when you have loved and cared for them, it is hard enough to part. It will help your peace of mind to know that they are safe within a legally binding contract. Explain to every potential owner that these clauses stand. If, after two years, the new owner is considering breeding, you, as their breeder, can write to The Kennel Club and ask for the endorsements to be lifted.

Sometimes The Kennel Club is slow in processing the papers, and they are not returned before the puppies are due to leave. In this case, draw up a statement yourself, recording the fact that the Endorsement will stand. Make sure that this statement is signed and fully understood by the new owner.

Selling Your Puppies

You have every right to question and assess each potential buyer with extreme care, and you must do so. You do not have to sell to anyone unless you so wish.

The first selling contact should be the puppy registration hot line (see **Useful Addresses**). Inform them as soon as you are sure that your bitch is in whelp and telephone again when the litter has arrived.

You can also advertise in the dog press or even in a local paper, but remember that the responsibility to make certain that the puppies find secure and happy homes rests with you.

Help for the New Owner

Provide the new owner with all the information you can.

Some breeders offer a year's subscription to the Irish Terrier Association, or at least give a list of Association events and shows. Encourage the new owner to join one of the breed clubs. The Irish Terrier Association has a wonderful Fun Day for dogs and their owners – in that order. There is a puppy parade, racing, musical chairs and even disco dog dancing! The children have fun with their pets, and it is a very happy day. It is a good idea to encourage the idea of supporting the breed, and gives you enormous pleasure to meet other Irish Terriers and see your puppies again.

It is also a good idea to have a 'puppy pack' for the new owner, containing the essential papers and some that are not essential, but useful:

- Detailed sample *diet sheet*, giving the exact amounts and times of feeding. Puppies going off alone for the first time to new surrounding may easily become unsettled – a long car journey often makes them travel sick – and it is vital to keep the food familiar, at least.
- The *pedigree*, and any necessary registration paperwork.
- Immunisation certificate.
- Worming certificate.
- *Information leaflets* about the breed, particularly with regard to *grooming and coat maintenance*.
- A list of useful addresses.

Resting the Bitch

Some bitches are upset when their puppies leave home. It is tactful to space out the partings rather than have all the puppies leaving on the same day. You need time to talk to each new owner and also to settle the bitch, who may fret.

Other bitches will have had enough of the puppies and will be shamelessly glad to get rid of them. If the bitch has been in an outdoor kennel with a puppy run, she will probably be longing to come back indoors. She should be very well and in excellent health. Some breeders think that a litter is good for a bitch, and that she can look in top condition again very quickly.

Once the puppies are established and independent, your bitch will need a proper period of rest. As soon as she has recovered, she can resume her life as before her pregnancy. Her diet should be back to normal and, although she may fuss and ask for more, do not overfeed her. She will try to persuade you that four meals a day are better than one.

Do not mate her again for 18 months at least, especially if she had a large litter. In any case, you will want to see how the puppies have developed. Be very careful to keep her away from male dogs when she is in season. Hormone treatments can prevent oestrus, but may prove depressing and have other side-effects.

The Older Bitch

The Kennel Club will not register the puppies of a bitch over eight years old. It is sensible and safe to have her spayed when her breeding life is over. Bitches come on heat for the whole of their lives, which can be difficult to manage. Another great advantage is that a spayed bitch will not develop pyometra (see chapter 11), a serious and life-threatening disease requiring immediate veterinary attention that can strike older bitches.

Managing Your Kennel

One difficult problem about breeding is keeping your dogs to a manageable number. It is very tempting to run on puppies and keep all your retired bitches and stud dogs. You will have been through a great deal together, but often it is neither fair nor practical to keep them all. Most breeders try to establish a small network of people who prefer to take on older dogs.

Irish Terriers love and need a proper family, and do not like just to be part of a pack or out in kennels. If they can be placed locally, you can still meet, which is fun for everybody. I am always very touched to see the joy with which the 'oldies' greet their breeders at the various Irish Terrier events. They never forget, but climb back into their 'new' cars with equal joy.

Never part with a beloved veteran who has given you the best years of his or her life. The heartbreak for you both is simply not worth it. If choices have to be made, a younger spayed bitch or older puppy who is not shaping up as well as you had hoped will prove the easier option.

A word of warning: try to space the ages of the dogs you keep. The youngsters cheer up the oldies, who in turn hand on the family style and good manners. You must avoid the terrible sadness of everyone growing old and reaching the end of their lives together.

Chapter Ten

Feeding Your Irish Terrier

The dog is a carnivore (meat or flesh eater) and its teeth, digestive system and feral predatory nature are designed to support this. All breeds today are descended from the wolf, which is by preference carnivorous. Having said this, wolves can adapt to an omnivorous diet and feral dogs, unlike feral cats, can digest almost anything that is edible. Nevertheless, under ideal circumstances the main protein and fat supply for a wolf comes from the carcass of an animal, so the meat content provides these most important elements of a dog's diet.

When puppies help with the gardening, take care they don't eat unsuitable foods.

Elements of the diet
Proteins

Proteins are made up of essential amino acids; without them, the diet would be deficient. This protein provides the 'building blocks' necessary for bodily growth (and therefore of great importance for the young dog) and the repair of the tissues (the healing process). These systems are linked, which is why the young recover more quickly than the old. Protein can also be used as a source of energy in times of starvation.

In addition, there are some more specific uses for protein in the body. Warning to those who insist on feeding their dogs on vegetarian diets: some vegetable proteins, soya beans for example, are more helpful then others in their amino acid content, but a proprietary brand prepared vegetarian diet would be more satisfactory, as the essential nutrients are correctly balanced in such diets.

Fats

Fat plays an important role in the diet, mainly as a source of energy – it contains twice as much as protein. The body stores energy in a specific form of fat that is more readily available (metabolised) than energy in protein (muscle) and would always be used up first.

Fat has other important functions in the body chemistry. Some groups of essential vitamins are linked with fat in order to be absorbed and stored. Fat forms part of the blood-clotting mechanism of the body and contributes to other vital processes.

It is clear from this that fat is essential for a balanced, healthy diet but, in terms of quantity, it should be about one quarter the amount of protein.

Carbohydrates

Carbohydrates are the third element of the diet. They have no absolutely essential role in the dog's metabolism which, as we have seen, relies mainly on protein and fat. In the wild, dogs would eat little or no carbohydrate.

However, cereal and vegetables contain the forms of sugars and starches that can be converted into energy or body fat. This is sometimes helpful for lactating bitches or for convalescent dogs. It is also much cheaper than high protein food. Also, some vegetable cell walls, although not digestible, are useful in supplying bulk and roughage to aid the movement of food through the digestive tract.

Carbohydrates give variety and add a few tasty morsels to a dog's diet. We'd be lost without them as rewards and titbits.

Vitamins

It has been researched and established that dogs require a total of 13 vitamins in their diet, albeit in very small quantities. Vitamins are chemicals necessary to the smooth running of the body processes. Vitamins A, D, E and K are actually stored in the liver, while B and C are not. Each has a vital role in some specific body function or metabolic process.

Symptoms of deficiency relate to the role that particular vitamin plays. For example, the lack of Vitamin A could affect the eyesight and the immune system. Lack of vitamin C would produced scurvy-like symptoms with an irritated, bleeding skin, as it did in the sailors of old. Most dogs can produce vitamin C for themselves, but it is present in most brand foods as a precaution for those who cannot.

There is not a great deal of highly specialised knowledge about the effect of the lack of various other vitamins. The very obvious one, once prevalent among undernourished children, is the lack of vitamin D, which causes rickets and affects the growth of the bones.

Your veterinary surgeon will be very aware that the prolonged use of antibiotics can suppress the uptake of vitamin K. Normally this vitamin is produced in the gut and contributes to the vital blood-clotting system. Without it, there is a danger of spontaneous haemorrhage.

Much work has been and is still being done concerning the use of vitamins in preventing various conditions, such as hip dysplasia (unknown in Irish Terriers), but at present it is in something of a state of flux.

I must emphasise again that only small amounts of these vitamins are necessary, and overdosing your dog can cause a condition called hypervitaminosis. In any case, diagnosing your dog's needs can be fairly hit and miss, so it's best left to an expert. Dog food manufacturers ensure a balance of vitamins and minerals in their products.

"Hey – yours looks nicer than mine!"

Minerals

In the complex chemistry of the body, minerals play a vital part and need to be present in the diet in sufficient amounts.

The level or ratio of calcium and phosphorus needs to be balanced. Domestic dogs, unlike their wild ancestors, often lack calcium as they do not have the opportunity to hunt and crunch up the bones of their prey. The dog's teeth and jaws were especially adapted for this purpose. The long canines enable it to crush bone.

Because of their rapid growth, puppies need the correct calcium/phosphorus ratio in their diet. They get this more easily from milk or even cheese than from a supplement, although cheese makes some puppies sick. It is possible to overdose a puppy on mineral supplements, as with vitamins.

Other minerals, such as iron and copper, play key roles in maintaining haemoglobin (red cell) levels in the blood. Sodium and potassium affect the nervous system. Iodine is essential for the correct working of the thyroid gland which, in turn, affects all the energy-releasing (metabolic) processes of the body. Manganese, cobalt and selenium have smaller, but equally essential, parts to play, while zinc aids the repair or healing process.

Supplements

If your dog is being fed on a balanced diet and is eating well it is not necessary to supplement the feed with vitamins and minerals. It is tempting to buy these supplements as they are usually on prominent display in pet shops and you somehow feel 'the more, the merrier'. This is absolutely not so and, as we have seen, too much of some vitamins, especially the fat-soluble ones, can be dangerous. For instance, X-rays have shown that too much vitamin A somehow weakens the structure of the bones. Excessive vitamin D can cause a build-up of calcium in the blood.

Even the long-term feeding on a food with a high vitamin content can cause hypervitaminosis, which is far more common today than hypovitaminosis (vitamin deficiency). The levels are too high in the long term, and you may have to vary the food with one less rich in supplements.

Puppies and lactating bitches need more calcium and the addition of sterilised bone flour is recommended. This should be given with cold liver oil (vitamin D) to facilitate the absorption of the extra calcium.

Discuss the details with your vet to make sure you are not overdoing the vitamins. However, there is no risk of overdoing the B group and this, in the form of yeast tablets, can prove a great appetiser and pick-me-up after an illness.

Proprietary dog food

The pet food industry is much older than you probably imagine. James Spratt first introduced specialised dog biscuits into Great Britain in 1866. He won the support of some of the leading breeders of the day, including Charles Cruft, who went on to found the famous dog show that still bears his name.

There is so much knowledge today about the dietary needs of both humans and other animals that I sometimes wonder how on earth we managed before. I have no doubt that, in our ever-imperfect world, all these new, specialised and often vastly expensive diets have their own built-in disadvantages. The pet food industry is now a multi-million pound international concern. It is highly competitive and vast sums of money are spent on research and promotion. Adjustments and refinements are being made constantly and there are now special diets for puppies, mature and older dogs. There are also diets for dogs with special needs, such as invalids or obese dogs. That puppies need to be fed differently from mature dogs is a matter of common sense, but the difference today is that the diets are based on scientific research and many an old wives' tale has been disproved.

Whether these 'perfect' foods equip a dog to cope with life as it really is in the long-term will be interesting to see. Are we in danger of producing dogs who can eat nothing but perfectly balanced food and react with allergies and enteritis to everything else? Most dogs scavenge, given half the chance, and need digestive systems that can cope with bacteria and unusual items.

Without doubt, convenience food for all animals has made the keeping of pets, especially dogs, much more manageable and popular today. Not many of us could face the smell of tripe and offal in our pristine, modern kitchens. There are three main categories of prepared food: canned, semi-dry and dry. Each has been carefully researched and each in its way presents the correct dietary needs of the dog. Measures and tables indicate how much should be given, and it is important to follow the manufacturers' guidelines precisely. Never exceed the amount recommended, or your dog may have tummy upsets or put on too much weight.

It is also advisable to read the contents list, as most prepared foods come complete with all the necessary vitamins and minerals, rendering it both unnecessary and ill-advised to add supplements.

The amount of protein varies in the various brands. Some have an all-meat content and are more expensive than those with a higher cereal content. Many come with instructions to include a cereal mixer with the canned food. This provides carbohydrate energy, which is much cheaper than meat, and the dry biscuits or large pellets give the dog something to chew, which is good for teeth and gums and encourages the dog to eat more slowly.

Irish Terriers' dietary needs vary throughout their lives.
Zuleika at 20 weeks. Photo: Marc Henrie

Canned food

This is still the most popular form of dog food in Great Britain, although dry food has taken a commanding lead in the United States of America. It has a high water content (as much as 70–80%), making it smell and taste good to the dog, if not to you!

The disadvantage is that cans are heavy to carry and take up a considerable amount of storage space. However, they do keep. In a cool place, they can be stored safely for months – even a year. They also need to be opened with a can-opener or require a sharp tug on a tag-opener. This is not a problem if you are feeding one dog but can be very hard on the fingers and wrists if you have several. It is also time-consuming. You need a long spoon to empty the contents and break it up into smaller pieces. Always put the food on an easy-clean surface, as some dogs are messy eaters and soft food can slip off the plate. On the whole, Irish Terriers are neat feeders and make a real point of cleaning their beards afterwards – usually on the door mat, if the food is moist and sticks.

I always think that canned food is slightly addictive, and nothing else ever seems to taste as good to dogs. It is useful for dogs who are getting over an illness or refusing to eat. They can often be tempted with a can and the protein is usually digested easily and less difficult to chew and swallow. It is important to realise that, once a can is opened, it will not stay fresh, even for a day, unless stored in the refrigerator. You can buy plastic tops or use clingfilm to seal the cans and protect the other food from the strong smell.

Semi-dry food

This is a halfway house between canned and fresh food and the dry mixes. It is supposed to have the good taste and easy digestibility of the former and the convenience of the latter. It has an unusual texture, rather like soft candle wax. It appears very clean and odourless, but the dogs seem to enjoy it enough.

The water content is 25–30% and the pieces, which usually come in transparent, sealed envelopes, look like either minced meat or chunks of meat. You need to read the contents label to discover exactly what the feed contains, as it is by no means only meat. Poultry and bone meal are sometimes constituents, as is soya bean meal. Vitamin and mineral levels are adequate; there is no need for extra to be given.

Semi-dry foods contain preservatives so do not require constant refrigeration. However, once the packet is open the contents dry out very quickly. Any leftovers can be stored in an air-tight tin. These foods contain sugar, so are not suitable for diabetic dogs. They are more concentrated than dry food, which means that less bulk is required. There will be far less mess than with canned food. Like canned food, semi-dry foods are useful for convalescent dogs or lactating bitches, because they are easily digested. They usually need to be used up within four months, but check the date on the packet. Vitamin content will deteriorate after this time and the food will become less nutritionally sound.

Dry food

Sometimes, dogs who have been fed on other types of food are not pleased to be given dry food. It is less palatable and takes longer to eat. Some dogs eat only a little at a time and, for one dog alone, the bowl can be left down all day. This seems to take some of the joy out of dinner time, but it is the last word in convenience food. It is easy to see the immense saving of labour in the use of dry food in large kennels.

The best dry foods are not cheap but, as the water content is as low as 8%, you are paying only for the actual food. This is as good or better value in the end.

You can add some gravy or cooked vegetables in a soup, or even water, to dry food to make it more tempting. Once wet, any uneaten food will not keep and needs to be thrown out. It turns into a mushy porridge which dogs, on the whole, do not like to eat anyway.

Some dry foods need to be soaked. These tend to be special diets and come in the form of thin, flat pieces or flakes. They are usually highly concentrated and well-balanced diets. As they do not have to be chewed, they are not as good for teeth and gums as the dry, chunky pieces.

Fodder mites Like semi-dry foods, dry foods have a shelf life of about four months, but it is necessary to check the dates on the sacks. If kept too long, dry food can attract fodder mites and so be spoiled. You may not be able to see the mites, but there is a change in the smell of the food. It is extremely important to use the sacks in strict rotation and keep the bins clean, regularly scrubbed out and carefully dried.

Storage Dry foods come in large, strong plastic or paper sacks in various sizes. These can be stacked neatly in a dry place, ideally indoors, as the food can attract mice or rats if stored in an outside garage or shed. Depending on how much you need, bulk buying is obviously cheaper. Large sacks are not always easy to handle or carry, so a small hand-trolley or wheelbarrow is an essential aid. You should store at least the sack in use in a metal bin with a tight lid. The smell of dry food is not pleasant in a kitchen cupboard.

Lizzie.

Fresh food

Some pet shops offer packs of frozen dog meat to be stored in a home freezer but not, it is suggested, with food for human consumption. In no way is it a balanced diet; it should be treated simply as a packet of frozen meat. It is heavy to carry and bulky to store, but considerably cheaper than dry foods. Some kennels and dog owners use a combined feeding programme involving dry food supplemented with frozen meat packs. Remember that any food that has been frozen and then thawed deteriorates more quickly than fresh food. On no account should it be refrozen.

This food consists mainly of offal, such as tripe (the stomach lining of cattle), heart, liver and spleen (melts). It should be thawed carefully overnight. Although tripe is sometimes fed raw, the food should generally be cooked well through for at least 20 minutes to kill any parasites in the meat that could affect the dogs. The tapeworm is one of the most common.

Cooking and preparing, dishing and carefully washing the bowls takes much longer than it does for dry food, and the smell is horrible and seems to hang about. However, it is possible to get a proper régime going in which you cook enough raw food for the week. The correct amount for each day can then be measured into plastic bags and carefully stored in a freezer. Each bag can then be thawed and emptied out into the dog bowl as required.

It is necessary to vary the type of meat as the protein and vitamin content varies considerably. Too much of one type could cause a tummy upset, and some dogs are less tolerant of lights (internal organs) and liver in large quantities.

Eggs provide an excellent source of protein. They can be mixed with a feed, either raw or hard-boiled. Chicken too is a good protein, but neither chicken nor egg has enough fat for balanced diet. On the other hand, minced beef contains a high percentage of fat.

It is difficult to provide all the correct ingredients in a palatable form using meat packs alone. They are probably most useful as a supplement to dry or semi-dry foods.

You need a good biscuit mixer with a meat diet. Check the packaging to ensure that the mineral and vitamin content is correct for the size of the dog. Ideally, the proportion of meat to carbohydrate should be 50/50, but slightly more meat if offal is used, as the protein is less concentrated.

It is possible to provide carbohydrates in other forms, such as rice, potatoes (not approved of by some breeders), oats, wholemeal pasta or brown bread. Should you do this, there is a chance that the vitamins and minerals will be insufficient. You can remedy this with a sprinkling of the correct substitute over the food.

All vegetables should be cooked before being added to the meat. This makes them more digestible, and the dog is less likely to suffer from flatulence or diarrhoea. Roast vegetables are best – carrots, turnips, swedes and so on – as they bulk up the volume of food without making the dog put on too much weight. Some dogs refuse vegetables, although Irish Terriers are good eaters on the whole. You need to mix the vegetables in well with the meat, or an over-fussy dog will sort them out and leave them in the dish, licked clean and tidy.

Except for the odd occasion, green vegetables are not advisable, especially cabbage, sprouts and broccoli. While providing low-calorie bulk, they also create gasses in the gut, which is not pleasant. Onions are not recommended, as many dogs seem to produce allergic symptoms when they eat them.

Vegetarian Diets

Some vegetarians like their dogs to be strict vegetarians too. This is perfectly sound, provided that the diet is varied and well planned. Dogs are not natural vegetarians, so any diet based entirely on vegetable products must be constantly supplemented with the necessary vitamins and minerals. A good biscuit mixer that provides some good, hard chewing is a help.

One problem is that the protein in vegetables lacks certain essential amino acids. Soya beans provide a good source but can cause diarrhoea if given in large quantities. Sources of linoeic acid, such as eggs and Cheddar cheese, convert into the amino acids so essential for the dog's health. Corn oil is another good source, and is also thought to be good for the dog's coat. It can be stirred into the food – you would need to check the amount with your vet.

As you can see, preparing a vegetarian diet for your dog is not a simple matter. In addition, many of the ingredients would have to be bought in a health shop, which can be expensive and inconvenient. For this reason, I recommend the vegetarian diets produced by certain pet-food manufacturers as a safe and simple option. Like all pet products today, they have been carefully researched and will meet all your dog's requirements.

It is difficult to switch a dog accustomed to a meat-based diet to a vegetarian one. There is no problem if dogs are used to it from puppyhood but older dogs seem to crave meat and may become restless and unsettled. Fussy eaters may need careful persuading. If your vet has recommended a special vegetarian diet because your dog is unwell it can prove especially difficult. You need to resort to tricks, such as sprinkling the dinner with yeast powder or mixing in some scrambled egg. You can give your dog cooked fish, but there is a serious danger from small, sharp bones. You need to break it down with a fork and look very carefully; however, fish is always tricky.

White or brown bread can be fed to dogs. Today's white bread, made from unbleached flour, is safe for them.

Fluids

Drinking water

A large dish of fresh, cool drinking water should always be available for your dog. Always have water and a bowl in the car and on any outing that entails being away from home for even an hour or so. Dogs suffer terribly from thirst and a day on the beach or a long, hot journey can be agony for a thirsty dog. Irish Terriers, being lively and very 'on the go', soon reach the stage of being overheated, panting and distressed. It seems extraordinary

"That's all very interesting, but where's my dinner?"

that sometimes they refuse to drink at once when in this state. Leave the bowl down, however – they will drink it eventually.

As has been mentioned before, dogs fed on dry food are especially prone to thirst.

Milk

Some dogs can tolerate milk but, although valuable as a source of calcium, it can cause loose stools or even diarrhoea. If your dog is already receiving all the calcium necessary for health, milk is optional. Dogs usually love it, and a saucer of milk with the cat can be a great treat. Milk should not be left standing to turn sour, a particular danger in hot weather. Some breeders think it is best given after a meal.

Titbits and Treats

Irish Terriers are rarely overweight and I have never seen one that I could call obese. Even neutered dogs and spayed bitches seem to keep remarkably trim. Therefore, there is not quite the same anxiety about little 'smackerals' between meals making them fat as there is with some other breeds.

Having said that, it can be very irritating to have a dog fussing and worrying you by constantly asking for titbits. Irish Terriers soon learn where their biscuits are kept and even a hand on the door can bring them scurrying to show you the way. They know exactly about the fridge, the pantry, the box of chocolates on your desk or the Polo mints in your pocket. So be warned – it may be charming to sit down with your puppy and share a biscuit, but be sure that it will never be forgotten. Irish Terriers are wonderful, funny dogs and will try everything to persuade you – staring, panting, holding up a paw, whimpering – they will stop at nothing.

Children love to feed dogs and passing morsels from the table (especially the bits they don't like!) is an old trick. We've all done it, I'm sure, but it is to be discouraged. Children should not be eating while dogs are hovering around the table. Having washed their hands, they should not touch the dogs until they have finished.

You need to decide exactly what sort of régime is right for you and your terrier and stick to it. If you are very disciplined about food and time, no doubt your dog will be disciplined too. But Irish Terriers adapt completely to their families. If you are less organised and let life run on, your Irish Terrier will be perfectly happy to swing with you. Given his huge sense of enjoyment, provided that his basic needs are met the variations of lifestyle will be up to you.

By tradition, in our house treats are always thrown for the dogs to catch. The dogs become very expert at fielding them from impossible angles. If you do this, have a word to tell them clearly when the game is over and there are no more biscuits. We use 'finished', which is clearly understood.

Kennel dogs, provided that they have plenty of human company, are no trouble. Their natural energy keeps them on their toes and, with a daily walk or play outside their run, they maintain their correct weight. Little rewards or treats for helpful behaviour or when they go back into their kennels would doubtless be enjoyed.

Types of treat

Sugar is bad for teeth – chocolates and sweet biscuits should not be given. Chocolate drops are marginally better, but it is better only to give favoured dog biscuits.

Most dogs, given the chance, are chocolate addicts. We've had the odd 'accident'. Not least memorable was one Christmas when the tree was stripped of sweets. The papers were licked clean and left flattened out on the floor. Although no Irish Terrier worth his salt would eat the wrappings, the excess sugar is likely to make them sick.

A piece of carrot is a good treat, but not all dogs will take it. As rewards for puppies they can be useful during early training sessions.

Bones and chews

Dogs undoubtedly love chewing bones. It is good for teeth and gums and gives great psychological satisfaction. It was common in the past to give dogs maorrow bones or the large [roasted] leg bones of beef. These are hard and thick enough to be safe.

No dog should ever be left unsupervised with a bone, as they are always potentially dangerous. Pieces of crunched bone can be swallowed and spike the throat or become compacted in the gut. Left in the garden, bones very soon attract flies or are buried by the dogs in large, unsightly holes. Indoors, even on a washable floor, they can be messy.

Cooked bones of any sort are extremely dangerous, as they flake and splinter more easily when chewed and can stick in the throat or gut. Chop and chicken bones are deadly dangerous. A dog found retching and gagging with the remains of a chicken carcass has almost certainly got a bone stuck in its throat. If you cannot see the bone to remove it you will need to visit your vet as soon as possible.

If the bones have already disappeared, some people think it a good idea to give the dog bread or rice. This may aid a safe passage through the gut, but you need to be very watchful. Any signs of vomiting or pains in the stomach should be investigated immediately by your vet.

With all the potential hazards of bones it is much more sensible to give your dog special dog chews. Nylabone do a large, very popular and varied range. These chews have the same advantage in preventing the build-up of tartar on the teeth and are much more hygienic – though we have had them returned to the house in an interesting state, having been buried in the garden for several days.

Many pet shops sell a range of rawhide chews and even pigs' ears, which look disgusting but are loved by dogs. These can be rather fatty. It is not really possible to have them indoors as they may stain carpets or make floors very slippery.

One warning about bones or much-favoured chews: dogs can become extremely possessive about them. Even the best-mannered of dogs will seldom share a bone with another dog. Children should be taught never to approach a dog with a bone: an intuitive snap would alarm everyone, including the dog. Teach your puppy right from the start to give up a chew (see chapter 8) and remember that bones and chews are 'special' and should be treated with respect.

Other treats

There are plenty more dog treats in varying shapes and colours. They are very expensive and delicious and make excellent presents or rewards – and can be fattening if fed to excess. They do not, unfortunately, take long to swallow. some are fortified with vitamins and minerals but, for the most part, they are just for fun.

Dental Care

Most vets have hand-outs on dental care in their surgeries and the whole idea of dental hygiene for dogs is assuming increasing importance. Cream of tartar has always been used to clean dogs' teeth, but today special toothpaste and specially designed toothbrushes are on sale. If essential, it is possible (though not recommended) to use ordinary toothbrushes and toothpaste, although foaming paste is more difficult to rinse away. It may be difficult to persuade old dogs to open their mouths and put up with brushing, but young dogs are easier to convince.

More dogs are surviving into old age now, and this is when correct dental hygiene since puppyhood really pays off.

Food allergies

As with humans, food allergies caused by sensitivity to food additives are an increasing cause for concern. Pet food manufacturers have gone to tremendous lengths to make their products as safe and allergy-free as possible.

There is a distinct difference between an allergic reaction and a reaction of intolerance to a certain food. If a dog cannot tolerate a food it will react almost immediately or within hours with vomiting and/or diarrhoea. This means that the dog's metabolism is unable to cope with, or process, the food. The more food taken, the more violent the reaction. A food allergy, on the other hand, takes longer between consumption and reaction. It takes about 10 days for the body to produce the antibodies that cause the allergic response. Even a tiny amount of the food (allergen) will trigger it off.

A wide range of symptoms can be caused by food allergies: mainly itchy skin which can become sore and weeping, vomiting or diarrhoea. Husky, heavy breathing, wheezing and coughing are other fairly common symptoms. Note that these are far more likely to have other causes. For example, fleas can cause serious skin discomfort and chest or bronchitic infections can distress the breathing.

It is difficult to trace the allergen, not only because of the time lag before the reaction but also because, if the dog's diet is varied, it is difficult to isolate the offending ingredient. You will need the help of your vet to supervise the procedure. It is a serious process that needs careful monitoring. The dog has to be fed for some time on a hypoallergenic diet, consisting mainly of proteins not usually in the dog's diet. A diet of rice and lamb is often the starting point. If there is no allergic reaction, the various elements of the previous diet are added one by one. Time has to be given to test each item as to whether there is an allergic reaction.

Sometimes the cause is not in the food itself but in the extras the dog may be receiving, such as fruit, chocolate or sweet biscuits. To complicate the matter, very similar allergic reactions can be caused by factors other than food. It has been known for an owner to go through the whole food drill only to find out eventually that the itching is caused by a certain nettle or the powder used to wash the dog's blanket.

Assuming that you find the cause of the food allergy, it is then a matter of adjusting the dog's diet accordingly. Dogs seem to have no awareness of what makes them sick or causes an allergic response. If it tastes good they will just go on eating the food.

Fussy eaters

Although it is unusual among Irish Terriers, some dog remain fussy eaters throughout their lives. This can be a nuisance, especially at times of stress when the dog really should be eating well. Recovering from an illness, after whelping, settling into a new environment or coping with an owner's absence are all made much more difficult if the dog is always having to be persuaded to eat.

Show dogs that need to be in prime condition for a show can, if they are fussy eaters, suddenly start leaving half their dinner and consequently lose weight. Breeders and show owners resort to any ruse by feeding them small and more frequent meals, warming the food and even feeding them by hand as one might a sick dog.

Puppies fed entirely on one type of food are far more difficult to introduce or change to other foods. One could say that they are less adventurous feeders, as it seems that preferences for certain foods are learnt early. Older dogs who have always been fed on canned food may take a little persuading to change to dry.

To make a change, introduce the dog to the new food gradually, putting a few pieces into the original food. Over the next few weeks, increase the ratio in favour of the new food.

Initially dogs are attracted to food by smell so, if you can make the dry food smell good by adding meat gravy or soup made from vegetables or even a sprinkling of sugar, it should make it more tempting. You need to be strict about cutting out any extras so that the dog is hungry when you give it the food. Leave the food down for half an hour or so and, if it is still untouched, try to steel yourself to make your dog miss a meal. Present the food again the the next meal time. Terriers can be very persuasive and will keep telling you it is the wrong food. We have had sulks, sighs, and walking around the bowl picking out minute pieces and leaving them strewn about on the floor. You have to decide whether it is worth persevering with the change unless, of course, it has been recommended by your vet for a specific reason.

Some dogs are better fed alone. Again, this is not usual Irish Terrier behaviour, but a shy or nervous dog settling into a new household may find a busy kitchen or other dogs feeding nearby a little off-putting. You can try putting the bowl down in the garden, but ants, flies and other animals make it unwise to leave it around outside. Find a quiet place and put down the bowl, telling the dog to eat. We were enchanted by an old dog who was so well trained that he would not eat until we tapped the bowl and said, "Begin – good boy!"

Some young dogs are put off feeding if they happen to get a fright just as they settle down to eat. A door banging, a saucepan clattering to the floor or a loud clap of thunder can temporarily upset them. It should not last – thankfully, Irish Terriers are greedy by nature.

If a dog is missing meals or off its food for more than a day or two you need to see your vet, as the dog is probably unwell. Sometimes there is a problem in the mouth, perhaps an ulcer or tooth abscess producing a reluctant feeder, but dogs rarely starve themselves as cats sometimes do.

Obesity

As with humans, more and more dogs are becoming obese today. According to a recent survey, up to a third of dogs in Britain are considered overweight. You can weigh your dog and compare it with The Kennel Club Breed Standard, but a good rule of thumb is that, unless you can feel the rib cage easily, the dog is too fat.

Obesity brings a whole list of health problems to dogs. The life expectancy of obese dogs is shorter, and heart disease, diabetes and other life-threatening diseases are more common among them. They often have problems with their joints through carrying the burden of extra weight and are more accident-prone, for instance when attempting to jump into or out of the car. Should they need surgery, they are more at risk from anaesthetic. In extreme cases, their quality of life is seriously diminished as they can neither run nor enjoy their walks. They are far less appealing to have around and never attract the same amount of attention and affection. It always seems very unfair. I have to say that Irish Terriers, with their built-in energy and natural restlessness, are rarely overweight – and I have never seen one I could call *unhappily* overweight!

The two categories most likely to put on weight are spayed bitches and neutered males. Bitches have more fatty issue in their bodies than dogs in any case and for this reason are more likely to run to fat from the age of six or seven.

To keep a dog at its correct weight sounds like a simple equation: the dog's energy requirement should equal the intake of carbohydrate and fat. Anything more than enough will be stored in the body as surplus fat. Once the intake of carbohydrate and fats has been reduced, the dog's weight should come down, but the real difficulty is to keep it there. Increased exercise is a necessary part of the programme to maintain the weight loss. It is easier to slim a dog using a commercial low-calorie package because the quantities are explained precisely. It is more difficult to judge quantities and ensure that the nutritional content is adequate if you are giving home-cooked food.

Your vet may well recommend a special obesity diet. These are helpful because the quantity of food remains the same so that the dog will not feel half starved. The food contains more fibre or bulk, which has a lower calorie content but fills up the spaces. Most obesity diets reduce the calorie intake to 60% of the original. This is quite considerable, and you need to harden your heart against anything extra. Nothing but water should be given to drink.

You need to begin by weighing your dog and fixing the target weight, which is the weight set by the Breed Standard, taking your dog's age into consideration. You will need to weigh your dog regularly to check the effectiveness of the diet. It is difficult for a dog to stand on the bathroom scales alone, although some do manage. It is better to weigh yourself first, then lift the dog and weigh the two of you together. Subtract your own weight from that of the dog. I can well imagine there will be times when neither weight pleases!

Keep a careful note or a progress chart. It may take several months to reach the target weight and after

Bright Penny of Brackenwood at 11 weeks. It is probably easier to use a proprietary puppy food at this stage.

that a certain amount of vigilance, including a weekly weigh-in, is necessary.

If you decide against a special diet and simply reduce the amount of the food generally given you may find you have a very hungry, worried dog. He will probably try to scavenge or even steal and may fuss and worry around you.

Remember: *It is much easier to prevent obesity than to struggle to cure it.*

Underweight
Weighing your dog regularly would also indicate a sudden or gradual weight loss which might need investigating. However, some dogs are naturally thin although perfectly healthy. This should not be regarded as a problem.

Special Diets
The large range of diets for special conditions is growing every year. Vets sometimes complain that it is difficult to keep up. At a simple level, sensible adjustments can be made to diet all through the dog's life if you feel the situation calls for it. Cold weather calls for more food; less can be given during a very hot summer.

The invalid
If the dog has been ill, every effort should be made to persuade him to eat. Sometimes a high-quality cat food works, or home-cooked liver or chicken served warm. Feed him by hand if it helps; your invalid will want a lot of special attention. After a gastro-intestinal attack, light food should be given in small quantities three or four times a day. Scrambled egg, rice, chicken and pasta are good.

Probiotic products

A probiotic product introduces back into the gut bacteria that aid digestion. The bacteria can be destroyed by the prolonged use of certain antibiotics. These antibiotics, while dealing with infections, can also suppress the necessary beneficial bacteria in the body. Probiotic products are available in pet shops and it is easiest to mix them with your dog's food. Live yoghurt has the same effect, provided that your dog is not allergic or intolerant to lactose.

Constipation

After an attack of diarrhoea the natural digestive rhythm can become unsettled, causing the dog to become constipated. You can add bran or any high-fibre ingredient to the diet, which produces more bulk and aids digestion.

Sometimes older dogs, who tend anyway to suffer from constipation, should be put on to canned food. It is easier to digest than dry food and the high water content helps to prevent constipation.

Life stage diets

There is an excellent range of life-stage diets for puppies and elderly dogs. Not only are these nutritionally ideal but they have chunks of the right size for young or elderly teeth. All you need are the bowls and a scoop measure to indicate the right amount each time.

Puppies

Puppies are especially liable to have tummy upsets during weaning. This is around the sixth week, when they are being put on to solid food. Even a puppy being introduced to the best complete puppy food can suddenly produce loose stools and seem unsettled. Following your vet's advice, you should change the food and give your puppy very small quantities at a time (see **Allergies**).

Puppies with diarrhoea are always bad news. Your vet will need to check that they do not become dehydrated through loss of fluid. Plenty of drinking water should be freely available at all times, not least to deter constipation.

Older dogs

Kidney failure: As dogs grow older their kidneys function less efficiently. They urinate more frequently and lose more body fluid as a consequence.

Your vet may decide that your dog should be put on a special nephritis diet to stabilise the condition. For maximum benefit, nothing but this diet should be provided. While providing a high protein content, it supplies enough fat and carbohydrate to prevent the serious weight loss often associated with kidney failure.

If you wish to make up your own diet for your dog from home-cooked food, you will need help from your vet, who will probably suggest chicken as the basic protein. In this case, you will have to give vitamin supplements as well. For instance, a Vitamin B deficiency can cause mouth sores, and this can be counteracted by the addition of yeast in powder form to your dog's diet.

Another sign of kidney failure is bad breath. Having first made sure that this is not caused by tooth and gum problems, your vet will conduct various tests and, with a clear diagnosis and correct feeding, your dog should recover and go on for several more years. If this condition is not diagnosed, the dog may go off its food and even start to vomit.

Heart failure: An ageing dog is likely to develop progressive heart failure. This condition too can be helped by changes in the diet. Food containing sodium (high levels of salt) should be avoided. These include bread, most prepared dog foods and any processed food.

Your vet will advise on the best diet for your dog. He will probably recommend a specially prepared complete food which will relieve you of the worry of preparing one yourself. It will almost certainly contain addition potassium and vitamin B, which is recommended for heart failure.

Diuretics are often prescribed for dogs with heart problems. They expel fluids from the body which tend to build up when the heart is pumping less efficiently.

Diabetes Mellitus: This metabolic disease, also known as sugar diabetes, is more common in older bitches than in dogs. It is caused by a deficiency of the hormone insulin, which is secreted in the pancreas gland. Insulin controls the uptake of glucose in the blood and, when it is insufficient, glucose builds up in the blood and is flushed out by the kidneys in urine and lost to the body. This urine has a characteristically sickly sweet smell. The body will then use its fat stores as a source of energy, so the dog will appear to be enormously hungry and thirsty. If the condition is not diagnosed, the dog will start to vomit and, ultimately, go into a diabetic coma. This is extremely dangerous and life-threatening.

The treatment of diabetes requires careful monitoring (see chapter 11) and very specific medication, but much can be done to help the dog's general condition and health through adjustments to the diet. She must not be given anything containing sugar.

If your dog is overweight, a special high-fibre diet should be given. Slimming her down will help to stabilise the sugar (glucose) concentration in the blood and may even reduce the dose of insulin required. However, if she has lost weight she will need building up. You could try a puppy food to encourage her to eat.

Frequent small feeds are better than the usual one or two meals a day. The fluctuations in blood sugar levels after feeding will then be less extreme.

Other enzymes produced by the pancreas assist digestion. If the balance is incorrect through a malfunction of the pancreas, the dog will fail to absorb her food correctly. She may be eating well and seem hungry, but the food will do her no good at all. She will lose weight and condition. Your vet will need samples of faeces to test for which enzymes need to be supplemented. Once diagnosed, these will need to be given regularly, for a long time.

Chapter Eleven

Health Care

Choosing a Vet

All veterinary surgeons undergo the same basic training, so choosing one is probably mostly about convenience and personal sympathy. You need someone in whom you have the utmost confidence. There will doubtless be times when you are worried and distressed about your dog. A good understanding with your vet is a great help. Ask around – personal recommendations are helpful.

If you live in the country, it is usually better to find a 'small animal' vet who is not too involved in treating farm animals. His or her practice will probably be more geared up to cats and dogs. Like doctors, vets would find it impossible to keep up-to-date in all fields, so most tend to specialise to some degree.

Try to find someone local. A long journey to the vet can prove harrowing with a sick dog, especially through traffic. I crossed London for 20 years to see the vet I knew and trusted. When she retired I vowed 'never again' and was amazed how much easier and less time-consuming it was. As I have said, Irish Terriers as a breed are remarkably sound and hardy. You are unlikely to be letting yourself in for lengthy ongoing treatment of any kind. When we arrive for the annual immunisation shots, my vet always says, "Had a good year, you lot?" not having seen us since last time.

However, puppies need careful attention and older dogs, too, may need more frequent checking. You may like to introduce yourself to the vet and have a good look around before your puppy arrives. Vets are busy, so keep it short. You are, of course, free to change your mind. Arrange for a check-up visit for your puppy and plan the immunisation programme, booking the dates well in advance.

If you are at all worried about your pup, do not hesitate to ring up for advice and take him in at once, if necessary. Some pups are prone to diarrhoea caused by the change of environment and diet. Having to settle and get used to new people may also prove upsetting and trigger off a tummy upset. Puppies can become dangerously dehydrated very quickly, so you need to seek advice immediately.

If you are interested in homeopathic treatment, you need to ask whether the practice offers alternative medicine as part of its service. If not, you can obtain a list of sympathetic vets from various homeopathic associations.

Health Insurance

Now is the time to make sure a health policy is in place. There are many schemes on offer. They vary, and you need to read the small print carefully. No policy covers every expense, nor will it provide total cover. They all expect you to pay the first £30 or so of each bill. Routine check-ups and immunisations are never included. However, insurance is an enormous security when you are faced with a sudden and expensive operation or high-tech treatment. The policy should cover third party liability. Some companies allow you to pay the premium in monthly instalments, which can be a great help if you have several dogs.

Your vet will advise you and, as his secretary will probably send in the forms for you, it may be as well to purchase a policy familiar to the practice. Most vets ask for payment immediately after each visit and it may be some time before you are reimbursed by your insurance company, so you should take this into your financial calculations.

You have every right to ask about costs before you launch into scans, pathology tests, ECGs and X-rays. Vets are immensely well equipped now, so be very cautious before you consent to a run of investigatory tests which may tell you little that you did not know already.

Immunisation
Immunisation is offered against the following diseases:

Distemper
Those of us old enough to remember the horrors of distemper can feel nothing but relief that puppies no longer die from it in droves. It is a viral disease spread by contact with the urine or saliva of an infected animal. The first symptoms are a dry nose, runny eyes and the appearance of being generally off-colour. If the disease is not overcome at this stage, it

Puppies like feet, but infections can be brought into the home on shoes.
Make sure your puppies are vaccinated as soon as possible.

will become increasingly serious, causing a high temperature, vomiting and even fits. There is not much you can do at this stage except try to keep the temperature down. We used to dose our dogs on raw eggs beaten up with brandy (prairie oysters) and sit with them night and day. It took them weeks to recover.

Canine Hepatitis

This is another serious disease which fortunately can now be controlled by vaccination. It attacks the liver and there are signs of jaundice, when the gums and mouth appear yellowish. The eyes can become opaque-looking and rather blue. Puppies are especially vulnerable and the survival rate is not good. There is no direct treatment. The temperature rises rapidly and can reach 40°C (104°F). There is a sudden and huge loss of weight and the dog is in a state of collapse. The blood-clotting system is affected and there may be internal haemorrhages. Should the dog miraculously survive, recovery and weight gain are extremely slow. The dog will go on being infectious for up to six months.

Leptospirosis

Again, this deadly disease can only be prevented by vaccination and seldom, if ever, cured. It should always be included in the immunisation plan. It is a bacterial disease affecting the kidneys, causing permanent damage and renal failure. Antibiotics can help if a dog is suspected of carrying leptospirosis, but there is sure to be some long-term damage to the kidneys, leading to renal failure. There is a human equivalent called Weils disease.

One distressing thing about leptospirosis is that very often a desperately sick dog appears to rally suddenly and seems much better. This may last for a day and then turn into the final collapse, when all hope is lost.

Leptospirosis is thought to be carried by rats, and any dog swimming in pools or streams in the country is at risk.

Parvovirus

Most of us had never encountered parvovirus until the start of the serious epidemic in 1980. It is a virus affecting the heart muscles, causing sudden death. Symptoms include vomiting, diarrhoea and dehydration. Until it was brought under control, hundreds of dogs, especially puppies, died. There was no direct or satisfactory treatment and it took time to produce a dog-specific vaccine. It is highly recommended that this should be administered routinely, as the virus is extremely resistant and can remain active in the soil for some time.

Rabies

This dreaded virus can attack most animals (including humans) and is transmitted through infected saliva entering the body. The central nervous system is affected. The symptoms are terrifying and the consequences dire.

In Great Britain we have strict quarantine laws regarding the entry of animals into this country and are therefore so far free from rabies. Dogs in Europe are vaccinated against the disease, but not so thousands of animals such as foxes, feral cats and badgers, all of which can catch and carry rabies. Countries in the Far East have no control whatsoever.

In some cases it takes weeks before the symptoms become obvious. It is not only a bite from an infected animal that is dangerous, but saliva can enter through a cut or graze on the skin. Extreme care is necessary. If there has been any contact with a rabid animal you should seek medical advice.

Kennel Cough

This is a troublesome condition, but not usually dangerous or life-threatening. It occurs mainly when dogs are kennelled together, and show dogs spending time with other dogs are especially prone.

The main symptom is a loud, rasping cough which seems to become even more distressing at night. The cough is at its worst for only about a week, but it can persist for much longer. Dogs affected can cough to the point of gagging and retching and will sometimes vomit up food. They appear less ill than you would expect, although it can develop into bronchio-pneumonia in very young or very old dogs. This is a far more serious condition, probably requiring a course of antibiotics.

A vaccine providing reasonable protection is available, but the cause can be complicated, with a spectrum of organisms involved. Unlike most vaccines, it is given intra-nasally (through the nostrils with a spray). Usually two doses are advised, given about a month apart, followed by an annual booster.

Breed Faults

As I have said before, Irish Terriers are blessedly free from hereditary breed faults. Absolutely no certificates and X-rays are required to confirm or deny some of the dreadful conditions found in other breeds. As my vet says: "There isn't a lot to go wrong with them." We owe a great debt of gratitude to past breeders who have done so much to preserve the health and happiness of this true working terrier.

Nevertheless, the breeder may ask you to sign a Warranty and Disclaimer (see sample in chapter 6 page 66). Certain cases that have recently been brought and won by owners against breeders – not, I must emphasise, Irish Terrier owners – have made this a sensible precaution.

Routine Care

Some health and general maintenance problems can be dealt with as part of the grooming and routine care.

Ears

Ears should be kept clean and trimmed, especially around the opening. Any sticky burrs and barley grass seeds should be removed. There is a danger that they can work their way into the ear, causing severe discomfort, and they would then have to be removed by a vet.

Various fungal conditions can attack the ear and the problem may then be compounded by bacterial infections. These cause the ears to smell very unpleasant and the dog will scratch constantly. It is sometimes made even worse by the presence of ear mites. Your vet will make a proper examination and prescribe medication. Never poke about inside an ear with an orange stick or cotton bud. It could be painful and do more harm then good.

It is quite a knack to put drops into an ear. Pull the ear flap gently forwards and upwards and squeeze in the number of drops prescribed. Massage behind the ears, holding them upwards, to dispense the medicine evenly, and prevent the dog from

shaking his ears. It can be a nuisance, as dogs tend to want to rub it off, and furniture can become soiled in the process.

Irish Terriers have neat, light ears, so they are not as prone to infections as breeds with thick, heavy ears. Only very rarely do they produce the typically terrier complaint of overly-narrow ear canals, prone to infection – I have heard of only one case in 40 years. This condition requires fairly radical surgery (lateral wall resection) and would be considered a serious breed fault.

Ears should be kept clean and trimmed, especially around the openings. Photo: Pete's Photographics.

The correct set of the ears in Irish Terriers is hard to achieve. A puppy with a perfect ear set can lose it while teething, which is exasperating. It is quite legitimate to encourage the ears back into place by sticking the tips down on the the head, just above the eyes. You would need instruction from a breeder. Once the ears have gone into place, they can be released.

Eyes

Older dogs tend to produce a slight discharge in the corner of their eyes. It is very simple to clean the eye with cotton wool dipped in a mild saline solution. Start in the corner of the eye and work outwards. Use two separate pieces of cotton wool, one for each eye.

If the eyes seem sticky you may need prescribed eye drops. After you have instilled them, hold the dog's head to prevent him from rubbing them off immediately.

More acute infections may need immediate veterinary treatment.

Feet

Irish Terriers' feet are neat and compact, and produce few problems. Irish Terriers are very fussy and careful about their feet but it is sensible to inspect them during grooming. A small stone or compacted mud can be trapped between the pads. This should be removed, as it causes limping and is painful. It helps to soak the foot in a bowl of water to soften the mud. Check around each toe and nail bed regularly. Dogs' feet are vulnerable to thorns and prickle, broken glass and crushed cans.

Dogs' feet can also be very vulnerable to stinging nettles. If stung, they may sit and worry their paws – even pulling out tufts of hair. My dogs soon learn to recognise nettles at a hundred paces and avoid them. There are creams to soothe the stinging.

Nails should be checked and trimmed routinely. City dogs walking regularly on pavements tend to wear their nails down, so their nails do not need to be cut as often as those of country dogs.

A guillotine cutter is best. Make sure it is sharp, and keep the foot steady. If the clippers are blunt and twist the nail it is extremely painful. Irish Terriers never forget, so a simple routine could then become a life-long battle. Only the tip should be trimmed off, or the nail will bleed. If this should happen, a dab with a styptic pencil will stop the bleeding at once.

Puppies' claws should be kept short – again, only the clear tip should be trimmed. If their nails were left long they could scratch and hurt the bitch, making her less keen to feed them, and the scratches could become infected and sore.

Most puppies will have had their dew claws (rather thumb-like claws on the inside of the front legs) removed. If they are still present, make sure you keep them very short, as the nails tend to curve and can catch and bleed or grow back into the skin.

Anal gland impaction

On either side of the anus are the anal glands – scent glands that mark out each individual dog's faeces. These sometimes become blocked (impacted) and have to be emptied; otherwise the dog becomes uncomfortable. Dogs tend to scoot on their bottoms; an action not; as sometimes thought, caused by worm infestation. Some breeders empty the anal glands themselves, but it requires some experience, so you may be happier to ask your vet to do it.

External Parasites
Ticks

Ticks are more a problem of the countryside, especially in areas where there are sheep and deer. They transfer easily to dogs, and then attach themselves to the skin by their mouth parts. They suck the body fluids, at which stage you will notice a round, swollen, greyish lump, about the size of a pea. It is particularly repulsive, but do not pull to remove it, as the body will detach, leaving the head and mouth under the skin. These can cause itching and irritation. There are chemical sprays, but a

Ticks can be a problem of the countryside, especially where there are sheep or deer.

smear of Vaseline is equally effective in causing the tick to drop off in one piece, as it smothers it.

In some areas of Europe and in countries outside Europe, ticks can be associated with severe illness and chronic infection. One of these, Lyme disease, which causes fever and problems in the joints, can be transmitted to humans. Lyme disease can also cause blindness in dogs.

Lice

You may be horrified to find when you take him for his first check-up that your puppy has lice. Do not be alarmed; this is not unknown, though not a sign of good kennel management. On discovering the eggs (nits) your vet may prescribe a powder or medicated shampoo. Both remedies are quickly effective.

Dog lice stay with dogs. There are two species, both of which attach to the skin and feed on the body fluids. They transfer through direct contact with other dogs. They can cause considerable irritation, but are not dangerous and are easily eradicated.

As well as beds, dogs and cats sometimes share fleas.

Fleas

Fleas are a much greater problem. With centrally heated houses and more carpets and furnishings, fleas can survive and prosper throughout the year, not just in summer. Part of their life-cycle can be spent off the dog and bedding, so carpets and furniture can become infested. It is an on-going problem, as a dog can pick up fleas at any stage of its life. They cause considerable discomfort and the dog will scratch continuously and even bite itself to try to relieve the itching. This can cause skin lesions, which sometimes become infected and sore. The dog can also become allergic to the fleas' saliva, which can cause a spotty, itchy and unpleasant rash on the skin.

Keep a flea comb as part of your grooming kit. Run it regularly across the coat, following the lie of the fur. You will probably find signs of flea dirt rather than the actual fleas. These tiny black specks – in fact, dried blood from the dog – collect into the comb and are easily spotted. Concentrate on the thick hair at the base of the tail – a favoured place for fleas. Do this outside in case a flea jumps off your dog and disappears into your carpet.

Flea control, especially in a hot summer, can become part of daily dog care. Blankets and soft beds need to be washed frequently, and special cleaning and vacuuming around the area is necessary.

Several powders and sprays are available. Read the instructions carefully, as they may be harmful to cats and toxic to fish. This is a serious problem if the dog swims in a pond or river. Cats and dog share fleas but cats require their own special sprays. Other remedies are appearing, and it is now possible to give tablets in the food which apparently deter fleas. There are special flea collars and drops which you apply to your dog's neck. There is even a pill, given weekly, which renders the fleas infertile!

Be aware that all these remedies imply a fair amount of chemical interference. They should be used sparingly and never as a cocktail.

Mites

Mites are too small to be seen by the naked eye. If your dog seems to scratch frequently and produces what looks like dandruff, this is likely to be the cheytiella mange mite. This mite can cause an itchy rash in humans, which is often diagnosed as an 'allergy to dogs'. This is quite untrue. All that is required is a special treatment shampoo from your vet. You will need to use it several times on the dog and have your carpets treated.

Scabies

Sarcoptic mange, called Scabies, has become a problem, especially in places where foxes are about. It is a very itchy rash, mainly on the face, ears and legs, which can develop into serious skin lesions. Mites may or may not be involved. Treatment involves using a sponge-on liquid preparation. Without treatment, it is irreversible and debilitating. Foxes die slow and painful deaths from it.

Demodectic Mange

Demodectic mange is caused by another species of mite. There is hair loss, mainly around the eyes and on the legs. It is not generally itchy but the bald patches can become infected and painful. This mite is generally passed from bitch to puppies. Treatment is as for scabies.

Ringworm

Ringworm is misnamed, because no parasite is involved. It is a skin fungus and is more common in cats than in dogs. It is serious in that it is contagious to humans, causing the same characteristic circular, red patches as it does on dogs and cats. It is easily cured by applying the correct antibiotic.

Internal Parasites

Roundworms

Your vet will advise you of the correct procedure in worming your puppy. This is of vital importance, as the eggs of the roundworm (Toxocara canis) can be dangerous to humans. These may be passed out in dog faeces and remain alive in the soil for up to two years. it is important that children do not play where dogs or cats defecate, as not all the animals will have been wormed regularly. Children should be taught to wash their hands before eating.

The main danger, although it occurs extremely rarely, is that, should a human being ingest the eggs of the roundworm, the larvae hatch inside the body. They can move around (a process called *visceral laval migrans*) and, should they reach the eyes, blindness could occur.

All Irish Terrier breeders take infinite care to follow veterinary instructions to keep their breeding bitches worm-free. This is vitally important, as puppies can become infected in the uterus. There are standard procedures that need to be followed to the letter.

Puppies too are dosed regularly from about three weeks until weaning. Thereafter, throughout life, they should be wormed at least once, or even twice, a year. Modern veterinary medicine has made it all very easy. Tablets are given, usually with food and, quite unlike the old days, there are not upset tummies or other side effects.

Roundworms are easy to recognise, but it is highly unlikely that you will ever see one. They are white, rather like thin spaghetti.

Tapeworms

There are several species of tapeworm, but each has the same flat ribbon shape and complex life cycle involving an intermediate host. A common one, *Dipylidum caninum*, spends part of its life cycle inside the flea. It has to be swallowed by the dog, probably during self-grooming. Only then can the worm establish itself in the dog's gut.

Another species of tapeworm, *Echinococcus granulosis*, can be a problem to both dogs and humans. The intermediate host is the sheep, and the eggs enter the body when the meat is eaten. The eggs form a type of cyst (hydatid cyst) in the body's organs. These can become quite large and make the dog ill. Dogs should never be given raw sheep meat, as that is the source of the infection.

Note that most remedies against roundworm are not effective against tapeworm.

Dental Care
Cleaning

We have looked at the need for regular cleaning with a toothbrush and toothpaste to keep the mouth fresh and remove the build-up of tartar. If tartar is allowed to build up it causes a gap between the tooth and gum. Food then can get caught in this, and an infection begins. This can lead to loss of teeth and a great deal of pain, and the dog's general health may suffer. Your vet will make routine checks and may advise the removal of tartar under anaesthetic.

Shedding

Puppies lose their teeth somewhere between 14 weeks and six months. They will chew and chew in an effort to be rid of the milk teeth and encourage the adult ones to emerge. Nylabone toys and chews are a help, but occasionally a milk tooth may need to be removed. You may find that the gums bleed and are very tender.

To many a breeder's despair, puppies' ears can suddenly collapse, prick upwards or move askew in response to the irritation of teething. With luck, they will settle down into the correct position again, but not always.

Other Conditions and Emergencies
Arthritis

Because Irish Terriers are fairly light and well balanced in body weight and bone structure they do not usually suffer much from general wear and tear of the joints. Also, they are very seldom overweight. They may become stiffer in the hindlegs as they grow older, but the chronic joint problems so prevalent in other breeds are almost unknown.

Arthritis often occurs after an injury to the joint, ligaments or tendons. Your vet may advise an X-ray or you could, with his consent, look at alternative therapies such as acupuncture and herbal treatments. These take a long-term view, but can prove very effective. There are also remedies to control the pain.

Cold and damp make the condition seem worse.

Another form of arthritis is caused by an infection, either bacterial or viral. This condition requires a period of rest to allow the body to overcome the infection. Exercise at this point could damage the joints.

It is very important at all stages of a dog's life to rest an injury for the prescribed time. This will help to avoid the onset of arthritis later in life.

Bites (Dog)

Bites are most likely to come from other dogs and need to be watched with care, as they can become infected. If they are bleeding freely you need to bathe them in a solution of antiseptic, dust on some wound powder and press gently to stop the bleeding.

A bad bite is a veterinary emergency and you may have to quieten and comfort a very shocked dog. A torn ear will bleed profusely and the bleeding is difficult to stop. On the whole, vets do not like to stitch ears as it involves cutting back the cartilage first. This is quite a major procedure and, unless the dog is a show dog, it is not worth doing. The wound will heal eventually, but the ear may need to be bandaged firmly against the head for a week or two.

You do find the odd problem ear that never quite heals and seems to bleed again if the dog shakes its head vigorously, scratches or rubs up against something. This is a great nuisance and very messy. You need to press the ear firmly between two dressings (or even your handkerchief) until the bleeding stops.

Some bad bites may be stitched or strapped with a butterfly bandage, or sometimes even clamped. However, the healing process starts from the inside, not from the skin. Where there is a likelihood of infection it is important for the wound to drain properly.

Bites (Snake)

The only poisonous snake in Great Britain is the adder but, in other parts of the world, snakes are a serious problem to all animals. The British/European adder lives mainly in sandy heathland throughout the country, and is more likely to be seen on hot summer days.

Should your dog be bitten by an adder, get him home or to the car as quickly as possible. Carry him if you can manage to, or make a sling with a coat or anorak so that two people can do it together. It is a good idea to keep him as quiet as possible. Apply ice cubes or a packet of frozen peas to the area around the bite. Give him a dose of antihistamine (Piriton, for example) and ring your vet at once.

If you regularly exercise your dog in an area such as the New Forest, where adders are common, it is a sensible precaution to keep antihistamine tablets with you. You may have to dose your own or someone else's dog.

Burns and scalds

The first-aid procedure is always to apply cold water to the burn. This will help to draw out the heat. A foot or leg can be put into a bucket of cold water. Other parts of the body can be hosed or sluiced with cold water from a jug or pan. This needs to be kept up for at least 15 minutes, though in winter the dog may become very cold and shivery. Ring your vet, who will advise you. Cover the dog in wet towels in the car, but again be aware of his temperature in winter. If the burn is severe, he may be very shocked and need a lot of reassurance.

There are no specific burns units for the treatment of dogs. Keeping the burn clean and cool with saline dressings while healing takes place is the normal procedure. Scarring and hair loss are almost inevitable if the burn is severe.

Cancer

The incidence of cancer in all dogs, as in people, is fairly high. However, the figures could be distorted by the increase in the number of elderly dogs. It is particularly sad if a young dog becomes ill with the disease.

Research, especially in the United States, is forging ahead and every year there is an improvement in the possibility of curative treatment and ways of coping with symptoms. You do, however, need to make some hard decisions. Most dogs will come through an operation and probably recover well. Whether you can go ahead with radio or chemotherapy is another matter. Quality of life is an overriding consideration. The exhaustion and other side-effects often accompanying treatment should be taken into account. If the dog is old, it is especially unfair.

Constipation

The most common causes for this are dietary and remedies have already been suggested in chapter 9.

Consult your vet if the difficulty persists, as there may be other reasons. If the dog is straining and in severe pain he will almost certainly have something caught low down in the back passage. Do not give a laxative, as this can produce dangerous tearing and haemorrhage, but see your vet immediately. A spiked piece of bone or, as happened to one of mine, a small stick may be caught and need to be removed, either manually or surgically.

Coughing

Coughing is one of those common symptoms that can have various causes, varying in seriousness. You should consult your vet about any cough that lasts for more than a day. You could try a soothing linctus: Benelyn is suitable.

One fairly common reason for coughing, Kennel Cough, is described on page 133.

A sore throat and infected tonsils can cause coughing or, on the other hand, coughing can cause a sore throat. It is hard to sort out cause and effect but, either way, antibiotics usually deal with the problem quickly.

A sudden violent attack of coughing and retching should be considered an emergency. It is likely that something has got stuck in the dog's throat or far back in the roof of the mouth. You can try to look, but this will probably distress the dog more. Do not delay, but get to your vet as soon as possible.

If there is a strange smell, it could be that your dog has drunk poison or disinfectant. This too could be dangerous.

Sometimes, especially in old age, the dog may produce a 'heart cough'. This tends to happen when the heart is working less efficiently and may have become slightly enlarged. It could even be pressing on the oesophagus (wind-pipe), causing a constant dry cough. Modern drugs do much to alleviate the discomfort.

Ringworm and other conditions also may cause the dog to cough frequently. It is advisable to check with your vet.

Cuts

Cuts usually happen to feet, and vary in seriousness. They always seem to occur when you are miles from home or the car, and profuse bleeding is always alarming to watch.

Some dog owners keep a 5cm crepe bandage in their pockets for this very emergency. It is certainly sensible to have something in the car to use as strapping – I once had to tear up a towel. This prevents the blood from going everywhere.

As for bites, bathe the cut with a mild antiseptic and sprinkle wound powder, which will help it to heal more quickly, on to an antiseptic dressing. Hold it firmly against the cut until the bleeding has more or less stopped, and bandage it securely.

It is difficult to bandage a foot efficiently and your best efforts with an old sack and elastoplast strapping will probably unravel. Your vet will have the correct dressing and even a 'boot' if necessary. It is best for him (or her) to instruct you, as the wound must be kept clean and dry.

There will be a lot of scolding "No, no!", as your dog will want to remove the strapping. It is imperative that he does not, as licking may keep the cut open and therefore more likely to become infected.

A clean, deep cut anywhere on the body is sometimes sutured (stitched) or the edges held together with special strapping.

A healthy dog should heal quickly, but it does require management to avoid set-backs.

Cystitis

Cystitis is an inflammation of the bladder, usually caused by an infection. However, there can be more serious implications involving kidney stones or a tumour.

The dog will urinate frequently, or at least try to. There may be signs of strain and discomfort and there could be blood in the urine.

Your vet will probably ask for a specimen. This you can collect in a flat dish – an old saucer is ideal for bitches. Slip it under her as she squats down. Dogs are more difficult to catch, but you need to persevere – try using a jug.

Put the specimen in a screw-top bottle.

Diabetes

Diabetes is caused by the failure of the pancreas to produce enough insulin to control the sugar levels in the blood. It is most prevalent in older bitches and is difficult to treat (stabilise) if the bitch is unspayed, because of hormone variations. General symptoms are excessive thirst and subsequent urinating, plus an increased appetite.

Your vet will need a urine specimen for diagnosis. Modifying the diet is sometimes sufficient to control the condition but, in more severe cases, daily or even twice daily injections of insulin may be necessary. Your vet will instruct you on how to cope; it is not a problem. Reading the blood sugar count on the special kit provided and giving the injections is very straightforward.

We had a diabetic bitch for many years. The only real problem was chasing her first thing in the morning with a saucer poised (see **Cystitis** above). She objected to the saucer and would hang on as long as possible. I would trail behind through summer dew or winter frost in dressing-gown and Wellington boots.

Diarrhoea

Diarrhoea indicates that there is some sort of trouble in the dog's digestive system. This could be in the small or large bowel. The attacks may be mild and require no more treatment than a day without food. If they are more severe and accompanied by vomiting the dog, and particularly the puppy, may become dehydrated and need intravenous fluids.

Your vet will require a description of the dog's faeces to help the diagnosis. A black stool indicates some internal bleeding and the dog should be seen by your vet immediately. Puppies can be in real danger. There are many and varied causes of diarrhoea, not least the emergence of the new type of dog who can eat only his one perfect balanced food (see chapter 10) and is upset by one Brussels sprout or a chocolate biscuit.

Irish Terriers love to scavenge and will tip out a bin and eat the contents very happily, often with no good consequence to their digestions. Various forms of bacterial food poisoning such as salmonella cause severe upsets. Some viral infections such as parvovirus produce similar symptoms. Food intolerance and allergies can cause chronic diarrhoea, as can stress and shock. Like humans, dogs can suffer from colitis and other related symptoms of an irritable bowel.

Diarrhoea can also be one of several symptoms when a dog is simply failing to thrive. This requires skilled veterinary diagnosis and care.

Recovery from an attack of diarrhoea involves the gut having time to recover. Giving the dog small, light meals several times a day – boiled rice, white bread and a little chicken or boiled egg – is a good way to begin.

Drowning

It is essential to drain the water out quickly by holding the dog upside-down by its hind legs. You can try artificial respiration by placing the dog on its side on the ground. Pull the tongue forward to be sure the air passage is free. Place one hand on top of the other and press firmly against the rib cage. Continue to press and release every five seconds in a regular rhythm. With luck, this will restart the breathing. If this is unsuccessful, you could try mouth-to-mouth resuscitation.

Electrocution

It is essential to disconnect all electrical equipment when it is not in use if there is a puppy around. Puppies will chew anything, so a live electrical cable is a deadly hazard. If the worst happens, turn off the power at the mains, if possible, before attempting to remove your dog. Never touch him directly with your hand, as you too will then receive the electrical shock. A wooden stick, rolling-pin or broom should be used to prise him away if you cannot find the mains switch quickly. You may have to give artificial respiration (see above) and treat the dog for shock.

Eclampsia

This condition, also known as 'milk fever', occurs when a lactating bitch's calcium level drops suddenly and is described in detail in chapter 9.

Fits

Fits can be very distressing to watch, especially as there is not much you can do to help. The dog will collapse and suddenly become rigid, clenching his jaws and sometimes frothing at the mouth. He may cry and whimper and the feet may jerk and paddle. Sometimes the bladder and bowels will empty involuntarily. The fit could be brief and over in seconds or last up to half an hour.

Keep the dog warm and quiet in a darkened room and allow him to recover in his own time. He may appear confused and his eyes may seem unable to focus properly. Until he is fully conscious, do not attempt to restrain him or give any medicine. You could get bitten.

The reason for the fit is an irregular function of the brain, but the causes are many. Your vet will make a thorough investigation, and treatment and management are usually successful.

Hiccoughs and wind

Puppies are prone to hiccoughs, often when they are learning to lap from a dish. Curiously, as with babies, a small teaspoonful of gripe water in a little milk helps.

Old dogs often suffer from wind, and can become the proverbial social liabilities! You need to change or adjust the diet and even try giving three small meals rather then one large one each day. Gripe water has been known to help, especially if the dog looks slightly bloated. Charcoal biscuits and Forgastrin, which contains bismuth and charcoal, may help.

Warning: Should your dog appear bloated and seem distressed, especially after food, it is a real **emergency**. Ring your vet and get there quickly. The dog could need immediate treatment for gastric dilation torsion (a twisted gut), which is a high-risk state.

Hypoglycaemia

This condition is seen mainly in over-worked gundogs. The dog seems to stagger and become confused. Give him something sweet – a piece of chocolate or some glucose water is ideal – and he will recover immediately.

Mastitis

This is inflammation of the milk glands in a lactating bitch and its remedies are discussed fully in chapter 9.

Metritis (Pyometra)

This condition is most likely to occur in older, unspayed bitches, although neutering is no guarantee against it. The danger time is four to six weeks after the bitch has been on heat. Fluid, pus and general debris accumulate in the uterus. The bitch becomes ill, depressed, often feverish and vomits. There may be a vaginal discharge, which could be white or brownish red.

This is a very sick bitch and you need to contact your vet at once. An ovarian hysterectomy will almost certainly be necessary to save her life.

Endometriosis, which is an inflammation of the lining of the uterus, may respond to antibiotics and not require surgery.

Poisoning

This is a real hazard to dogs, especially puppies who, like children, chew anything. Scavenging and rooting about, favourite Irish Terrier pastimes, are also potentially dangerous.

The dog will show signs of extreme distress, sometimes retching and vomiting, and may even collapse. Seek your vet's advice at once.

It is not always easy to find the cause, and some poisons take time to show any effect. You will need to give your vet as much information as possible – any chewed remains, dug-up plants or specimens of vomit should be shown to him or her.

Take extreme care with all garden poison: slug pellets, rat poison and weedkiller are deadly. Aim to find other methods of control and have a poison-free garden. Antifreeze is lethal and, unfortunately, dogs seem to like it. Keep all medicines under lock and key. Screw-top bottles may baffle children, but puppies chew them up very easily and swallow the pills, often with dire consequences.

Road Traffic Accidents

Dogs loose on a road are at deadly risk from the ever-increasing amount of traffic. Should you see or become involved in an accident in which a dog has been hit, exercise extreme care when approaching the animal. He will almost certainly be in a state of pain and panic and may well bite you. Use a belt or lead as a noose around his neck to guide him off the road. Beware of oncoming cars, as you might be hit or cause an accident.

Should the dog be lying on the road, again approach with care. Kneel down and put your arms underneath him and, keeping him as flat as possible, remove him to the side of the road. If you have a coat or blanket, ease it under the dog and, with help, you can lift him to safety in the blanket. Wrap him up and keep him warm until the police arrive.

All accidents in which a dog is struck must by law be reported to the police. The police will advise you about veterinary services if you are in an unfamiliar area.

Stings (Wasp and Bee)

Despite being stung frequently, every Irish Terrier I have ever known has been an inveterate bee and wasp hunter. One used to spend the entire summer 'frozen' like a pointer with her head in the bee-covered mallow bush. There would be the odd 'kill' and the odd sting, which would send her scurrying off shaking her head, but not for long. Back she would go to the hunt again.

Stings are not generally dangerous to dogs unless they are in the mouth, when there is a danger of swelling and blocking of the airway. Should this begin to happen, ring your vet at once. A sting on the ear or foot can be counteracted by a wasp spray such as Waspeze, but this cannot be used near the eyes or in the mouth. Piriton can help, but only with your vet's permission.

Ideally, dogs should learn to avoid stinging insects, but they seem to think the fun outweighs the risk.

Homeopathic Remedies

Most vets today are very knowledgeable about homeopathy. Alternative medicine is becoming as popular in the treatment of animals as in humans. You have only to ask and a fistful of leaflets will be put into your hands – and it is difficult to know where to begin.

What is Homeopathy?

Homeopathy has been in use since the time of Hypocrites but, in its modern form, has evolved from the work of a Halinemann, a German chemist who lived over 200 years ago. He discovered that small doses of Chincona (from which quinine is derived), if taken in small doses, produced the symptoms of malaria. When given to sufferers in similar small doses it helped them to recover. He went on to test other substances in widespread use, such as Arsenic and Belladonna, with equal success.

The results of these experiments suggested to Halinemann that the body's own defences were stimulated into action by a very small substance that 'mimicked' a disease. Hence the idea that 'like may be cured by like'. Indeed, the efficacy of the drug seemed to be enhanced by the smallness of the dose, which prevented unpleasant or harmful side effects.

Because of the small doses, homeopathy is a very safe and natural way to treat health problems from which our pets may suffer. It promotes good health because of the body's own powers of self-regulation and self-healing. It is often very successful when used to treat chronic conditions that have responded to no other cure. To give your dog homeopathic remedies is to be assured that the treatment is safe, free from side effects and environmentally friendly.

Most homeopathic remedies come in the form of powders or tablets. It is preferable to give them between meals without food. If this proves difficult they can be given on small pieces of food or crushed, if it is a tablet, between two spoons and tipped on to the back of the tongue.

Try to handle the remedy as little as possible. If you have to touch it, make sure your hands are clean and dry.

Tablets should be stored in a dry, cool place, away from the sunlight, and kept in the containers in which they are supplied. This would be a paper box or glass phail or bottle – *not* a plastic bottle or bag, as the remedy could react to plastic.

Dosage

The dosage of homeopathic remedies is very different according to whether the remedy is for an acute onset of symptoms or for a long-standing or chronic condition. Instructions need to be followed carefully.

Most pharmacists stock a range of homeopathic remedies and cures suitable for both humans and animals. If the dog's condition is serious, or if the symptoms persist, it is always advisable to contact a vet.

A basic First Aid kit suggested by the Homeopathic Development Foundation Ltd includes the following:

- *Arnica* For bruising, wasp and bee stings; before and after tooth extraction.
- *Arconite* For fright and shock; for the onset of feverish condition.
- *Arsen Alb* For vomiting and diarrhoea; for the chilly dog who cannot settle and has constant thirst for small amounts of water.

- *Calendula and Hypericum Mother Tincture Combination*   An invaluable antiseptic and mouthwash.
- *Gelsemium*   For timidity and nervousness; for feverish and restless states.
- *Ignatia*   For pining, for instance in boarding kennels.
- *Nux Vom*   For poor appetites; for digestive upsets and constipation; for the touchy, irritable dog.
- *Scullcap and Valerium*   Sometimes given to dogs at shows to increase the 'feel-good' factor.
- *Sulphur*   For skin conditions such as eczema. The animal constantly seeks a cool place in which to lie.

The Last Years

Irish Terriers tend to live for a long time, their lifespan averaging and often exceeding 12 years. This is a large chunk of your own life, and I often think Irish Terriers' last few years are the most precious of all. They know so much about you and follow the annual round of events with family and friends with ever-increasing enjoyment and understanding. Then, suddenly, the hair on face and eyes seems lighter, they no longer hear the doorbell or leap as high as they did to catch a ball – and you know that the last phase has begun.

As with puppies, you need to be very watchful and attentive to an older dog's general health. If he seems off-colour, it is sensible to have him checked by your vet rather than wait and see, as you might well do with a younger dog.

Special diets (see chapter 10) are available for older dogs. These are easy to digest and have all the necessary food elements. However, you may have trouble convincing your old-timer that they taste as good as his usual dinner. Teeth need regular attention but, if he has always had them cleaned and scaled, problems should be minimal. If his mouth smells he should have his teeth checked at once.

He may show signs of stiffness and weakness in his back legs, and may need a leg-up into the car or even out of

Breezy Bryony, still enjoying life at 14.

The elder statesman.

bed. Deafness and decreasing sight make it even more necessary to supervise him when out and about. He will not need very long walks, and will probably sleep more.

Old dogs often develop heart problems, which can be anything from a murmur to a gradually increasing failure of function. Rarely is there a full cardiac arrest. With regular checks your vet will undoubtedly pick up the warning signs. There is effective medication to prolong and improve the dog's quality of life. Panting, collapse and general distress usually indicate a severe heart problem. You can often feel the heart 'bouncing' by placing your hand under the chest. You need to contact your vet immediately if this happens.

Kidney problems generally respond well to treatment, especially if diagnosed early. Excessive drinking and jaundice are typical signs.

Wetting is not uncommon, especially in older, spayed bitches. It has to be managed tactfully, without embarrassing her and making her miserable.

Any lumps and bumps that appear, especially if they are around the mammary glands in bitches, should be checked immediately by your vet. Most will be harmless fatty cysts but your vet may decide that surgery, cryosurgery (freezing the tumour) or even chemotherapy is advisable if the lump proves malignant.

You need to decide just how much medical interference is right and proper for your elderly dogs. It is neither wise nor fair to subject them to elaborate, ongoing treatment which may have painful side-effects and is by no means a certain cure.

My dogs have all become extremely stubborn and wilful in old age. Irish Terriers will never give up; they keep on calling the shots to the end. Refusing to walk on the lead (and

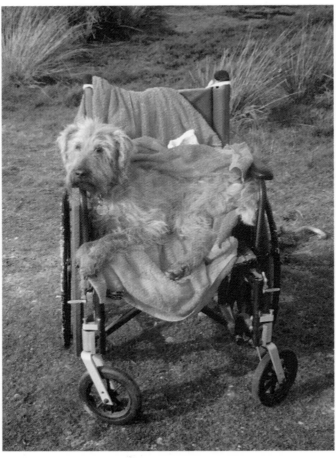

Becky, aged 14, taking things easy.

then lagging miles behind or even sitting down), insisting on the front seat of the car, barking to be fed hours before time – all these are fairly standard behaviour. You have to love and admire their fighting spirit.

Sadly, the time does come when the old dog's quality of life is no longer sustainable. You may need to rely on your vet's advice as to the proper time to have him put to sleep, but sometimes only you know best. It's not easy – no, worse than that, it's a terrible ordeal that simply has to be faced.

Whether you decide to take your dog to the surgery or ask the vet to come to your house is up to you. Be prepared for tears and heartbreak, but be assured that your vet has seen it all before, doubtless many times, and will not be surprised. You may wish to stay and hold your dog, but would surely be forgiven if this proved unmanageable.

The injection is given into a vein in the leg in the same way as an anaesthetic. It is a much stronger drug, and the dog appears to relax and fall asleep almost immediately. It is very peaceful and your dog will feel no distress.

Your vet will advise you about the arrangements to dispose of the body. You may wish to bury him in your own garden. Alternatively, there are animal cemeteries where your dog may be buried. They can also arrange for a cremation, after which the ashes are returned to you in a casket.

It is not at all unnatural to mourn for your Irish Terrier. Individuals and families differ, and you need to find the right way to cope with your grief. It is important, for only then will you be able to come to terms with your loss. Other family dogs or, when you feel stronger, a new puppy can prove the ultimate comfort. No dog can ever replace another but in time he will become a beloved companion and character in his own right.

Follow my leader.

For Bunch
An Irish Terrier

When Someone Dies
Who Lit the Day,
Gave Reason,
Opened the Soul,
The Eyes,
With Incandescent Joy,
A rare Sweetness, Honesty and Feeling
Made us touch Truth
In an Inexplicable Way,
Was a gentler kind
Of Love and Mysticism,
A Universal Spirit;

Then We may die a little more,
But Give Thanks
And are closer to God.

James H Jackson, 1998

Chapter Twelve Showing Your Irish Terrier

If you have a really good puppy that you have either bred yourself or bought in, you may decide to try him or her in the show ring. Ask other breeders to cast an expert eye over your dog. It can be very difficult to be unbiased, as we all tend to think, quite understandably, that our dogs are without compare!

Showing should and can be fun for the whole family, but it does involve a great deal of time and work with your dog, early starts on show days, often long journeys and late, exhausted returns home. Have I put you off already?

Ch Montelle Sunarise (Rufus) untrimmed.

Shows are of enormous importance in maintaining standards in the breed as they provide an opportunity for dogs of the same breed to compete against each other. Hopefully the dog who conforms best to the Breed Standard and performs well in the ring on the day will be the Judge's choice. Breed type, temperament, general health and sheer showmanship are also important considerations in selecting the winners. It is vital for the good of the breed that the best specimens are chosen, as they will come through for the breeding stock of the next generation.

There will always be conflicts of opinion. One judge will favour a dog who may not appeal, for whatever reason, to an equally reputable judge on another day. It is the name of the game; you have, above all, to be a good sport and not become too disgruntled and disappointed.

By showing your dog you are making a great gesture of support for the breed. With a numerically small breed like the Irish Terrier, every entry counts and is important. Every enthusiastic supporter at the ringside is important, too. Shows provide a showcase – a shop window, if you like, for the breed. An enthusiastic crowd at the ringside and a good entry of quality dogs and bitches being expertly shown is of tremendous value as promotion for the breed.

The ring also provides a place for breeders to study and compare each other's stock. Pet owners are delighted and inspired to see how their dogs should look and newcomers are informed about and attracted to the breed.

However fierce the competition and whatever the importance of winning, all of us, breeders and non-breeders alike, have an important part to play. In supporting as many of the shows as we possibly can we are helping to present the breed and keep the Irish Terrier in the public eye.

Preparation

Visiting shows

Before embarking on showing, it is sensible to visit some shows and get the feel of how things are done. This is an excellent chance to meet and speak to some of the breeders and exhibitors and you may also find the chance to speak to beginners and owners like yourself.

You will be fascinated to see how the breed performs in the ring as you study the expert handling. It is not as easy as it looks and has to be an exercise in concentration and partnership between handler and dog.

The Irish Terrier Association runs an annual Fun Day to which owners may bring their pet dogs. There are races and competitions and a puppy parade. The children show their dogs in a special class for junior handlers. It is always a very happy occasion and a 'must ' for newcomers to the breed.

One important tip: it is better not to speak to exhibitors before they show their dogs. They are bound to be tense and concentrating on preparing their dogs, and you will receive a much more sympathetic ear when the judging is over.

You may gain some valuable insights into how the judges make their decisions, and will doubtless hear what the exhibitors thought about it! Don't be put off by the amount of controversy, especially at the bigger shows. It is difficult to assess top quality dogs and, at this level, it can be very much a matter of the Judge's personal taste. It is all part of the game – if sometimes exasperating and disappointing.

Dog press

Before you begin showing, you need to keep up with the dog press. In Great Britain, the weekly papers *Our Dogs* and *Dog World* can be ordered from your newsagent and will give you all the information you need about shows and show results. There are special columns and articles of interest about most breeds that will give you a real source of knowledge and insight into how the world of showing dogs works.

Ringcraft classes

No puppy under six months can be shown so you will have time to learn the first steps of ring behaviour. Ringcraft classes are a must. Like obedience classes, they are run by your local dog training group, although you may find some private individual trainers. The Kennel Club has a list and local vets are usually helpful with names and addresses.

Ch Trackways Booger Red with Peter Bell
at Birmingham Dog Show 1991.

Types of Show

There are various types of show, ranging from the small, unbenched shows to the full-scale, all-day Championship Shows.

You should begin with the Open and Exemption Shows. You will need to learn a great deal at these smaller, more friendly shows to gain the experience and confidence to tackle a Championship Show.

You will need to plan show visits well ahead of the show. Make sure that your dog is registered with The Kennel Club and all the transfer papers, where necessary, are in order (see chapters 7 and 9). Send a stamped, addressed envelope to the Show Secretary, whose address will be given in advertisements for the show, and you will be sent a schedule for any of the advertised shows. If the show is run by one of the breed societies, the Hon Secretary of the society will send the required schedule and entry forms.

Only Exemption Shows accept entries on the day. Open Shows require registration four weeks before the show and Championship Shows, six weeks before. It is very important to have the form with the Secretary on the day stated in the schedule. Rules tend to be followed strictly and your late entry will be refused. It is probably sensible to ask the Post Office for a Certificate of Posting when you send off the entry form and make sure it is properly signed by the Post Office staff in case your entry is lost. This is the only proof of posting that The Kennel Club will accept.

Benching

Most Championship Shows are benched, which means that each dog is allotted a space, usually within a row of wooden cubicles, where he can be kept when resting throughout the show. Breeds are located together in blocks, usually as close as possible to the ring where they will be shown.

Far more breeders and exhibitors today like to bring their own dog boxes or cages, which they put on to the bench. The dog will be comfortable and in familiar surroundings, but cannot be seen so well by the public. From this point of view, cages are better than solid boxes, but there have been rare occasions when the dog has caught his teeth on the wire. Care and supervision are absolute necessities.

You will need a special benching chain which attaches to a strong collar. It is sensible to have a name disc, which should be worn by the dog at all times except in the ring. No dog should be left on the bench with a slip collar only. It is not secure enough. A long benching chain is also a potential hazard as it can get wound round legs or, worse still, necks.

Make sure your dog is comfortable on Vet Bed, with a water bowl and blanket. For a younger dog, some chews or favourite toys are a good idea, as it can be a long, tedious day.

Most owners would not dream of leaving their dogs unattended, which is a good reason for taking the family along to help.

Once the dog has settled, you can always ask a neighbour to keep an eye on your dog, but remember that your dog is always your responsibility. Sadly, as with other aspects of life, it is increasingly less safe to leave a dog unattended, and there have been cases within other breeds of tampering and interference.

Penmore Patsy on the bench at a show.

Show Kit

Some people have the knack of travelling light but, for most of us, a small trolley on which to carry our show kit is an enormous help. It can be tucked tidily under the bench when not in use, and it does save the back.

You may want to take and set up your own grooming table, and have a neat bag for your grooming kit. You may also have a zip-up bag into which you can stack various 'bits' that might be handy, such as a roll of kitchen paper, a cloth and bottle of water, a towel, a plastic bag for collecting the rubbish and bags for cleaning up after your dog.

First aid

A small first aid box is a good idea, with plasters, antiseptic wipes and cream, a pair of tweezers (I once spent an agonising day with a splinter under my nail) and some simple dressings. Panadol or Neurofen are a good stand-by for a headache.

For the dogs, you might take some tummy-settling tables, and Waspeze and Piriton in case of insect bites, which can be a major hazard at summer shows. Some breeders give a herbal tablet before the show (Scullcap Valerium).

If it is very hot – and sometimes benching tents become humid and over-heated even with the flaps tied back – a travelling coat or spare towel can be soaked in cold water and wrapped round your dog to cool him. You will not want to do this until after showing, as it might affect his coat.

If you are attending an unbenched show, do not leave your dog in a hot car. It is extremely cruel, and a potential death trap (see chapter 8). If you do, you will be severely reprimanded by the organisers, who could report you to The Kennel Club, in which case you might well be disciplined. Some shows refuse to accept any future entries from owners whose dogs have been found in distress.

Food for the day

Always take a picnic, which should last throughout the day. Bars and restaurant tents are always crowded and you may not be able to leave your dog for long enough to stand in a queue.

Have a cool box with drinks for you both. Take far more than you might expect to need. You may be grateful for a final drink in the car park before setting out for home, and there are always thirsty friends.

Give your dog his usual feed at the usual time, but sharing a few sandwiches with you after the showing adds some spice to the day for him.

Hints on Showing

Timing

Be sure to arrive at the show in plenty of time. There will certainly be crowds of people all trying to get through the same gate at the car park. Make a careful note of where you parked or, like me, you will be frantic at the end of a long, tiring day, having forgotten where you left the car!

Once you have been to a particular show and know the way around it all seems quite straightforward, but finding the right entrance, staircase, lift, ring and bench, or the right marquee from a car park three fields away, can be a nightmare if you are in a hurry. You need to remain calm and must not let an attack of show nerves and general exasperation get the better of you.

In the ring

You will probably have been to ringcraft classes and by now you should have learned the basic technique of showing your dog. Learn all you can about moving around within the group.

You need to have eyes everywhere, and be one step ahead all the time. It is easy at first to be intimidated and crowded out by more experienced owners and probably more assertive dogs. You need to be able to find and keep your own pace, at which both you and your dog feel most comfortable. Never push other dogs around in the ring. It is not good sportsmanship, and you want to establish a reputation as a fair competitor.

The pace

Terriers walk briskly in the ring. It is almost a trot and is the stride that shows the dogs off best. Each dog has a different pace, which alters slightly as he grows older. It is a matter of great expertise and experience to pace your dog correctly. This is where a friend's expert eye is a great help to set the stride correctly.

Class walking around at the Bournemouth Show.

Your walking pace to match your dogs will probably feel much faster than it looks from the ringside. Be sure to wear comfortable shoes.

Do not expect a young dog to behave like an adult. Most of the judges under whom you will show know and love terriers and many are breeders themselves. They will understand precisely that a young terrier can be bouncy in the ring and will doubtless make suitable allowances. It is pointless to lose your cool or your confidence. Irish Terriers recognise this at once and play up accordingly, just for the joke! A few deep breaths can be very calming.

Presentation

You need to present yourself and your dog to the best possible advantage. Your clothes must be neat and suitable. It is not a compliment to your dog, however well prepared he is, or to the judge and the whole show scene, if you appear in a grubby T-shirt and scruffy jeans.

One of our smarter judges is known to match her suits to the breed she is judging: green, orange, brown and beige for Irish, black, white and red for Scotties. She, for one, would certainly notice your appearance in the ring.

You need to look good and present a harmonious picture with your dog. Try not to slouch and drop your head forward. It looks apologetic and you want to convey your belief that you will go home with the best dog in the world, whatever the judge decides.

Most judging follows a similar pattern, and a steward will assist the proceedings. Do not be late for your arrival at the ring.

Keep a watchful eye on the Judge and react quickly to instructions. You will be asked to walk around in a circle and line up for the judge to study and compare the entries. Each dog will then be examined separately and you will probably be asked to lift your dog on

Irish Terrier line-up at the Bournemouth Show.

to the judging table, although some judges prefer to examine exhibits on the ground. Teeth, eyes, ears, coat, and paws will be examined, and the judge will probably run his hand over the dog's back. Hold your dog's head up lightly and stand aside to allow the judge free access.

You may be asked some questions: your dog's name, age, or anything the judge wishes to comment upon. Keep your replies short and to the point. You may distract and even irritate the judge if you talk too much.

You may be asked to walk your dog away from and back towards the judge, who will be looking for a strong, smooth, balanced action.

Ringcraft classes will have prepared you both for the judging procedures. Be quick and decisive about the line-ups and move immediately up or down the line as the Judge instructs you.

The dogs show stance is important, and a concentrated, collected and controlled programme from both of you will impress the judge most.

It always seems a shame to me that such lively, amusing, charming dogs should have to behave so uncharacteristically quietly in the ring. However, no dog that is leaping about can be seen properly, and showing is a very special, separate activity, more like a stage performance than everyday behaviour.

Some people, mainly those I call 'old-fashioned terrier men', love to square the dogs up to face one another down, declaring that it displays the true, assertive terrier spirit. This may be so, and undoubtedly it makes the dogs look smart and on their toes in the ring. However, with the public generally so terrified of 'dangerous' dogs, the slightest 'Grrrrr...' in the ring is too easily mistaken for aggressive and unreliable behaviour. Nothing could be further from the truth but, frankly, I do not think it does the breed any good at all in today's climate of opinion.

Titbits

Titbits, in the form of small biscuits or dog treats, are permitted in the ring and can be helpful if they encourage alertness and do not distract your dog or any other dog from giving his best performance. Every judge likes to feel he or she is being wooed by the dog. The eagerness, the slight tail wag, the bold stance softened by the beautiful, deep kindness in the eye – all these are irresistible attractions, winning immediate approval. All these qualities can be lost if the main focus of interest is the contents of your pocket.

Handlers

Irish Terriers, especially the dogs, are sometimes shown by professional handlers. There is always much argument about the fairness and suitability of engaging professionals to handle dogs, in case it should adversely affect the chances of 'ordinary' competitors. They certainly seem to win frequently, which can be depressing, as we all like to feel we are in with a fair chance. I think they are a great asset, as they set a very high standard in the ring. The dogs are always well presented and expertly handled. The handlers are smartly dressed in suits and ties, which sets the dogs off well.

I have seen several dogs with full champion potential just not quite make it when being shown by their breeders. Once given to a handler they seemed to find that extra form and sparkle and were spotted immediately by the Judge.

Most handlers are devoted to their charges, and it is easy to see that the affection and respect is mutual. I was talking to one the other day who was handling his first Irish. His enthusiasm was unbounded: "I've handled so many breeds, but she is a dream ticket. She's *so* bright – she really has brains to burn."

Handlers' fees are a matter of personal arrangement and adjustments are often made according to the amount of time involved. Kennelling fees are charged if the dog spends time before the show with the handler and is prepared by him for showing. Once a good working relationship is established, however, it is not uncommon for the breeder to pass the dog over to the handler at the show.

Occasionally a professional handler will advertise in a dog paper but, for the most part, finding a good handler is a matter of personal observation in the ring and word of mouth. If you decide to approach one, be a little careful, as other breeders and owners may already be involved. There is a certain etiquette to be followed and you must not seem to be interfering with established arrangements.

If you find you have a real flair for showing, you may decide to become a handler. This is very much a matter of gaining experience, becoming known and building up a sound working knowledge of the whole show scene. Your reputation will depend not only on winning but also on your reliability, kindness towards the dogs you handle, and good sportsmanship.

Preparation for the Show

There are as many opinions as there are breeders and owners about the best routine for running up to a show. Your dog has to appear in peak show condition on the day.

Coats

Preparation depends on the time of year and the condition and type of the individual coat. This, as we have seen, varies rather. The lighter, wheaten oat tends to be softer and to grow more quickly than the red or red-gold coat.

177

Timing is everything, and you will need to study the coat to be sure that it has grown through sufficiently not to need any major attention on the day of the show. It also depends on whether there are several shows coming up, in which case there will be less preparation once the coat is established in good show order.

There is a tendency today to show the dogs with very closely stripped coats. Some people criticise this, as it makes show dogs look rather different from the average pet. In the days when dogs were usually kept in outdoor kennels, which were probably unheated, no dog was stripped out so closely. It is probably a matter of fashion, and the dogs do look very smart, but it seems a little unfair that a dog who would have looked perfect a few years ago now appears 'woolly' in the ring in comparison with the more fashionable short look of today.

Show trimming the Irish Terrier

The following section, written be Connie Birch, is reproduced here by kind permission of the Irish Terrier Association:

Grooming tools required:

- Stripping knife with fine serrated edge. Not a razor edge, for use on head, ears, etc. (Mars 341).
- Stripping knife with coarser serrations for removing long rough coat on body (Mars 328).
- Steel grooming comb, half close teeth, half open set teeth.
- Pair of 18cm (7in) hairdressing scissors kept solely for trimming purposes
- Hindes Terrier Palm brush.

Make sure the dog is in good physical condition, as only healthy skin and coat will trim out well and re-grow successfully. If the skin is dry and coat poor, feed one teaspoon of Vitapet oil daily. Worm every three months as a routine,

Trimming must commence well ahead of the show date to obtain a first class trim and a coat of the correct length. Irish Terriers are best given as little last-minute trimming as possible as the coat colour is temporarily lightened and ones efforts become very obvious.

If starting with a dog 'in the rough' with dead coat, one should commence approximately 8–10 weeks before the show. Some coats grow more quickly than others and you will have to time your own dog, making note of when you consider he looks his best after re-growing his new coat.

With the coarser stripping knife, strip out all dead coat from the whole dog, taking great care only to remove straggly dead coat from the legs and whiskers. To do this, take the coarse stripping knife and, with the thumb, push the hair into the serrations, grip the hair with a slight sliding action with the knife almost flat against the body, and pull the dead hair out all over the body. Using the fine end of the grooming comb, after the initial removal of all the dead hair has been completed, rake through the soft undercoat to remove surplus 'wool'. Rake in this manner several times a week, avoiding leg hair and whiskers. This will encourage the hard new coat. Only ever comb leg hair and whiskers sufficiently to avoid matting and to remove dead coat.

About 3–4 weeks before the show, trim the head, ears, side and front of neck and shoulders Refer to figs 12.1–12.3. Trim with fine stripping knife the top and side of the skull, in front of the ears, and shape the eyebrows. The latter is not easy to explain and I would suggest the novice looks well at an expertly prepared terrier.

The whole expression of an Irish Terrier can be made or marred by the manner in which the eyebrows are trimmed and shaped. Trim the ears very closely both inside and out and scissor out and around the orifice of the ear, taking care to prevent cut hair from entering the ear canal. A smear of Vaseline will avoid scratching. Try to avoid scissoring the edges of the ears as the colour will lighten. Take an imaginary line from the corner of the eye to the corner of the mouth and then trim all hair from behind this line, under the jaw, from the front of the neck down to the breast bone and then, less closely, down

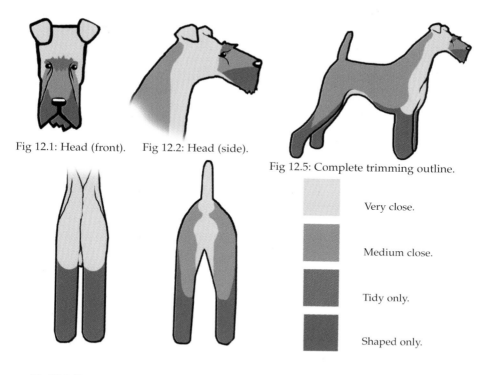

Fig 12.1: Head (front).   Fig 12.2: Head (side).

Fig 12.5: Complete trimming outline.

Very close.

Medium close.

Tidy only.

Shaped only.

Fig 12.3: Front.   Fig 12.4: Back.

between the front legs, tidying out out excess hair. Trim the sides of the neck and shoulders as shown in the illustration. Very carefully remove all light-coloured fluffy hair from the whiskers on top and bottom jaw.

An Irish Terrier should not be left too much whisker as it softens the expression. Trim away only excessive hair under and in front of the eyes, but *never* trim away so much as to make the foreface 'pinch in' in front of the eyes. The trimming lines must at all times blend one to the other. Abrupt lines anywhere are ugly.

With the coarser stripping knife, tidy over the ribs and remove any surplus long hair on the underside of the brisket. Use scissors or sharp clipper on the private parts and underline beneath the ribs, but do not accentuate the tuck-up. Trim the tail closely at the back and sides and a little less closely on the front. Watch for a natural thin patch half-way up the tail and avoid trimming here. Do not make the tail over-thin – this unbalances the overall picture. Refer to fig 12.4 and proceed to trim with the fine stripping knife the rear end of the dog. Trim very closely under the tail and outwards to where the coat swirls. Trim down either side of the tail and over the buttocks and across to the swirl again. Carefully trim this swirl down or carefully scissor down but do not attempt to get rid of it. Remove all hair from inside the thigh and around the private parts. Shorten feathering from the crotch to the hock joints. Shape from the point of the hock to the ground either side in a perfectly straight line. Remove rough hair from the thighs, carefully merging it in with the body coat. Leave a little more on over the stifle joint. Trim all hair from between the pads on the underside of the feet. Trim around the outer edge of the feet to give neat, small feet, but do not expose nails.

The front legs require very careful attention. They must look straight from every angle. See fig 12.3.

Work for the most part on the back line of the leg hair, removing all hair that spoils the straight line from elbow to floor. Remove surplus hair from the elbow joint, as to leave this can make the dog look wrong in front. Remove with scissors all hair from between the pads on the underside of the foot. Carefully trim excess coat from foot and trim around the base to give neat, small feet, but be careful not to expose nails. Remove the heavier growth of hair that will often be found around the ankles and overlooked.

One week before the show the cheeks and under jawline will probably require tidying. The 'frill' down the side of the neck should be trimmed in the direction of the growth of the hair, upwards from the shoulder to behind the ears. Do not make it bare. Trim down from the base of the skull to the top of the neck, graduating the light towards the withers and running into the back without any abrupt break. See diagram 12.5. Trim the sides of the neck if necessary. Be very conservative about trimming here as the colour will be lost and there will not be time for it to re-grow. The night before the show, carefully groom legs and then wash them.

At the show, watch your classes and make sure your dog has had a chance to relieve himself. Groom the dog well to remove dust from the coat and coax the leg hair and whiskers into position with the Palm brush. Use the grooming comb sparingly, if at all. Give yourself plenty of time.

All this will require a lot of practice, but will be found most rewarding. After the show continue going over the coat or it becomes untidy. Your dog should remain smart for quite a few shows before he will need to be stripped out again.

Bathing

Soap and water is considered likely to soften the coat and is not recommended too close to show day, if at all. Your dog must, however, be clean and fresh, with nose, ears, eyes and mouth spotless.

Have a bottle of saline solution and some cotton wool handy to wipe away any gunge around the eyes. Be very gentle when you clean the ears. Most vets recommend only surface cleaning, as you can damage the delicate skin if you use a cotton wool bud inside the ear. Saline solution or ear wipes are recommended.

Feeding

It is not wise to feed your dog before the show. He will appear less alert, and you will not be thanked for a mess in the ring. There are exercise areas, so be sure your dog has relieved himself before being shown, and clean up after him.

Classes and Procedures

Classes

Some breeds include other categories but, for Irish Terriers, the main classes are as follows, dogs and bitches being shown separately:

Puppy 6–12 months.

Junior 12–18 months.

Novice (mainly at club shows) For any dog who has not won a Challenge Certificate or a First Prize at an Open or Championship Show (all puppy classes excepted).

Post Graduate For any dog who has not won a Challenge Certificate or five or more other wins.

Limit For any dog who has not won three Challenge Certificates or seven or more First Prizes in any other shows.

Open For all dogs of the breed for which the class is provided that are eligible for entry at the show. In other words, entrants are usually those who have won their way through to this level and, although it is open to all, absolute beginners will probably find they are out of their depth.

These are summaries, and the definitions of classes will be listed clearly in the show schedule.

You need to read the instructions carefully and be sure that you are entered for the correct class. For instance, if you win a class with an over-age puppy, your win will be cancelled by The Kennel Club. If you realise you have made a mistake on your entry form, go to the Show Secretary immediately – preferably on arrival – to see if it can be sorted out.

When starting off with your puppy, it is wise to work your way through the classes in the correct progression. This will give your dog his best chance in the ring. As I have said before, Irish Terriers tend to be slow developers both in terms of appearance and settled, steady behaviour. A puppy who looks good in Junior may look a positive baby in Novice. The Judge, too, will be less lenient about giddy behaviour in adult classes.

Procedures

At an Open Show, all class winners compete for Best of Breed (BOB) but, if the classes are split, the Best Dog and Best Bitch are decided first and then compete for BOB.

At a Championship Show the Dog Challenge Certificate (CC) and the Dog Reserve Challenge Certificate (RCC) are decided, and the same procedure is followed for the bitches. They then compete for BOB.

The Best Puppy is chosen from the winners of the Puppy and Junior classes.

The BOB winner will then go into the Group Classes and compete with BOB winners of other terrier breeds.

If you are fortunate enough to have an Irish Terrier who competes and wins well (and luck does sometimes come into it!) you need to aim for three CCs under three different judges. This would make your dog a champion, and you would then be entitled to put 'Ch' before his name.

This is a very general explanation of show categories and procedures. There is a great deal more to learn. When in doubt, ask the established experts and listen to their advice. Never imagine you know it all. Part of the fascination of showing is the on-going learning process, not just in the ring but in your knowledge of the breed and your own dog or dogs in particular. The judge will give a written report about your dog if he is placed first or second, which can be

Showing indoors: (left) Ben's Heir Ben and (right) Shaun of Lymehills.

ITA Open Show 1996: (left) BIS Tanwell Gaelic Treasure and (right) BOS and BP Tanwell Gaelic Venture.
Judge: Billy Semple

most helpful and encouraging.

Try to build a reputation for fair play and good sportsmanship. Nobody forces you to enter your dog under any particular judge. It is a common courtesy to accept the decision and not to spoil another dog's win by disgruntled comments or open criticism. There will always be another judge and another day. A smile and a handshake looks good in the ring and is right for our breed.

One real pitfall to be avoided at all costs is to imagine that you have the perfect dog. No such dog ever existed, but seeing your dog every day, knowing his character and adoring him as an individual can make you 'kennel blind'. In the long run, this is self-defeating. To quote from *Irish Terriers* by Edna Howard Jones:

It is only by looking at your dog with clear eyes and with the courage to admit his failings that you are likely to eventually eliminate faults and breed a dog worthy of top honours.

Ch Trackways Booger Red in the Terrier Group line-up.

Try to make the day enjoyable for your dog. Whatever the result, praise him to the sky if he has done his best for you. Irish Terriers are acutely conscious of your mood and to show your disappointment or cross temper is simply not fair.

Spayed bitches and neutered dogs

Until recently no neutered dog or spayed bitch could be shown under Kennel Club rules. This has now been reversed and, with a written application to The Kennel Club, permission may be given. It is early days and too soon to tell if this new ruling will have any effect. Whether it is worth showing a dog or bitch with no possible breeding potential is debatable, [although the exhibit will probably still have relatives who can be bred from to produce similar characteristics].

Junior Handling

A great deal of fun and experience can be gained by youngsters entering the Junior Handling classes. Many top handlers, breeders and judges started as junior handlers. It is certainly a valuable means of gaining early experience in the dog scene, making friends and learning to be a good competitor.

Keeping Records

It is very satisfying to keep a record in a special notebook of each occasion your dog appears at a show. It is interesting and a quick way to check the state of play of your dog's show career. However vivid the occasion may seem at the time, after a year or two you will find an accurate record,

Crufts 1980: Ch Ben's Heir Ben (first), Ch Major Generla of Montelle (second) and Ch Tanwell Lucky Tim (third).

written down, a useful reminder. Some breeders make a special scrap book with pictures and comments. This is an enormous help to people like me when chasing information about the breed. It also provides a small tribute to the dogs who have contributed something to the breed and given you much pleasure and pride.

Judging

How to become a judge

You may well ask, because no-one is sure!

You would normally have been around for some time and shown a great interest in and support for the breed. You would have joined one or all the breed societies and put in a fair amount of work at their various functions and shows. You may have attended all lectures and seminars held in connection with the breed. You would also have done some stewarding at shows.

As your knowledge increases, you may let it be known that you are interested in judging, or you may simply be invited. It helps if you are an owner or, better still, a breeder or handler and known on the show

Enniskellin Dragoon on the judging table.

circuit. Any work in the dog charity field or connection with other terrier breeds would be considered a plus.

Firstly, you would be proposed, put up for discussion and voted upon by the breed society committees. If accepted, your name would be put on the B List, which is for small shows only. With good judging to your credit, you will move up to the A2 and eventually the A1 list, which includes the top terrier judges. This is a slow process, and may take years. Not just the number of shows, but also the actual number of dogs you have judged (minus the absentees) will be considered.

All judges on the A list have to be approved by The Kennel Club, and a good character reference is the starting place, along with good standing within the breed. Having said that, I sometimes think that judges are born, not made. You *can* learn but, if you do not have that instinctive flair, the 'stockman's eye', probably you will never become more than an undistinguished judge. It is not just a matter of picking out faults: that is the lowest form of judging. You need to be able to see and judge the dog *as a whole*, including how he moves.

Your fingers when you examine the dog should tell you all about him. This is a curious and intuitive skill, rather like a good doctor with a patient. Remember, above all, that you are there to uphold and interpret the Kennel Club Breed Standard as specified by the founders of our breed and judge that particular dog on that particular day.

Do not be in a hurry. Give yourself time to grow into the job or even to decide if it is really for you. Judging carries huge responsibility, both on an individual level and for the effect your judgement will have on the breed in terms of bringing forward the best dogs. You need to feel absolutely sure that it is something you can manage with flair and competence. Remember that attached to each dog's lead is a person who has invested much in the dog you are judging. There is bound to be disappointment and frequent criticism and you will have to be able to keep your head and not be swayed by any consideration other than the worth of the dogs in front of you.

Prepare yourself carefully by learning all you can. Study the breed standards, go to shows, watching and asking advice from senior judges, attend seminars and use every occasion when there is a dog to look at as an imaginary judging session. Any dog of any breed will do. Rather like breeding, judging is an on-going learning curve throughout your career. You will never know it all!

Judging record

From the very first judging appointment that comes through the post you will need to make a very careful record and keep it in a special folder. The Kennel Club expects you to keep all letters, schedules, catalogues and judges' books where all entries, even the absentees, are carefully marked up.

Reply to any invitation to judge within 14 days as, if you are unable to accept, you must allow the Secretary maximum time to find a substitute. Read the invitation carefully, noting exactly what costs or accommodation arrangements, if any, are being offered.

When the Secretary sends a confirmation of your engagement, this is now a binding contract which can only be broken in extreme circumstances. Should the worst occur, you would have to write to the Secretary who, in turn, would send your letter on to The Kennel Club.

Plan your judging appointments carefully, especially at the beginning. You should not overdo one area, but try to move around the country, gaining as wide an experience as possible. Make sure you have an up-to-date *Kennel Club Show Guide and Rules*. The *Kennel Club Year Book* is another useful publication.

A week or so before the show, you should receive instructions from the Secretary, which should be clear and precise. Car park tickets and judge's badges are often included.

Make quite sure, by checking the map, that you know where you are heading, and make some sort of time plan before you set out.

The day of the show

Arrive in plenty of time but not, if it is a Breed Show, with hours to spare. A frantic committee will be setting up the show and will not know what to do with you. It is not correct to spend the time talking to exhibitors.

Dress tidily and suitably (see page 175), making sure that your shoes are 'trusted friends'. You will be on your feet for a long time and you must be comfortable.

When you arrive find the Secretary, who will doubtless be relieved to see you. You will probably be offered coffee. Take the time to sit quietly and go over the judging book.

When you meet your Ring Steward, discuss how you will place the dogs. Walk around your ring and see if there are any problems. You may be horrified to know that most judges have stories of finding glass, drawing pins, nails or potholes in the ring. You may also like to move the ringside chairs back a little.

It is not always up to the Judge, but at some shows there may be a last-minute decision about the weather. Irish Terriers look best and show well on grass but, if the weather is showery and cold, it is often necessary to move the ring indoors. Decide what you want to do and try to stick with your decision. At Breed Shows there will be cups and trophies to be set up on tables, the shop and the raffle, which make changing the layout of the show much more difficult.

The hardships of showing outdoors.

Try to start judging on time. It is a good idea to set some sort of pace on your judging. It is a mistake to start too slowly and then find yourself rushing through the bitch classes. Keep up a steady drive through the judging. There should not be long pauses when nothing seems to happen.

You want the dogs to look good and there should always be a slight sense of drama. Part of your job is to provide a piece of theatre for the ringside audience. It has to be a show.

Once you have judged all the dogs, pick out the number for which you have prize cards and possibly another two. Bring out every dog you want to see again – the others should leave the ring. Be very sure you have not overlooked anyone.

Ask the remaining exhibitors to move their dogs around the ring again. You can compare their movement as they walk together in the group. It gives you time to think, and the dogs will settle better if they have been walked around.

Many judges say that the first prize is usually obvious; it is the other placings that are more difficult. You need to have absorbed the Breed Standard fully, because this is your yardstick. There may be room for interpretation, but not for personal preferences. Remember always that, just as important as type, quality, soundness and general health, the dog must *be* an Irish Terrier. He must exude the essence and character of the breed: the jauntiness, intelligence and spark must be obvious.

Showmanship is an important factor; it is, after all, a show! A dog who looks unhappy, nervous, too aggressive or just plain bored should never win over one who is showing well and responding to his handler.

The dogs are lined up with the first five placings from left to right. Before you make your final line-up, be sure in your own mind. Unless you spot a mistake, do not change the placings. This is not the moment for changing your mind. It is unfair, and you would never be forgiven.

Withholding certificates

The decision to withhold prize cards or CCs is one that you may very occasionally have to make. For whatever reason (usually lack of quality) it is up to you to decide, but you will need to make a written report to the Show Secretary with a full explanation.

Incidents in the ring

If there is any sort of 'incident' in your ring that you feel needs sorting out, do not hesitate to ask your Steward for the Show Manager to be brought in. This is an unusual and unlikely occurrence, but be prepared. Fainting or illness sometimes strikes. I remember one incident when an exhibitor, after a long morning waiting for his breed – which couldn't possibly have been Irish Terriers! – was obviously in No Fit State. I did feel that, when he was asked to leave, it was more in sympathy than in anger. He reeled out, saying: "Thank God I was spotted in time, for I'm sure I'm not capable!" I'm afraid there was laughter.

Signing the certificates

The Kennel Club Challenge, Reserve Challenge and Best of Breed Certificates must be signed by you before they are handed to the winners. You can fill in the owner's name and the registered Kennel Club name of the dog after the lap of honour. These are moments of great pride and often emotion for exhibitors and dogs. You, as Judge, must share in this and remain there, supportive and interested to the end. Handshakes and congratulations are in order, and even a word and pat or two for the 'real' winners.

Good Manners in the Ring

All judges develop their individual styles and it surprises me how much they can alter the atmosphere in their rings.

Scrupulous courtesy is essential. Never forget to say "Please" and "Thank you". Every exhibitor has paid you the compliment of wanting to show under you and has paid the fee! Each deserves your full attention, fair appraisal, sound guidance in the ring and unfailing politeness. I remember when judges called everyone "Sir" or "Madam". A little formality is no bad thing as it helps to create the right feeling of quiet authority and everyone being 'equal before the law'.

Always speak clearly. Indoor shows in particular can be noisy, and it adds to the exhibitors' general anxiety if they cannot hear instructions.

You are in charge of the ring – never allow yourself to be bossed about. A novice judge in a ring full of experienced exhibitors with an over-eager steward can begin to feel pressurised. You must remain confident and always in control. You set the pace. It is your right and part of your role as Judge. Aim to become one of those judges who create a happy ring and exhibitors will be pleased to show under you whether they do well or not. After all, not every dog can win.

Never forget to thank your stewards and the secretary. It makes a huge difference and, if praise is justified, be generous.

Be fair in your show reports. They should be helpful, not just a catalogue of faults you have been clever enough to spot.

Tact and discretion are the key words. However vast your knowledge or skilled your judgement, these are the qualities that will cement your reputation as a fair and first-class judge. You will always attract a good entry and be able to make a real contribution to the general good of the breed.

In conclusion...

Judging requires great stamina and concentration. You may be offered a break and at a Breed Show there is usually the Judges' Luncheon where you can quite legitimately ask to be left in peace and quiet. You will never be asked to sit down with exhibitors. However, the task is arduous and the responsibility great.

You need to be absolutely honest with yourself and know when to retire. Lapses of concentration and undue exhaustion are good indicators. It can be sad, but you should finish knowing that you have done your best, made a real and positive contribution to the show scene and left your mark on your own beloved breed.

Chapter Thirteen Associations, Clubs and Societies

We are fortunate, in Irish Terriers, to have several excellent breed associations or clubs which are all well founded, long standing and efficiently organised. The elected Committees with their particular sets of rules, verified by The Kennel Club, do a tremendous job, providing a focal point for the management of breed affairs. This is a crucial role not only for 'internal' breed matters, but because it enables us to play a full part in the dog scene.

Whether in liaising with The Kennel Club, presenting a case to the Government or supporting charities or research, the breed clubs have an essential part to play.

By far the largest group is the Irish Terrier Association. Founded in 1911, its main objective has always been to encourage the breeding of really good, and constantly improving, Irish Terriers. It should provide opportunities for breeders and owners to meet one another and share in the companionship and pleasure of enjoying and promoting the breed.

The Irish Terrier Association (ITA)

Edna Howard Jones of the ITA told the story of the Irish Terrier Association in Dog World *in 1981 on the occasion of the Associations 70th Anniversary:*

1911–1981

Quote: *The origin of the Irish Terrier Association is carefully recorded on the first page of the enormous leather bound minute book with the Association's name inscribed in gold on the cover.* The initial meeting is described as *an informal meeting of Irish Terrier Fanciers* and was held at the Horticultural Hall, Vincents Square, London, on January 5, 1911. It was very well attended and the outcome was that arrangements should be made for a general meeting to be held at Crufts (then held at the Agricultural Hall, Islington), on February 8 with Miss Paul and Colonel Ireland acting as Honorary Secretaries *pro tem.*

This meeting too was very well attended. Dr Twamley was voted to the Chair and a strong committee elected, one of whose members will still be remembered by some of us today: the late Mr O T Walters, who was one of our best known breeders and judges and who became a member of The Kennel Club Committee.

The Marquis of Breadalbane KG was elected President and an illustrious list of Vice-Presidents followed whose names included the Earl of Lonsdale, Lord Breville, HM the Maharajah of Juid, Lord Dewar, Major General Sir Foster Newland and others, testifying to the enormous popularity of the breed in the days when King Edward VII owned an Irish Terrier called Jack. Irish Terriers were immortalised by the beautiful paintings of Maud Earle who captured their distinctive style and character as no other artist has or, for that matter, could.

Miss Paul and Colonel Ireland were elected as Joint Honorary Secretaries and Treasurers.

Disapproval

Before the inauguration of the Association, the only breed club had been the Irish Terrier Club and the formation of another was an expression of disapproval of its policies; obviously there had been personality clashes. Two facts bear this out in the first set of rules drawn up by the Association: (1) that no committee member of the Irish Terrier Association could be a member of any other breed club committee and (2): that whereas the Irish Terrier Club had drawn up a list of club judges (none of the founders of the ITA were on this list) the ITA made a rule *that no list of club judges be made or entertained*. In later years these rules were rescinded and in any case when membership dwindled so sadly in the 1930s and the Irish Terrier Club had ceased to exist, they would have been redundant anyway.

With Miss Paul and Colonel Ireland still Joint Secretaries and Dr Twamley as Chairman the Association flourished and membership rose to 84 in the first year.

No mention is made of the outbreak of the 1914 war until 1916, when it is recorded that a subscription of five guineas had been sent to The Kennel Club Ambulance Car Fund, but the Year Books for 1914 and 1916 carry the Union Jack and the Royal Standard on the cover and on the 1915 issue there is a group of the flags of the Allies in colour. This issue makes the first reference to the difficulties of holding shows and to other restrictions but urges members to keep their best stock and keep going to a reasonable extent.

Battling on

By 1917 all shows were stopped and it was decided that all members who had paid their subscriptions for that year should remain members for the duration of the war and for the first year of peace without further payment. With a substantial balance in their current account and £100 invested in War Loans the Association battled on.

In 1920 Miss Paul sadly reports the death of her Co-Secretary and Treasurer Colonel Sir Robert Ireland who had been on active service from 1914 to 1919. In her 1919 report, Miss Paul said she had suggested at the AGM that as the future of the Association was assured she would retire but, in her words: "The members present very kindly expressed their wish that I should continue in office and for the time being I agreed to do so." She remained in office until 1925 and her beautiful handwriting and well expressed minutes which fill so many pages are an example to us all. She owned some of the most famous Irish Terriers of the day including Ch Paymaster, Post Boy, Postman and her last champion that some of us still remember, Ch Eton Boy.

In 1923 the Marquis of Breadalbane died and the Earl of Lonsdale became President. He remained in office until his death and was always interested in the breed and our affairs. I wrote to him each year when I became Secretary, giving a report of our activities, and his courteous replies are still in my possession.

Declining

In 1925 Miss Paul finally resigned and Mr O Hamlin was elected as Secretary and Treasurer with Mr W Green as chairman. His term of office was brief and in 1928 Mrs Catherine Taylor succeeded him. Annual statements were published for the next six years showing the balance sheet, cup wins and a list of members (by now much depleted), but no reports were given.

In 1933 Lady Dent took on the duties with Colonel Colenso as Chairman. In her first report are signs that the breed was declining, as indeed it was, and she appealed to all members 'to take as active a part as possible in the affairs of the Association; otherwise with such fierce competition from other breeds the work of the Association will become impossible and one of the oldest indigenous national breeds will disappear from the show ring.' She also expressed the hope that the members would take advantage of the new Kennel Club regulation under which a whole litter may be registered for 7s 6d ($37^1/_2$p) and thus help to increase the number of CCs granted.

In 1935 Mr Stanley Warden was elected Chairman as Colonel Colenso wished to resign. I remember attending my first AGM with Mr G I N Henry from whom I purchased my first two Irish Terrier bitches. There Lady Dent said it was difficult for her to remain in office but nowhere is the fact recorded that Lady Dent resigned and I was elected. What happened was that Lady Dent wrote to Mr Warden handing in her resignation and it was proposed by letter that I should be asked to take office.

No one came!

There are no minutes for the 1936 AGM, as no one came to Olympia in response to my hand-written (!) notices except Lady Dent, and at the 1937 AGM when there were four people present I reported this fact and the impossibility of enacting any business.

I must record here that the 1936 episode dampened even my ardent enthusiasm and I wondered if it was worth trying to continue. My Chairman, Mr Stanley Warden, gave me as much encouragement as he could.

By 1938 things were shaping better and new members came along willing to serve on the committee. Then came the war and all I had to do was to pay The Kennel Club the fee for the maintenance of title.

In 1946 a report was printed to cover the years 1939–1945 in an endeavour to give continuity to the Association's affairs. We now had some 50 members and Mr G D Moore, whose wife owned the famous Russetone Kennel, became our Chairman with Lady Dent as President.

Distinguished

In 1961 we celebrated our Golden Jubilee with a championship show held in the Home Park, Windsor, by permission of the Chairman and Committee of Windsor Championship Show, on Friday, June 30, the day before Windsor. We held a luncheon there with several distinguished guests including Nord Northesk, Dr Esther Rickards and Dr Muller, president of the Netherlands Irish Terrier Association. Dr Aubrey Ireland judged the excellent entry of 63 dogs. It was a very hot day I remember.

In 1966 Lady Dent wished to retire as President. In her place Mrs Landseer-Jones was elected and she is our President today. We are all so grateful to her for carrying out her presidential duties so gracefully and so thoroughly.

In 1968 Mr Moore resigned and Mr Harry Quick served as our Chairman until 1974 when our present Chairman, Mr Arthur Long, was elected. No-one could have the interest of the breed more at heart than he has, and the Association is so well served with its present committee.

Mrs Jackson produces a wonderful Year Book for us and in addition to our ever-increasing membership here we have a long list of overseas members.

This is our history. The future is bright. We have group wins here and abroad to be proud of. We are financially sound and there are many willing to help and work for the good of our breed and it is time for the handwriting in the minute book to change.

The ITA today

(Updated by the author)

Since 1981 the Association has gone from strength to strength. The membership has increased enormously and we have enough overseas members to warrant a special Overseas Secretary, Mrs Helen Crawley. Miss Ann Bradly took over as Secretary of the Association when Edna Howard Jones, after 47 years as Secretary, became our President. Mrs Connie Birch and Mr Stephen Parkhurst were successive Chairmen, followed by our present Chairman, Dr Alex Noonan.

The committee which is elected from names put forward and voted upon at the AGM is outstandingly able. I have never known a committee that works harder and there is a wider circle of friends and family who turn out to functions and provide a supporting back-up team for which we are enormously grateful.

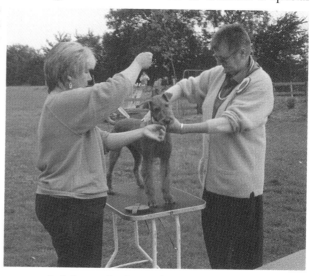

Judging at the Open Show at Roade, 1994.

Shows

The committee organises an important Championship Breed Show each year in June at Burford in the Cotswolds. It is a chance to entertain our friends and overseas members in a lovely setting.

The Open Show is at Roade in Northamptonshire in September. This is a more recent show, but is picking up fast in interest and support. It is followed in the afternoon by the Fun Day, which was considered a great innovation at first, but has become very popular with pet owners. It has proved what we always suspected, that to enjoy the real Irish character you have to see them at play. There are races and competitions, a puppy parade, disco dog dancing, a raffle, a photograph competition, an agility course and, believe it or

Fun Day at Roade, September 1994.

not, an obedience competition! It is enormous fun and a great opportunity to meet the puppies and have a quiet word with the 'oldies'. It is not to be missed and the children and dogs love it.

Discovering Dogs

A recent and very popular development of the dog scene is Discovering Dogs, organised by The Kennel Club. An area is set aside at Crufts for dogs to be seen and handled by the public. Each breed has an exhibition space, and the sociable Irish have an enjoyable, if exhausting, day. A special, separate Discovering Dogs exhibition in London in November

Irish Terriers at 'Discovering Dogs', Crufts 1995.

is held with the sole intention of providing an opportunity for prospective pet owners to meet the dogs and decide which breed is for them. The respective breed clubs organise and present the breeds on these occasions.

AGM

The AGM held each year in March is an important occasion. Committee members are proposed, elected or re-elected. We often combine the 'business' part of the day with a question and answer forum or a stripping and trimming demonstration, which is of interest to members.

Catering at ITA occasions is always excellent (we have some 'pros' on the Committee) and the high standard of hospitality and welcome established over many years by our late President Edna Howard Jones is still very much part of the Association's 'credo'.

Hot line

There is a Puppy Hot Line (see chapter 6) and every member of the Committee is always delighted to come forward with advice and help for pet owners.

Hand stripping class award – Rufus trimmed correctly. Photo: Tracy Morgan

Funds

Raffles, tombolas and sales are the usual way of boosting funds at the various functions. The Committee runs the breed stand at Crufts. Very acceptable gifts and memorabilia, stripping knives, books and pamphlets are on sale there, and a great deal of advice is available if you need it.

Legacies

The Association has had the good fortune to receive two quite considerable legacies which are administered by a separate committee of trustees. We have already undertaken several projects for the general good of the breed and are most grateful to our Benefactors Mr and Mrs Long and Miss Christapherson.

Year Book

One of the great prides of the Association is the annual Year Book. Edited by our Secretary Ann Bradley it is the proverbial 'good read'. There is news of the breed shows and breed affairs and articles, both amusing and touching, from members all over the world. It is much admired as a publication and of great interest to all Irish Terrier fanciers. It is included in the membership fee.

I was elected President in 1994 and Mrs Cynthia Jackson is Vice-President. We are delighted and proud to have Mrs Ferelith Somerfield as our Patron.

The North of England Irish Terrier Club
*Current Hon Secretary, **Paul Livesey**, writes:*

The Club was formed at a meeting held at the Manchester Show in March 1906. It has remained active since, although with some interruptions caused by world and other events, and has been predominantly centred in the Manchester area. Those present at the inaugural meeting and the first Officers appointed represented many of the most influential breeders and exhibitors of the time. Throughout it has always concentrated on the practical aspects of breeding, preparing and handling Irish Terriers.

The first Chairman was F Breakell, owner of Ch Bonnet and Ch Killerney Sport, and among the founder members was F M Jowett, author of the definitive book about the breed and owner of many champions under his Crow Gill affix. Another member was Frank Clifton of Stockport, described by Jowett as having the strongest kennel in the breed. It is doubtful if so many champions have ever been owned at the same time by one exhibitor. No trivial claim considering his champions: Munster Grip, Charwoman, Mile End Kitty, Mile End Muddler, Mile End Barrister and Mile End Vixen, as well as several other Challenge Certificate (CC) winners.

Other members were T Ramsay-Ramsay, a Championship judge; J Oates, with his champions Ch Straight Tip and Ch Straight Pride; J Stanworth, owner of Ch Turf Commander; and A B Montgomery who had just started out with his first champion, Ch Celtic Bella, and was to prove such a force in the 1920s.

The Club was very active in the following years, supporting many shows around the Lancashire area. In 1909 Mrs O W Porritt, a member of the founding family of the Scapa international company, joined, making up her first champion, Ch Barlae Brickbat, and going on to breed and make under her Musbury affix Champions M Tip, M Demon, M Maureen and M Fionnuala. At this time club finances must have been healthy as they purchased six cups valued at 36 guineas. Minute books show that these cups were actively competed for, on a point basis, until world affairs interrupted things in November 1914.

The next record was of re-forming in March of 1922. John Wild was elected Secretary and was still in office in 1962. During this time the leading member was A B Montgomery with his first champion of the decade appropriately named Ch War Bonus, quickly followed by several under his Celtic affix. Other prominent members with champions were W Slater (Bolden); W Tottle (Tapton); T Yorke (Rambling) and N Galloway. Elected a member in 1925 was a certain George Barr of Chorley who, besides making up Ch Brantvale Belle, was to become of the greats amongst handlers of all terriers.

There have always been close links between the Club and Ireland and perhaps the most influential honorary member during the early 1920s was F Carson with his dog, Irish Leader, who was kennelled in the Manchester area during the problem years of communications between England and his Dublin home. In one nine-month period he is reputed to have serviced over a hundred bitches. A study of the pedigrees of champions at that time shows how successful he was and why he was in such demand. Bobby Grant is the only person I have known who saw the dog and he described him as one of the best.

The final record of the Club in this period was in March 1928. During the late 1920s and early 1930s activities seem to have centred on a joint North of England Airedale and Irish Terrier Club.

In December 1946, with the stabilisation of world events, the Club re-formed once again at a meeting in the Kings Arms, Bloom Street, Salford, which was to be home for the next 25 years. In 1947 the Club first applied to register with The Kennel Club and the Irish Terrier Club stood as sponsor. The Chairman, at that time, was the local canine celebrity, Jean Hopwood, with John Wild as Secretary. Members included Jack Tonge and his wife, later to succeed with their Chapeleas; B Gilliland and his Wogils; and Joe Farnworth, whose No Retreat had won every class from Puppy to Open and the CC and BOB at Manchester Show in 1934 and was later sold to a breeder in the United States of America where he continued his successes.

Soon to join the Club was that other great handler, Fred Roberts, making up literally in his own name Ch Robert Mair and having other champions, including those he handled for Edith Slater, President of the Club in 1949. He has the reputation, which I have never been able to verify, of qualifying a champion in six days with wins in the Scottish, Blackpool and Belfast shows.

In 1952 Tommy Evans joined, becoming Chairman in 1954. His famous Swinpens were only part of his story, since he continued the long-established close links with Irish breeders and in particular with the Teltowns of John Sweeney (father), and Gerry and Jimmy Sweeney (sons).

In the mid-1950s Charlie and Mavis Pollard joined and, after making up their Ch Depleach Kettledrum and Ch Micky Finn, have been successful with their Lynphens, particularly Ch L Express, so influential in the United States.

In 1957 the Club was awarded its first Championship Show, held at Rusholme Town Hall, Manchester, with Bobby Grant as judge. Despite the success of this event it was to be another 32 years before their next Championship Show.

Since the fifties there have been a string of successful members, Paddy Carroll being the most influential with his Carolmacs. He took his turn as Club Secretary as did other successful exhibitors, Beryl Bell and her Woodvilles and Ged Morrison with his Gedmors. Our current Chairman, Stan Brown, has made his mark with his Yewoods whilst Jill Livesey, joining in 1981, has left the job of Secretary from 1982 to the present to husband Paul, while she got on with making a success of her Riojems.

The Club currently has a membership of around 60 and runs popular shows twice a year. It holds a Championship Show every other year, alternating with the Ulster Club, maintaining the close links with their neighbours across the Irish Sea. My apologies to the many not mentioned here who have worked so hard and without whom there would have been no Club.

Southern Irish Terrier Society

My thanks to **Ursula Merrington** *(President) for writing this potted history.*
Application was made to The Kennel Club for registration of the Southern Irish Terrier Breeders Society in February 1931, and this was granted on 17 March 1931. The first President was Mr L H Twyford and the first Chairman Mr H Rose. In February 1935 the first application was made to change the title to the Southern Irish Terrier Society.

From the outbreak of war in 1939 until 15 August 1947 the Club was inactive but retained its title at The Kennel Club. After the war an announcement in the canine press quickly brought support from old members and the nucleus of the newborn club was formed by 1 May 1948. Through the untiring efforts of the Hon Secretary, Mr H Phipps, who retired shortly afterwards through ill health, membership grew rapidly.

The first post-war Open Show was held on 10 January 1948, when Mr E S Hertz judged the 108 entries. The Hon Secretary and Treasurer at the time was Mr A F Delmaine.

The first Southern Irish Terrier Society Championship Show was held on 27 March 1954 at Lime Grove Hall, Shepherds Bush, London. Ninety dogs were entered, making a total of 123 entries.

For several decades the Society was run very ably by Miss N Woodifield of the Pathfinders Irish Terriers, who was both Secretary and Treasurer.

Today the Society holds three shows a year: a Championship Show on the fist Saturday in October at Minstead Village Hall, Hampshire; an Open Show at New Park, Brockenhurst, within the Christchurch and New Forest Canine Society Open Show, at the end of July; and a Limited Show on the first Saturday in December at Dummer Village Hall, close to the M3 in Hampshire. This is also when the AGM is held.

The present Officers are Miss G S Langton (Chairman); Mrs June Symonds (Secretary); and Miss P McBride (Treasurer). They are assisted by an enthusiastic Committee. The current President is Mrs Ursula Merrington and the Vice President is Mrs Helen Crawley.

New members are always welcome.

The Irish Terrier Club of Scotland

Robert Crawford (Chairman) writes:

The Club was very active in the 1920s and 1930s, mainly thanks to the enthusiasm of Mrs Shaw of the Drumshaw affix (Secretary) and Mr A Martin (Chairman), who had some excellent wins.

Things became very quiet during the war but, in the 1950s, Mrs Shaw re-established the Club. Edna Howard Jones took a great interest, attending many of the AGMs and offering help and advice.

When Mrs Shaw retired, support and interest seemed to fall away, and the club was wound up by the Secretary, Mr J Stewart. The cups were sent to the Irish Terrier Association for safe keeping and presented as trophies at the Irish Terrier Association Breed Show.

In 1980 Ann and Robert Crawford went back to live in Scotland. His father had bred a successful line of Irish Terriers in the 1960s (the Adantons) and, having inherited the affix, Robert Crawford continued the family interest. This seemed the moment to re-establish the Club and rekindle the interest in the breed in Scotland.

The Crawfords started slowly, holding Fun Days at home for several years. There were training demonstrations, races and novelty events. There was lunch with wine and general good comradeship, and often 40–50 people and their dogs attended. They then canvassed opinion about re-starting the club and were delighted with the support they received. Soon there were more than 70 members, and they applied for and received Kennel Club approval in 1987.

Meanwhile, Robert Crawford was continuing his success with the Adantons. He bought in a Tannell bitch in the mid-1970s: Tannell Wood Anenome of Adanton. He mated her to Tommy Watterson's dog Ch Imperial Major to produce two lovely bitches, Adanton New Edition and A Irish Sequel. A Irish Vision has two CCs and 2 RCCs and his brother,

A Irish Choirboy, has already sired five Australian champions. Anne, a top breeder of pedigree donkeys, also plays a large part in the management of the dogs.

The Drumshaw line continues with Mrs John Stewart and has produced several champions.

The Irish Terrier Club of Scotland hold an Open Show each year in October, and the Fun Days continue. This summer 20 Irish Terriers and 'their' families watched an organised five-mile Ramble and picnicked in the grounds of the Duke of Hamilton's estate.

There is a strong feeling of conviviality and friendship within the Club. This is a sound basis to work on and progress to bigger and better things. Caroline Lamb is Secretary and a mainstay of the organising team.

The All Ireland Irish Terrier Club

It is sad that, although obviously Ireland was the original home of the 'red terriers', there are now probably fewer there than in Denmark. However, there are still some very ancient, distinguished lines and some great experts who, to quote Jimmy Sweeney, 'fell out of their cradles with Irish Terriers'.

The All Ireland Club is active and, in a recent booklet about the breed, reminds us that the *Madra Rua* (Gaelic for 'red dog') is associated with some legendary heroes such as Brian Boru. Irish Terriers were the favourites dogs of the cottiers: hardy, plucky terriers, big enough to guard the potato patch and kill the rats but not needing as much food as larger dogs. Above all, they were gentle and kind enough to live with children. Even today, dogs bred in Ireland have a character and cutting edge considered uniquely valuable.

The All Ireland Irish Terrier Club has strong links with the Irish Kennel Club and the well-known breeders are international judges.

In Conclusion...

Tracey Deegan Foley's poem *The Irish Terrier* expresses the genuine love and respect still felt for the 'Micks':

A friendly face, a fiery heart
A spirit – wild and free,
A temperament of solid gold,
There's no other dog for me.

A chestnut coat, so rich and red
His eyes as black as night,
His stature – sturdy, strong and hard,
He'll impress with all his might.

A friend for life, that's what he'll be,
So loyal and very proud,
This dog could never fail you,
He's a treasure in a crowd!

"My turn now!"

Chapter Fourteen
Irish Terrier Activities

Family Dogs

The great majority of Irish Terriers become family dogs. As we have seen, they have evolved down the ages as the ideal, hardy, all-round, medium-sized working terrier. They are bred in the bone to family life: sparky and assertive enough to be unsurpassed as guard dogs, but loving, gentle and loyal with 'their' people.

Irish Terriers love their creature comforts and fit in easily with all aspects of modern living. They travel well and take up less room and with their neat feet bring less mud into the family car. They do not moult and leave hair on the carpets. Trimmed and stripped two or three times a year, they are the neatest and cleanest of dogs to have around. They are equally suited to town and country living.

They are wonderfully adaptable and settle in quickly with changes of scene like family holidays. With their natural exuberance they are born participators in all aspects of family life. Every occasion is filled with amusement when the dog is around.

I remember winning an obstacle race at a County Sports Day with

Miss Bunch, then aged about two. She clambered over piles of tyres balanced on benches and a see-saw and ended, after a short sprint, with a great leap on to and over some hay bales. It was a spontaneous effort, quite unrehearsed, and performed by Miss Bunch with great attack and courage. But when we were supposed to give a winners' exhibition round, Miss Bunch decided to tiptoe gingerly around and take every possible care. She decided the see-saw was an outrage and refused to attempt it. She kept looking at me as if to say, "But surely you remember the silly thing tips up?" We laughed about it for days. It illustrates the Irish Terrier's ability to perform brilliantly when faced with an exciting new challenge but, once they have seen the pitfalls, they are not as biddable as some breeds at keeping on trying just for the sake of it.

Irish Terriers like to be as close as possible to 'their' humans.
Photo: Tracy Morgan

Children

Irish Terriers are wonderful playmates for children and, like many, many mothers, I am always grateful to our dear Ceiledh Mavourneen for the joyful loving care she gave my three children.

They are, of course, proper dogs, not little designer pets. Children must learn to respect them as living creatures, not animated toys to be pushed around. This is a valuable lesson for all children.

Gentle Companions

Once mature, they are gentle companions for the elderly and, with training, could become ideal Hearing Dogs

On the lake

199

Barney competing in Agility. Photo: In-Press Photography

and Pets As Therapy (PAT) dogs, which is something for the future without doubt.

Agility

I have mentioned in chapter 8 that Irish Terriers are 'naturals' at this activity, and many of them enjoy it. Remember, though, that the owner too has to be fit in order to keep up with the Irish Terrier!

Obedience

If you are a control freak, the average Irish Terrier is not for you. In general, they like to please, but are not programmed to blind obedience.

Dog training classes can be a help in achieving some sensible control both for your puppy's safety and your own peace of mind. Classes can be great fun, especially if the trainer has a sense of humour and takes a real interest in the dogs.

Basic obedience

Having learned the first basic commands (see chapter 8) you progress to simple obedience work. We find that this is increasingly popular with owners at our Fun Day.

Before you aim too high you will need to decide exactly how regularly you will be able to attend and how much time you can afford for practising between classes. Never be too proud to repeat a class if necessary. It is important that you both have a complete grasp of each stage. If you intend to enter competitions it does not look good either for you or your club if

Ch Tanwell Glint of Gold training in Agility.

you make too many errors. I never mind a bit if dogs make mistakes. It always seems rather endearing. However, for most people you will be seen as some sort of representative and being fully prepared is part of the deal. This takes time and commitment.

Another advantage, apart from the usefulness of classes, is that you will probably enjoy the friendship of other dogs and their owners, swap puppy adventures and even go out for walks together.

Well disciplined dogs help the not-always-positive general press image of the canine world. However exaggerated and unfair the criticism may be, the onus is on us. We must have manageable, well behaved dogs who are a joy to live with and a pleasure to know.

Irish Terriers may not always toe the line, but they understand very quickly when the limits have been set.

Competitive obedience

I do not think any terrier is an ideal candidate for competitive obedience although, with expert training and handling, the odd indiviual can excel. The Irish, with their famous sense of humour and flair for independent decision making, can be full of surprises.

You need to be very sure that your puppy and later adult dog enjoys not only the classes but the whole jolly round of competitions. Remember too, that Irish Terriers are slow to grow up and, whereas a year-old collie may be a reliable working dog already, a terrier will almost certainly be a fairly unfocused juvenile. You have to remain amused and never exasperated through being too highly competitive. The thrill of winning and coming home with cups and certificates must never be at the expense of your dog's natural enjoyment and right to a long and happily carefree puppyhood.

The visitor.

After teaching your puppy the first simple commands of Sit and Stay (see chapter 8) it is best to seek expert advice for help with more advanced training. Reading about it will help to prepare you as, although training methods may differ slightly, the basic moves remain the same. The other commands he will have to learn are Down and Stand, which again are dealt with in detail in chapter 8. There is a progression to the Recall, Heelwork and Retrieve, which would need some specialist advice. See **Useful Addresses**.

Field Training

It is interesting to note that Irish Terriers have frequently made excellent gundogs. With their general alertness and keen senses they can be trained to rough shoot or keep a line with the beaters. My daughter's dogs have always followed the guns, but I have to confess they do tend to bolt after rabbits and hares or disappear

A natural athlete.

into a hedgerow for the afternoon on happier and more varied pursuits.

Miss Joan Simcock, a well known judge and life-long admirer of Irish Terriers, assures me that it is simply a matter of training and they can become outstanding gundogs, both retrieving and flushing out with equal skill.

It is well to remember that, although their coats are warm and waterproof, Irish Terriers do not have the layer of fat and muscle bulk of the larger shooting dog. Too much wet and waiting about on frosty winter days can eventually cause health problems. A dog's waxed jacket should be considered not undignified but a necessity for a dog built for speed rather than for waiting around for hours in the rain and cold.

Mrs S O'Keefe with Barney, who wins prizes at Agility.
Photo: In-Press Photography
Below:
The country walk. Photo: Tracy Morgan

Chapter Fifteen Irish Terriers in Art and Writings

Irish Terriers in Art

One of the advantages of a breed as old and celebrated as the Irish Terrier is that there are a fair number of wonderful paintings, drawings, prints and memorabilia which have become highly collectable items, ranging from postcards and cigarette cards at one end of the market to pictures of great importance (and cost!) by famous artists at the other. Collecting is an increasingly popular pursuit.

Dr Alex Noonan, who shares with her sister Lindsay Williamson a fine collection of paintings, has kindly supplied the following information and illustrations.

Maud Earl (1864 –1943)

Maud Earl painted many important dogs of her day, among them those of King Edward VII, whose Irish Terrier was called Jack. Prints are available of some of the Irish Terrier paintings, such as *Dublin Fusiliers* (which was used as an advertisement for Black and White Whiskey) and *A Council of Perfection*. The originals fetch enormous prices.

Reuban Ward Binks (1880–1950)

Reuban Ward Binks painted mainly water colours of dogs belonging to Royalty and the landed gentry.

George Vernon Stokes (1873–1954)

There are several paintings of Irish Terriers reproduced largely for the design of cigarette and postcards.

William Hamilton Trood (1860–1889)

There is one very famous painting in particular entitled *Hot Pursuit* which figures an Irish prominent among several breeds.

Henry Crowther

Dr Noonan's own collection includes *Champion Eclipse*, painted by Henry Crowther in 1926. He painted dogs at shows, usually setting them in pastoral backgrounds.

E Aistrop

Again a painter who painted champions at shows. *Mile End Muddler* (see overleaf) is a beautiful head study painted at the turn of the century.

Lilian Cheviot (1890 –1922)

Lilian Cheviot studied at the Caldrons School of Animal Painting. Her works include a very compelling study of an Irish Terrier (see overleaf) with wonderfully expressive eyes that follow you like those of the Mona Lisa.

Eugenie Valter

One of two sisters who painted dogs in the early part of the century which were very popular for cards, calendars and post cards. *Faithful Friends* (see overleaf) is a charming head study of an Irish and Fox Terrier. It was used for a calendar in 1934.

Florence Jay (1905–1920)

A contemporary of Maud Earl, Florence Jay exhibited at the Royal Academy. She painted dogs, with special attention to expression and coat. Dr Noonan has one of Jay's Irish Terrier paintings.

Ch Eclipse, by H Crowther. Courtesy Dr A Noonan.

Ch Mile End Muddler by E Aistrop.

An Irish Terrier head study by Lilian Cheviot.

Arthur Wardle (1864–1949)

Arthur Wardle was a prolific painter of terriers, for which he is best known. Many of his studies were used subsequently for postcards, cigarette cards and *objets d'art* such as cigarette cases, boxes and power compacts.

The large auction of dog studies from his estate drew dealers to Sothebys from all over the world. There were four Irish Terriers, largely studies for other commissioned works. Dr Noonan acquired two of these works: one a full portrait (the head of which is often found on cards and *objets d'art*) and one of the 'Sleeping Dog' series.

Faithful Friends by Eugenie Valter

Other Collectables

Dr Noonan has a wonderful collection of postcards and cigarette cards.

There are other very collectable objects to be found. Some find their way into auctions or turn up in antique shops or stalls at dog shows: bronzes, pottery, enamel broaches, gold pins or broaches and even the rare china piece. Souvenirs and memorabilia abound today, with a large price range, from engraved crystal glasses to stickers of the 'I love' variety. The quality is variable but there are some lovely items which will doubtless become the collectors' pieces of the future.

Writings about Irish Terriers

So much has been written about Irish Terriers. Some of it sounds curiously dated but the essence and the message is always the same.

Jack London

Jack London, the famous American author who wrote *Call of the Wild* and *White Fang*, owned and loved Irish Terriers. His books *Jerry of the Islands* and *Michael Brother of Jerry*, now sadly out of print, are full of deep affection and enthusiasm for the breed. He wrote:

Jerry has been love-selected and courage-selected. His ancestors had been deliberately and consciously chosen by men, who, somewhere in the forgotten past, had taken the wild dog and made it into the thing they visioned and admired and desired it to be. It must never fight like a rat in a corner, because it must never be ratlike and slink in a corner. Retreat must be unthinkable. The dogs in the past who had retreated had been rejected by men.

They had not become Jerry's ancestors – the dogs selected for Jerry's ancestors had been the brave ones, the upstanding and out-dashing ones, who flew into the face of danger and battled and died, but who never gave ground... and since it is the way of kind to beget kind; Jerry was what Terrence (his father) was before him, and what Terrence's forefathers had been a long way back. And Jerry was a gentleman, which is to say a gentle dog – he had been so selected.

An Irish Terrier painting by Florence Jay.

An Irish Terrier postcard.

From a picture by Arthur Wardle.

F M Jowett

In 1914, F M Jowett wrote in *The Irish Terrier*:

The general appearance should be that of a hardy, game, stylish Terrier, built on the lines of speed and showing a graceful, symmetrical outline. There should be a distinct difference in build, as well as color, between an Irish Terrier and a Wire-haired Fox Terrier; the Irish Terrier being more on the leg, longer in body, and built more on racing lines, but at the same time having plenty of bone and substance all through, and not Whippety. The height at the shoulder should be approximately 18in; weight 25–27lb.

In the show ring, the Irish Terrier has a style and character all his own and walks up to his opponent and challenges him to a 'tread on the tail of his coat' in a manner that is distinctly characteristic of the breed.

He should look a hard workmanlike rough-and-ready customer, that can keep his end up at any kind of sports, either on land or water.

William Haynes

William Haynes wrote in *Irish Terriers* 1921:

We can assert positively that the breed came from the northern parts of Ireland, and from the first was racy in build and red or fawn in colour. These three facts added together make pretty positive proof of age in the race. It is shrewdly conjectured that the origin of this northern breed is to be found in the crossing of some terrier with the Irish Wolfhound, a big, coarse, wire-coated greyhound type of dog. This theory is well supported by the wire coat, the red colour and the racy build of the Irish Terrier. (And, might be added, would also account for his endurance and courage) – If, as seems very probable, he is an offshoot of the Irish Wolfhound, he can claim direct descent from the dog Adam, for the greyhound family is one of the oldest, if not the oldest, of all canine races.

An old print of Ch Mile End Muddler and
Ch Munster Grip.

Robert S Lemmon

In an article called 'The Irish Terrier' in *House and Garden*, June 1930 Robert S Lemmon wrote:

He has the quality of initiative developed to a high degree and tempered by an astonishing amount of brains. He has never suffered the fate which has overtaken some other breeds – sacrifice

A collection of Irish Terrier cigarette cards from Dr Noonan's collection.

More Irish Terrier cigarette cards from Dr Noonan's collection.

A colour postcard of an Irish Terrier.

of native intelligence or stamina on the altar of show-ring appearance. In fact, the process of refining through which he has passed since entering the show game has made him an even better dog inside than in his old days. He is still the gay, imaginative, do-or-die Irishman of yore.

It would be rather difficult to discover any legitimate canine accomplishment beyond the ability of a typical 'Mick'. He is an excellent house dog, guardian, children's playmate and all-around companion for young or old. You can teach him anything any dog can be expected to learn.

These are his more obvious characteristics. About the time you have come to realise them through personal experience you will begin to sense another and more subtle one which might be termed the instinct for wise action. Time after time you will see a fully mature Irish Terrier choose instantly the right course for the circumstances of the moment. Call it intuition, intelligence, instinct or what you will, there it is. Possibly it has something to do with the fire hidden deep in those dark eyes of his – a heritage, perhaps, from a land where the supernatural is woven into the fabric of all things.

D and G Kidd

From *How to Raise and Train an Irish Terrier*, 1965:

Speak to an Irish Terrier, and he will return your greeting with a singularly intense look from his deep, dark eyes. This penetrating expression reflects character, intelligence, sensitivity and a rich personality.

This is the Irish Terrier: he stands just below knee height, some 18in at the shoulders, large enough to repel an intruder but small enough to be picked up by his master and carried if need be.

His hard coat, wiry and dense, is solid in colour, either bright red, red-wheaten, or golden red. He is spirited, fearless, full of fun, ready to return affection in double measure…

It is heart-warming to see an Irish Terrier attempting to bridge the speech gap between animal and human, particularly in returning a show of affection: tail wagging, body wiggling, singing low throat sounds, squinting his eyes, and sometimes baring his teeth in a wide smile. He can't talk but he certainly can communicate.

Hubert Brown

From *Country Life* magazine, 1923:

The eye of the Daredevil is wonderfully expressive. It is tender and appealing, full of fealty and almost suppliant to his master; but it is shrewd and piercing, or grim and challenging, as circumstances are suspicious, or danger threatens. Always it is radiant with intelligence, but it blazes when the battle is on… None is hardier than the Irish Terrier, nor more adaptable. He graces the country estate and is quite at home in the city apartment. In character he is gentle as a doe with those he loves, and loyal and faithful unto death. He knows children and is one with them in spirit and in play.

Albert Payson Trehune

From a moving tribute, 'St Patrick's Pal', in the *Herald Tribune*:

The Irish Terrier is perhaps the finest dog on earth. He does not throw away his priceless devotion and loyalty on every stranger who may chirp to him. But to the death he is the comrade and protector, and exuberant playmate and sympathizing comforter of the human who has won his heart and respect.

He is an Irish gentleman of the deathless old school; a fiery, true gentleman, from the tips of his braced toes to the rough thatch of his crown. He is more; he has a heart three sizes too big for his shaggy body; a heart that is as white and clean as a Knight errant's.

He is no bully, but he will flinch not one hundredth of an inch from the fight that is forced on him, be the odds ever so impossible against him.

There is a psychic side of the Irish Terrier, too, found in almost no other dog; a tinge of the mysticism of the land of his ancestry.

Edna Howard Jones

From her book *Irish Terriers*:

Irish Terriers are such endearing dogs. Their deep affection and faithfulness to the owners is unusual for a dog that is lively and full of intelligence and very game. Their love for and gentleness with children is a very marked characteristic and it is a delight to watch them with babies and young children. They are very adaptable and excel as a family pet or as a one man dog. Few people who have owned a really typical 'Mick' ever desert the breed for another!

In another part of the book she records the following anecdote:

I do think the Birmingham Irish Terrier who caught a tram to the Park each morning is too good to miss. The dog lived some way from the Park, and only 'himself' knew how he discovered the right tram. Was it instinct, design or chance? Anyway, catch the tram he did with such regularity that the tramways sent an account to his master for his fares. He always walked home, which corresponds with the story of an Irish Terrier owned by a friend in Sussex some years ago. Her dog caught the bus to the Ashdown Forest, but never seemed to be able to catch the right bus home.

The Irish Digest

The following extract appeared in The Irish Digest in 1927:

By the mid 1890's the 'Irishman' had become a raging vogue, and not without reason.

He was a charming companion. He was devoted and plucky to a fault. Ever merry and bright he loved to romp. He was hard and wiry, took to water readily and was a demon ratter. He would travel incredible distances to seek the master of his devotion. He was patient and gentle with children and of very cleanly habits. A most striking characteristic was his dare-devil impetuous courage, regardless of consequences of the formidable appearance of an antagonist who dared to 'tread on the tail of his coat'.

He must never be denied exercise or work or may become quarrelsome with an irritable temper.

Edna Howard Jones with her last 'baby', Lulu.

Yet when well handled the Irish Terrier is the sweetest mannered dog in the world.

Great Western Railway Magazine

Another famous Irish Terrier, Tim, used to collect money for charities at Paddington Station. His story, which appears below, was published in the *Great Western Railway Magazine* in March 1901, and is quoted here by kind permission of the National Railway Museum, but it originally appeared in the *Temple Magazine*:

It was during this same month (May) that Tim was presented to the Queen [Victoria] by special command. A telegram from Windsor commanded him to be in readiness to enter Her Majesty's carriage on her arrival at Paddington. Tim was duly led into the presence of his Sovereign by his master. The Queen patted him tenderly, said kindly words to him, and placed a bright sovereign in his box.

Now Tim has a way of his own of showing gratitude for a special contribution. He does it by standing on his hind hegs and giving three barks, short, sharp and vigorous. But being a wise dog – almost human, as his master truly believes – he did not dare to bark in the presence of his queen. It was an occasion when respectful homage was required, and so he swung his head from one side to the other, and then let it rest on the floor of the carriage for a brief space. That was his bow.

Rowland Johns

Another charming early story about Irish Terriers comes from a book called *Let Dogs Delight* by Rowland Johns. In this his master, Mr Beal, says of him:

Pat is a brown Irish Terrier and he is nine years old. He is very clever and has brains, to a certain extent, like a human being. I am very strict with him but he is apt to be rather spoilt by the ladies. I will now relate some of Pat's doings...

He is up very early every morning and if he finds that the butcher's boy has overslept or has some difficulty in getting up on a cold morning, he goes to the bedroom, jumps on the bed and pulls all the bedclothes off the boy. Also, every morning at nine o' clock, he goes to the grocer's shop, without being sent, to fetch my daily paper and also fetches my wife's groceries in a basket. One day he had some pepper to bring home and some of it got up his nose so ever since that occasion nothing will induce him to bring pepper unless it is wrapped in two papers instead of one.

He can collect orders from custormers and deliver some of the meat, and the monthly account books and money are entrusted to him. If other dogs molest him when he is on his way, Pat will calmly lay his books or meat inside any cottage gate, fight and conquer the other dogs then collect his belongings and deliver them at the shop or house.

In the summer charabancs come here from Eastbourne and when they have a load of people to bring they ring me up on the telephone and say, "Will you send Pat to the Ram Inn to tell them that a charabanc will arrive for tea in half an hour's time!" I then write the message on a piece of paper and off Pat goes with it. On arriving at the inn he will try all the doors in order to obtain an entry but should these be closed he will get through an open window and will refuse to return until he is given an answer to bring back to me. The proprietor of this inn has given Pat a brass studded leather collar to which is fixed a brass plate with the following words engraved upon it: *Pat Beal, Messenger Boy, Firle*.

The butcher's shop in which I live is a branch and I am the Manager. Three or four times a week I go to Lewes; Pat always accompanies me in the cart. As soon as I draw up at the head shop in Lewes, Pat jumps down from the cart, enters the shop and takes the slaughterhouse keys from a nail in the wall; he then jumps back on the cart again and we proceed to the slaughterhouse. When wer arrive there, Pat takes the reins and leads the pony into the stable and when the killing is over I tell him we are ready for home and he again goes to the stable and leads the pony out to the cart.

Without a word of exaggeration, he is a wonderful dog. It just shows what kindness will do.

Lt Col E H Richardson

The following extract from *British War Dogs* by Lt Col E H Richardson features Keeper Macleod talking about the dogs under his control during World War I:

At that time Paddy was badly gassed in the front line and came right back to the section kennel, a distance of 17 kilometres. When he came in he was totally blind but went direct to his own kennel and lay there till I went to his assistance. In three hours he had his eyes open again and was a lively as ever...

At the same time, Paddy was in the wars again. He was led nearly up to the top of Passchendale Ridge with the infantry. He was along with an officer and a runner at a farmhouse which contained Germans. A German came out and took a revolver and shot the dog which was left on the field for dead. He had lain there a long time before he came to himself. He reported at Brigade Headquarters and word was sent to me to go and fetch him as he was badly hit.

Lt Col B J Hanley

The following account by Lt Col B J Hanley (Retd) appeared in *The Irish Terrier Yearbook*, 1984:

Prince, a faithful friend and companion of the 64th Regiment who started life with us about January 1912. He professed to be owned by one Pte Brown, but his life was lived more with men in the barrack rooms than in his master's quarters. True he occasionally lodged there for a night as fancy took him and his ablutions were usually performed by his mistress, Mrs Brown, accompanied by many scoldings for having stayed in Barracks where it was presumed he collected his soilings. Even in these days, nearly 15 years later, we remember him making his daily rounds of the barrack rooms where he made so many friends. He was a stout fellow and whatever he met, he never lowered his tail. He was always present on a march and whatever the length, he did two miles for every one we did if one must judge by the way he scampered in and out of the fields, sometimes in chase of a rabbit and sometimes just for the love of it. So he lived until August 1914 when war separated us from many of those peacetime friends. We went to France and Prince went to London with his mistress. He lived his city life for six weeks and what a tiresome six weeks for Prince. He was a soldier's dog, and only a soldier's life could he live, so who shall blame him for unceremoniously joining forces with the Queen's Westminsters as they marched through London on their way to France. It was thus that he found us again. On arrival with the Queen's Westminsters began a march to the line and behold their march brought them near to us on the occasion that they stopped for a night in Erkingham. Strange that Pte Brown should also pass through Erkingham on the one night of the 1460 days that we spent in France. His surprise on meeting Prince can be better imagined than explained and Prince soon settled the question of ownership.

Prince recommenced his life with the 64th. But a different life than in the days of old. Every night, almost with human knowledge, he scanned the faces of those who were borne out on the stretchers, lest by the chance he missed greeting an old comrade of peacetime days. Those wonderful brown Irish Terrier eyes contained a depth of pity and his tongue has licked many a cold face. Even on such roads as have become famous in history his tail never dropped. Menin Road and Hell Fire Corner, Devils Gate and Cemetery Walk were as well known to Prince as to those humans whose task carried them nightly over those danger spots to the trenches beyond. There was no hospital for him when he received his wound and only such succour as could be given by the unskilled hand of a transport sergeant was all he asked, and then with wound still only partially healed he came again to greet those going away and those who were left. Getting older but still performing his self-imposed duty brought him to that day when war ended abruptly. Surely Prince wondered why it stopped. He had done the same job for four years and this sudden change puzzled him. The 64th were going back to England and what about poor old Prince. He couldn't understand that dogs had to go into quarantine, neither could he understand that it was an expensive business for a poor man, but the difficulty was overcome by the RSPCA, who having heard of his services in France took him into quarantine and eventually returned him to his master. He was coming back to us as soon as his passage could be arranged, but death took him from us. What better tribute can we pay him than his noble head shall hang amongst those who knew him so well. There is no Tombstone to mark that place where his body lies, and none is necessary, for his life is deeply engraved on the hearts of those who knew him.

Stories of the courage and endurance of Irish Terriers during that war and the love and comfort they gave to the soldiers are legion. My book *Jack of the Great War* is based on these stories.

Lucy Jackson (the author!)

Lucy Jackson has written a string of books about Irish Terriers.

Jock of the Great War is a poignant and moving story about the courage and devotion to duty shown by dogs in the front line of battle during World War I. It is accurately researched and beautifully illustrated by Judy Tucker. Joanna Lumley wrote about it: "I have taken Jock into my heart forever" – and so will you!

Miss Bunch and her Friends tells of walking three Irish Terriers in a London Park. They lead the way, 'talk' to everyone, share the picnics, put up with the birds and scare the 'ladies in Yasmaks'. Their friends are equally adventure prone. It is a funny, gentle book which children love.

Painting on a leaf, signed 'Louisa'.

Stories of Breezy and Blanvey is about two old 'Irish rogues' who live on the edge of Hampstead Heath. They are always setting the world to right and usually win – apart from the odd come-uppance. They are so unmistakably Irish Terriers!

Ted and his Teddy Bear is a picture book for little ones. Beautifully illustrated by Lisa Kapper it tells how tiny Ted is given a big teddy bear to keep him company. He loses him for the winter and when the spring comes Ted has grown and is the 'Big Ted' now – a real, grown-up Irish Terrier.

The much loved little book *For Irish Terriers and Other Dogs Too* describes all the situations that make dogs so exasperating and endearing – especially the Irish.

The African Adventure of Finnegan O'Reilly is a story of love and loyalty, and Finn is unforgettable,

Alexandra Days

Paddy's Pay Dog is amusingly illustrated and tells of Paddy, who 'dances' as part of an aerobatic double act. On his day off he takes his pay in a purse and visits the barber, the pub and the cinema. After an adventure with some boys who try to steal his ice-cream he returns home to his pretty mistress with a posy – aah! It is full of the Irish Terrier generosity and fun.

Jilly Cooper

In Jilly Cooper's delightful book *The Canine Years* Clarissa's dog, the much-adored friend and walking companion was an Irish Terrier. She wrote to say, "They are absolutely fabulous dogs and so funny!"

Major Grambien Parry

Major Grambien Parry wrote *Murphy - a Message to Dog Lovers*, 1912. At Highway in Gloucestershire there is a walled cemetery with tiny headstones all in memory of his dogs. It is still beautifully kept by the present owners with a plaque on the wall. It is a tribute to the dogs, three of which were Irish Terriers. He wrote a charming account of his life with Murphy, one of his much loved Irish – his 'dear boy'.

Evelyn Howard

Evelyn Howard's book *The Dog that went to Heaven* is a charming story full of Irish Terrier wit and grit. Mike decides not to 'be dead' and returns through many adventures to be with his 'boss'. Its delightful illustrations are by L R Brightwell.

Beatrix Potter

Stumpy the brown terrier in Beatrix Potter's *Little Pig Robinson* is unmistakably an Irish Terrier.

I only met one person, a dog called Stumpy who was going the opposite way. He was carrying a paper parcel in his mouth.

Some dogs do not care for fish. Stumpy had been to the Butchers to buy mutton chops for himself and Bob and Percy and Miss Rose. Stumpy was a large, serious, well-balanced brown dog with a short tail. He lived with Bob the Retriever and Percy the cat and Miss Rose who kept house.

Stumpy had belonged to a very rich old gentleman, and when the old gentleman died he left money to Stumpy – ten shillings a week for the rest of Stumpy's life. So that was why Stumpy and Bob and Percy the Cat all lived together in a pretty little house.

Lindsay Williamson has written a charming sequel, telling the heroic tale of how Stumpy earned his mutton bone pension.

Monaghan

This poem by Monaghan usually appears with charming illustrations. I think that it illustrates something of the mystery and magic of Irish Terriers:

'Twas long ago, and long ago, he left the Wee Folks' ken
And wandered far, and very far, and ne'er returned again.
He travelled paths that led afield from haunt of Elf and Gnome
And found an alien harbour in the Other Peoples' home.
Then in and out, and thro' the years, – now by the light o' day –
Now by the link of elfin torch – now by the lanthorne's ray –
So have the Wee Folks quested on, ay, all their class and kin;
But never shall they win him since the Others took him in.
'Tis not the East Wind's sigh ye hear, 'tis not the Dead Lear's fall;
'Tis Elfin brogues a-flying, 'tis the Elfin questing-call
As ever on and on the Chase through Glen and Glade and Bog –
The Little People hunting for the Little Peoples' Dog,
The while this Dog, the Faeries' Dog, is fretting to and fro
Forever searching, scenting, for his Glens-of-Long Ago,
And ever shall be the Quest be keen, and ever fresh the scent
For lo, at dawn of Christmas Day the Faerie Gods relent
And for a trice a twelvemonth by the Faerie Rulers' whim
The Dog espies his people, and his People dance for him.

But look! The Day is breaking! And the Terrier is true
And waits once more, as evermore, the Christmas Rendezvous.
'Tis there he finds his Faeries underneath the Holly bough -
But, *Whist!… Be silent. Brothers!… I think he sees Them now!*

Songs of Leinster

Songs of Leinster is one of the best known dog poems in the language. These, the last verses say it all:

But he'd stick to me to his latest breath
An' he'd go with me to the gates of death;
He'd wait for a thousand years would he,
Scratchin' the door and whinin' for me
If meself were inside Purgat'ry.

So I laugh when I hear them make it plain
That dogs an' men ne'er meet again.
For all their talk, who'd listen to them,
With the soul in the shinin' eyes of him?
Would God be wastin' a dog like Tim?

Marie Noël

Lastly, I include a translation and adaption of Marie Noël's *Contes de Noël: Le Sixième Jour*:

As soon as the Irish Red Terrier was created, he nosed the hand of God. God patted him on the head.

"What is your wish, Dog?"

"Please, God, my wish is to live at Your home in Heaven, right on Your doorstep."

Said God: "Not in a thousand years. I have no need for a dog, since thieves are not yet in existence."

"When will they be?"

"Never. I am tired. I have been creating things for five days now, and it is time I took some rest. Here you are now, the best of all my creatures, my masterpiece. Better stop now. An artist should not overstrain himself. If I went on, I am certain I would fail. Go now, little Irish Red dog, go and be happy forever."

The little Irish Red heaved a deep sigh.

"What am I supposed to do on Earth?"

"You shall eat, and drink, and make friends, be fruitful and multiply"

The dog sighed sadly once more.

"Is that not enough? What other task do you require?"

"To wait on You, my Lord. Could you not take your abode on Earth?"

"No," said God, "definitely no. Of course I cannot. Settling on Earth to keep you company is totally and thoroughly impossible. I have numerous tasks to see to: Heaven, Stars, Angels, so many things needing attention."

The dog bowed his head in sorrow and walked away. Then he turned round and said:

"If only, Almighty God, if only there was in that place where you send me some kind of a master similar to You..."

"No," said God, "there isn't."

The dog said in a very small voice:

"Could you not try and make one... it might work..."

"This is out of the question," said God. "My task is completed. The whole world is now as I wished it to be. Never shall I be able to create a better creature than you. Were I to shape another being today, I can feel in my hands that it would be a failure."

"O Almighty God," said the dog, "what does it matter if it is only second best, as long as I can follow him where he goes, and stop when he stops..."

God was overwhelmed by such kind-heartedness, and He said:

"Let it be as you wish."

And he walked into his workshop and created Man.

NB: Man is a failure, of course, as God had guessed. It does not matter really, since the Irish dog is happy.

Chapter Sixteen

Anecdotes and Epilogue

Monarch of the shore.

Anecdotes

Talk to the owner of an Irish Terrier anywhere and the effect is always the same. The face lights up and the anecdotes begin to flow: "You wouldn't believe it…", "You should have seen…", "I was thunderstruck…"

Many of the stories are accompanied by gales of laughter and sometimes the odd tear.

All express the love, loyalty, pluck, intelligence, humour, waywardness and irresisitible charm of the breed.

Irish Terriers inevitably have a huge impact on the lives of their human companions, and the tales live on for ever. There are so many anecdotes that it is difficult to decide where to begin.

Miss Bunch

Our Miss Bunch, when not much more than a year old, showed incredible courage. We were out walking on the Pennington marshes when our old bitch, who was lagging behind, was charged by a young bullock. The old dog was stone deaf and quite unaware of the thundering hoofs and deadly danger. Miss Bunch appeared from nowhere and streaked across the bullock's nose, turned quickly and dashed back, cutting it off in its tracks. It gave us the time to rush up and beat the bullock off. We never knew how Bunch had even noticed what was happening, let alone understood and known exactly what to do. Without her intervention the old dog would undoubtedly have been trampled and killed.

Miss Bunch, now a rather frail old lady herself, is fiercely protective of the new puppy. Any squeak from real or imagined hurt when playing too roughly with friends in the park has Bunch thundering up to 'see off' those friends at once.

Guard Dogs

Irish Terriers are wonderful guard dogs. Jill Livesay was in India as a child. Their dog Rory was instinctively very protective of 'his' children and the family property. They had left him to guard the car one day when a thief (a rather well-endowed lady) pressed up against the car, making a long arm through the window. Rory leapt forward and held her there, pinned to the car 'by the bust'. In spite of a gathering crowd, he held on until the family returned.

Loyalty

Their loyalty is legendary. Miss Pravda was born in Prague and Susannah was her adored childhood pet. They went everywhere together. Tragically, when Miss Pravda was 12 the whole family was sent to a concentration camp for five long years. Susannah stayed with friends. When Miss Pravda returned she was by now a quite grown-up girl of 17. She was terrified that Susannah would not recognise her. Susannah hesitiated for only a moment – and then crawled across the floor on her belly, whining softly, and leapt into Miss Pravda's arms. She had not forgotten.

Clowns

Irish Terriers have great natural cheerfulness. Tom, Miss Gwen Fuige's family pet during the Second World War, went through the entire Blitz in London. His irrespressible high spirits kept up his family's morale, especially during the long hours in the air-raid shelter. "We were all right as long as Tom was there to make us laugh," she says. It has earned him a plaque in Battersea Dogs Home.

Pathfinders Pixie.

Social Animals

My brother's dog Jocky-Boy was well known and much loved by the whole village. Usually referred to as 'that Irish rogue', he turned up for all village occasions, making his presence felt with varying success. Funerals, weddings, sports days – he always knew when something was afoot. He used to ride on a small wooden platform attached to the bar of my brother's bicycle. His tricks (catching balls and sticks) earned money when he went 'busking' for the war effort.

Mischief

Hattie Manners was walked daily in Kensington Gardens. She loved to slip through the Palace railings and set the alarm bells ringing. Legend has it that, when Lady D was moving furniture, Hattie, back once more in the Palace grounds, was found by the removal men sitting comfortably on a pale-gold Royal sofa.

Endurance

Irish Terriers have great powers of recovery and endurance, as illustrated by Brandy's story. He was a rescue dog (most unusual for an Irish Terrier!) and no-one knew his origins. He had obviously had a bad start and was very nervous, completely unsocialised and quite unused to people.

With loving care and devotion from his owner Lisanne, Brandy settled down and became a star on the Obedience trial circuit. He won the Irish Terrier Association Cup one year. With his house brother, Ossie, he was a superb model for the Sandersons 'Check Collection' catalogue. In spite of his dreadful early start he was never vicious and, as Lisanne so movingly expressed it, "Everything he had he gave to us."

Erinsgold Shaunes Girl.

Ceiledh Mavourneen

But more than all, it is the tender care and deep affection they offer their human companions that makes them so unforgettable.

I have poignant memories of Ceiledh Mavourneen, who 'worshipped' and sustained my children all through their early years. She joined in with every game and soothed away every tear. She sat with them through mumps and measles, scarcely leaving the sick room.

She was a warm and loving focus of our lives and prompted the famous remark from my daughter, then aged five: "No, no, it's not just Lucy – you see, we all love the dogs best."

Could more be said?

Epilogue

"Well, if they're such great dogs, why don't we see more of them?"

A good question, and I admit we could do with a few more puppies around and a few more dogs in the show ring. But no Irish Terrier is a push-over and in an age of conformity and ultra-convenience, perhaps not everyone is prepared to give the time to a dog who tends to have an opinion on most things and would like you to agree!

I have to confess that this book was finished with our two new puppies Zuli and Bega in residence. I had forgotten the impact of pups on a household and Irish Terriers are the proverbial 'little tykes'. Forget the daffy dog on the television pulling long strands of loo paper with never a tear to be seen. We have ours shredded. No machine could get a closer cut and it takes only minutes! But the rewards far outweigh the mishaps and they are not really much wilder than other puppies – it just goes on for longer!

The contemporary scene does indeed look good. There are some beautiful dogs appearing and a solid body of skilled and dedicated breeders both in this country and Europe and also in America.

Increasing the numbers of a breed needs to be a slow and careful process. There is too much to lose, and a sudden peak in popularity spells disaster. No one within the breed would countenance that.

Whenever you see an Irish Terrier, do stop and talk – whether in snow or sunshine, town or country, the park or the beach, they are always 'at home', delighted with themselves and having a great time. You will probably receive a rapturous welcome and be invited to reveal or, better still, to share the contents of your bag or parcels.

Look into those wonderful dark eyes and see the famous 'fire' – the energy, the understanding, the joy in life.

Before you know it you will have joined the ever increasing happy band of those of us who **love Irish Terriers.**

The End

Appendix A

Irish Terrier Champions 1875–1918

Compiled by Paul Livesey

Name	Sex	Owner	No of CCs	Years of CCs
Sport (late Celt)	D	G Jamieson	1	1875
Spuds	D	G Jamieson	1	1877
Fly	B	H Mappleback	2	1878–79
Sporter	D	E F Despard	1	1879
Erin	B	W Graham	8	1879–82
Sting	B	R B & T S Carey	9	1879–84
Gripper	D	C Lamb	1	1882
Glory	B	W Graham	1	1882
Pagan II	D	J N R Pim/G R Krehl	3	1883–85
Peter Bolger	D	H Waterhouse	1	1883
Kitty	B	R F Godfrey	1	1883
Poppy	B	J N R Pim	6	1883–86
Playboy	D	J N R Pim	13	1884–86
Gaily	B	C Lamb	5	1884–88
Garryford	D	W Graham	6	1885–90
Batchelor	D	C J Barnett	7	1886–88
Extreme Carelessness	B	W Graham	11	1886–89
BA	D	H Sumner	4	1888–89
Ballyhooley	D	E A Wiener	4	1888–89
Breda Rattle	D	W Graham/G R Krehl	8	1888–90
Breadenhill	D	Dr Tennant	15	1891–94
Brickbat	D	E A Wiener	26	1889–94
Banford	B	J E Jessop	6	1889–90
Droleen	B	R B & T S Carey	2	1889–91
Bonnet (late Amusement)	B	F W Breakell	8	1890–91
Dan'el II	D	Capt Sladen	5	1891–92
Breda Mixer	D	W Graham	12	1892–96

Name	Sex	Owner	No of CCs	Years of CCs
Checkmate	D	G Mayall	3	1894–97
Ted Malone	D	Mrs Butcher	6	1894–98
Treasurer	D	T Wallace	4	1895–99
Breda Muddler (late Chapelier)	D	G Mayall	10	1895–98
Sarah Kidd	B	R B Smith	9	1895–97
Bolton Woods Mixer	D	S Wilson	30	1896–1901
Belfast Erin	B	F Gregg	8	1897–1901
Blue Nettle	B	J Craig	4	1897–98
Stackhouse Sportsman (late Mansfield Sportsman)	D	G B Waugh	3	1897–99
Kineton Biddy (late Bridget Kelly)	B	Dr W W Fenton	3	1897–98
Senela Heeate	B	C H Higson	4	1898–99
Charmian	B	G Mayall	3	1898–1900
Munster Grip	D	G Krehl	3	1899–1900
Muskerry Lass	B	J Craig	3	1899–1900
Scarlet Lancer	D	A P Simpson	3	1899
Charwoman	B	F Clifton	15	1899–1902
John Ridd	D	F W Westlake	4	1899–1901
Union Jack	D	A P Simpson	3	1900–01
Bloomfield Burgomaster	D	M Short	3	1900–01
Suffolk Bill	D		3	1900–01
Mile End Muddler	D	F Clifton	17	1900–03
Crow Gill Maureen	B	F M Jowett	3	1901–03
Mile End Vixen (late Barlae Vixen)	B	F Clifton	3	1901
Colin	D	F McNamee	3	1901
Kinswoman	B	R S Knox	4	1901
That's Trumps	B	Dr H J Twamley	3	1901–02
Winsom Lass	B	J Harrington	3	1901–03
Straight Tip	D	J Oates	17	1901–04
Lady Peggy	B	T Rigby	3	1901–02
Beeston Belle	B	W H Slater	8	1902–03
Bawn Beauty	B	Mrs L Butcher	8	1903–05
Bolton Woods Star (late Fulwood Frost)	B	J Watt	4	1903

Name	Sex	Owner	No of CCs	Years of CCs
Mile End Kitty	B	F Clifton	3	1903–07
Celtic Bella (late Greenfield Boreen)	B	A B Montgomery	3	1903
Mile End Barrister	D	F Clifton	16	1903–07
Bolton Woods Venus	B	S Wilson	3	1904
Mile End Peggy	B	F Clifton	5	1904–05
Mourne Prince	D	C Browne	4	1904–05
Kate Kearney	B	H H Wilson	3	1904
Fulwood Ferenze	D	J Watt	7	1905–06
Paymaster	D	Miss L A Paull	11	1905–07
Mullinger Kate	B	H H Wilson	5	1905
Beeston Betty	B	J Collis Walker	6	1906
Sir Edward	D	J Mitchell	3	1906–07
Redeemer	D	H Ridley	4	1906–08
Tipperary Tyke	D	Dr H J Twamley	3	1906–07
Crow Gill Patricia	B	F M Jowett	3	1906
Crow Gill Myra	B	F M Jowett	3	1907
Bloomfield Erin	B	M M Short	6	1907–09
Killarney Sport	D	F W Breakell	10	1907–10
Beauty's Boy	D	Mrs L Butcher	4	1908
Bloomfield Irene	B	G S Thomas	6	1908
Botanic Demon (late Bellingdom Bruiser)	D	W H Darker	22	1908–14
Bingley Beauty	B	J Barron	7	1908–09
Barlae Brickbat	D	W Prentice/Mrs O W Porritt	14	1909–13
Bolton Woods Authority	D	S Wilson	3	1909–10
Botanic Venus	B	W H Darker	5	1910
Tender and True	B	Dr H J Twamley	3	1910
Wicklow Mick	D	J R Evans	4	1910–11
Straight Pride	B	J Oates	6	1910–11
Musbury Tip	D	Mrs O W Porritt	4	1910–13
Proverb	B	Miss L A Paull	10	1911–14
Musbury Demon	D	Mrs O W Porritt	8	1912
Musbury Mavourneen (late Barlae Betty)	B	Mrs O W Porritt	3	1912–14

Name	Sex	Owner	No of CCs	Years of CCs
Barlock Beauty	B	T Barrett	3	1912
Bawnmore Fuss	B	H H Wilson	3	1912
Wicklow Munster	D	J R Evans	4	1913–14
Poplin	B	Miss L A Paull	3	1913
Botanic Gael	D	M Ballard	4	1913–14
Musbury Maureen	B	Mrs O W Porritt	6	1913–16
Musbury Fionnuala	B	Mrs O W Porritt	3	1913–14
Portia	B	Miss L A Paull	3	1913–14
Turf Commander	D	G Stanworth	4	1914
Double Shear	D	J P Lowrance	8	1914–16
My Lady Mountbac	B	M Ballard	10	1914–15
Wrose Badger	D	H H Wilson	9	1915–16
Botanic What a Lady	B	W H Darker	3	1916
Frontier Special	B	W E Thornber	4	1916
Brentmore Blinker	D	W A Pritchad	4	1916

Note: Some of the early Championships records are unclear. This particularly applies to the years 1890–1904, when first a points system was applied and then challenge wins in selected shows only counted towards achieving Champion status. Where there is any doubt whether a dog has qualified, the dog has been included in the list.

Appendix B

Irish Terrier Champions 1920–1997

Compiled by Paul Livesey

Name	Sex	Owner	No of CCs	Years of CCs
1920				
Kelvin Batchelor	D	N Galloway	5	1916–20
Excess Profit	D	N Galloway	3	1920
Celtic Molly	B	A B Montgomery	4	1920
War Bonus	D	A B Montgomery	3	1920
Celtic Colleen	B	A B Montgomery	3	1920
1921				
Boldon Bhoy	D	W Slater	4	1920–21
Wrose Startler	D	A B Montgomery	4	1920–21
Celtic Clare	B	A B Montgomery / J R Evans	4	1920–21
Celtic Batchelor	D	J E O'Neill	3	1921
Hilton Eirene	B	J F Hitchings	3	1921
1922				
Wacc	B	H G H Wellington	3	1921–22
Abermolly	B	A B Montgomery / O T Walters	4	1921–22
Peg O'The Ring	B	O T Walters	3	1921–22
Celtic Patriot	D	A B Montgomery	7	1921–24
Wrose Bouncer	D	Mrs R Kearns Franks	5	1921–23
Brentmoor Ballarat	B	W A Pritchard	4	1921–22
Celtic Playboy	D	A B Montgomery	6	1922
Celtic Rattler	D	A B Montgomery	3	1922
Boldon Bunty	B	W Slater	6	1922–24
1923				
Celtic Poppy	B	A B Montgomery	3	1922–23
Bloomfield Refugee	D	M Short	3	1922–23
Celtic Pal	D	A B Montgomery	7	1922–24

Name	Sex	Owner	No of CCs	Years of CCs
Celtic Judy	B	A B Montgomery	10	1923–24
Celtic Erin	B	P N Nissen	3	1923
Celtic Mutt	D	Lady Hehir	3	1923
Cringle Begorra	D	N Galloway/S Warburton	8	1923–29
Boy	D	E Perfect	5	1923–24
Bakarian My Lady	B	G A Betts	4	1923
1924				
Watchman	D	H G H Wellington/H R Brown	3	1923–24
Klu's Best	B	E G S Cardell	3	1923–24
Celtic Poplin	B	A B Montgomery	4	1923–24
Shore Road Batchelor	D	S Warburton/H H Wilson	3	1924
Tapton Surprise	D	W Tottle	4	1924–26
Hibernian Hard Dawn	D	J C Hirst	4	1924–28
Frank's Choice	B	J R Jackson	3	1924
1925				
Bakarian Judy	B	G A Betts	3	1924–25
Celtic Timothy	D	A B Montgomery/T McDaid	3	1924–25
Celtic Sweetheart	B	A B Montgomery	3	1924–25
Oval Lady	B	J C Hirst	3	1924–25
Galloper	D	W S Green	14	1925–27
Cotteridge Boozer	D	T Scott	4	1925
Culrathain Madcap	B	A R Anderson	4	1925
Rambling Rose	B	T Yorke	4	1925
Ratepayer	D	Dr C Preston Ball	3	1925
1926				
Bankhall Molly Bawn	B	T McDaid	3	1925–26
Gracious	B	W S Green	3	1925–26
Frankeen	B	H Clough/S Warburton	5	1925–26
Goldseeker	D	W S Green	3	1925–26
Rambling Sandie	D	T Yorke	4	1926
Eclipse	D	P W Vincent	3	1926

Name	Sex	Owner	No of CCs	Years of CCs
1927				
Frontier Optimist	D	G H Massey	3	1926–27
Goldtape	B	W S Green/F Calvert-Butler	6	1926–27
Goldthread	B	W S Green	8	1926–27
Dany Graig Top Gear	D	R Thomas	4	1927
Culbahn Chance	B	H H Wilson	3	1927
Tapton Rory	D	W Tottle	3	1927
Jugo	D	Dr M E Tressider	5	1927–28
1928				
Conspirator	D	J Connell	3	1927–28
Bright Eyes	B	R S Holland	3	1927–28
Brantvale Belle	B	G M Barr	4	1927–30
Prancer	D	Miss L A Paull	3	1927–28
Godetia	B	W S Green	3	1927–28
Acushla of Ennisfarne	B	Lady Hehir	4	1927–28
Uriah	D	H Clough/S Warburton	3	1928
Wrose Quids	D	H H Wilson	3	1928
1929				
Neatness	B	E T Poultney	3	1928–29
Culbahn Circe	B	F Calvert-Butler	5	1928–30
Hibernian Judy	B	J C Hirst	3	1928–29
Goldstick	D	W S Green	5	1929
1930				
Pegaway	B	Miss L A Paull	4	1929–31
Goldlace	B	W S Green	5	1920–30
Hibernian Malone	D	J C Hirst	4	1929–30
Culbahn Crusader	D	J R Jackson	3	1929–30
Ancon Avenger	D	D S Starring	3	1930
Strongheart Sensation	D	E Cohen	4	1930–31
1931				
New Inn Boy	D	Miss L V Walters	4	1930–31

Name	Sex	Owner	No of CCs	Years of CCs
Solid Man	D	F Calvert-Butler	13	1931–33
Hibernian Cora	B	J C Hirst	3	1931
Hibernian Aileen	B	J C Hirst	6	1931–33
1932				
Kelvin Felix	D	W Tottle	4	1930–32
Brantvale Belladonna	B	G M Barr	3	1932
The Saorstat	B	Dr A J Swanton	3	1932
1933				
Culbahn Coquette	B	J R Jackson	3	1932–33
Felstead Mischief	B	J F Hutchings	4	1933
Grandstunt	D	Dr A J Swanton	4	1933
1934				
Culbahn Creole	B	J R Jackson/Lady Dent	5	1933–34
Rarean Risky	B	T Hegarty	3	1933–34
Last of Begorra	B	J W North	3	1933–34
Culbahn Cuchullin	D	Mrs R Harrison/J McKay	4	1934
Culbahn Charming	B	J R Jackson	3	1934
Culbahn Costello	D	J R Jackson/T Edwards	6	1934–37
1935				
Eton Boy	D	R Everill	3	1933–35
Shore Road Topper	D	W S Green	3	1934–35
Culbahn Confidence	B	J R Jackson	3	1935
Slemish Stormer	D	R Grant	4	1935
Roeside Ramona	B	C P Lynch	4	1935
Culbahn Caustic	B	J R Jackson	3	1935
Merrey Maureen	B	Miss F M Simpson	3	1935–36
1936				
Slemish Splendid	D	R Grant	4	1935–36
Wolstanton Bridgeen	B	Mrs H Plant	4	1936
Kelvin Colleen	B	J F McKinstry	3	1936
Culbahn Chevalier	D	Mrs J J Walker	3	1936

Name	Sex	Owner	No of CCs	Years of CCs
1937				
Lavers Leader	D	H Phipps	4	1936–38
Ballinamodree	B	J R Jackson	3	1936–37
Culbahn Comeaway	B	J R Jackson	3	1936–37
Culbahn Cuagh	B	J R Jackson	3	1937
Red Dan	D	E P Slater	6	1937–39
Kelvin Glorious	B	J F McKinstry	3	1937
1938				
Hen's Heir	D	W J Gardiner	3	1936–38
Lisna Supreme	D	J Goff-Pimm / R Williamson	3	1937–38
Coalville Mike	D	Mrs G Heath	4	1938–39
Kelvin Acushla	B	J F McKinstry	3	1938
Kelvin Starette	B	J F McKinstry	3	1938
1939				
Sherry of the Mill	B	Mrs G D Moore	3	1938–39
Hoplite	D	Mrs E P Slater	3	1938–39
Drumfree	D	Lt Col C T C Plowden	3	1938–39
Russetone Whiskey	B	Mrs G D Moore	3	1939
Merrey Miranda	B	Miss F M Simpson	3	1939

Showing ceased during the Second World War

Name	Sex	Owner	No of CCs	Years of CCs
1947				
Russetone O'Shaunnessy	D	Mrs E M B Moore	4	1946–47
Russetone Simon	D	Mrs E M B Moore	3	1939–47
Safe Convoy	B	Mrs C E Birch	3	1946–47
Newpark Lovely Ann	B	F Dempster	3	1947

Name	Sex	Owner	No of CCs	Years of CCs
1948				
Brentwicke Paddy	D	Mrs G Lomas	3	1948
Redtack Michael	D	W M Aldersley	3	1947–48
Crackle of Cranmore	D	K Ingram	3	1947–48
Ichinose	D	J Mair	12	1948–53
Solid Marigold	B	G Clayton	4	1947–48
Nadder Deborah	B	Mrs E P Slater	4	1947–48
Lady Jane of Aira	B	Miss L Mitchell	3	1948
Culbahn Crona	B	O Fitzpatrick	3	1948
1949				
Culbahn Slemish Safeguard	D	J R Jackson	3	1948–49
Barney's Progeny	D	F Roberts/F Dempster	10	1948–50
Wogil Melody Maker	D	B Lilliland/T Drew	6	1949–50
Breezy Molly O'Shea	B	Mrs I V Shaw	3	1948–49
York Lass	B	R Williamson	3	1949
Aira Topsy	B	Mrs A G Hayes	4	1949
Russetone Nadder Bloom	B	Mrs G D Moore	3	1949
1950				
Wogil Antiville Taveron	D	B Gilliland/T Drew	5	1950
Russetone Wag	D	Mrs E M B Moore	3	1950
Brentwicke Nickie	B	Mrs G Lomas	3	1949–50
Russetone Wanton	B	Mrs E M B Moore	3	1950
Gracious Simonette	B	A J Williams	3	1950
Keillor Ever Sure	B	A Martin	4	1950–51
1951				
Roberty Maire	D	F Roberts	7	1950–52
Merrey Mascot	D	Miss F M Simpson	3	1949–51
Begorra Noble Dan	D	D B Aaron	4	1950–51
Keillor Effective	D	A Martin	4	1951
Pathfinders Bandleader	D	Miss N Woodifield/J S Pringle	3	1951
Oudenarde Farriers Galloper	D	Ms D & H Hamilton/Mrs M Temple	6	1950–52

Name	Sex	Owner	No of CCs	Years of CCs
Commissar Lass	B	Mrs E M Thompson	3	1950–51
Merrey Melissa	B	Miss F M Simpson	4	1950–53
Ballymakenny Dinkie	B	H Fairtlough	5	1951
Drumshaw Shealagh	B	Mrs I V Shaw	5	1951–52
Ballymakenny Pippa	B	H Fairtlough	5	1951–53
1952				
Bright Boy	D	T C Evans	3	1952
Howgill Henrietta	B	Mrs E S Howlett	3	1951–52
Brackenwood Herbtuppence	B	Miss M Abell	3	1952
Roeside Ranee	B	C P Lynch	3	1952
Tara of Innisfallen	B	Mrs I Blundell-Watts	4	1952–53
1953				
Arley O'Flynn	D	Miss M de Beaumont	3	1952–53
Drumcorrie Blarney	D	Miss M de Beaumont	3	1953
Somerton Sensational	D	J McIllhagga	3	1953
Chip Ryan	D	R Jordan	7	1953–59
Supine Lady	B	W Hyde	4	1951–54
Oudenarde Orangespark	B	Mrs D & Miss H Hamilton/Mrs M E Temple	4	1953
Tessie of Aira	B	Mrs A G Hayes	4	1953
1954				
Pathfinders Drummer Boy	D	Miss N Woodifield	6	1953–54
Begorra How's Zat	D	D B Aaron	3	1954
Somerton Sunstorm	D	J McIllhagga	3	1954
Pathfinders Nell of The Grand	B	Miss N Woodifield	4	1954
Culbahn Coronation	B	J R Jackson	3	1954
Tithebarn Same Again	B	J Noone	4	1954–55
Brackenwood Ballerina	B	Miss M Abell	4	1954–58

235

Name	Sex	Owner	No of CCs	Years of CCs
1955				
Culbahn Callboy	D	J R Jackson	3	1954–55
Drumcorrie Shamus	D	Miss M de Beaumont	4	1954–55
Brackenwood Midnight	D	Miss M Abell	3	1955
Merrey Maestro	D	Miss F M Simpson	4	1955–56
Begorra Dancer	B	D B Aaron	3	1955
Pathfinders Red Riding Hood of Aira	B	Miss N Woodifield	4	1955
1956				
Cheadle Boy	D	T A Howarth	3	1955–56
Russetone Slainnte	D	Mrs E M B Moore	3	1955–56
Somerton Solitaire	D	J McIllhagga	3	1956
Drumcorrie Simon	D	Miss M de Beaumont	7	1956–57
Peg the Rake of Aira	B	Misses C Harris & S M Medcalf	5	1955–59
Pathfinders Last Dance	B	Miss N Woodifield	3	1955–56
Somerton Sunvale	B	J McIllhaagga	3	1956
Drumcorrie Patsy	B	E Hertz	3	1956
1957				
Drumcorrie Piper	D	Miss M de Beaumont	4	1957
Merrey Milord	D	Miss F M Simpson	10	1957–60
Begorra How's Jenny	B	D B Aaron/Mrs S N Clayton	3	1955–56
Brackenwood Joyous Venture	B	Miss M Abell	5	1957
Brackenwood Fiona	B	Miss M Abell	3	1957
1958				
Pathfinders Quickstep	D	Miss N Woodifield	3	1957–58
Roeside Rallah	D	C P Lynch	3	1957–58
Pathfinders Two Step	D	Miss N Woodifield	9	1958–59
Meranti N'Changa Copper	B	Mrs N B Houlden	3	1957–58
Pathfinders Watlztime	B	Mrs M M Frost	6	1958–59
Oudenarde Irish Rose	B	Mrs D & Miss H Hamilton/Mrs M E Temple	7	1958–59
1959				
Oudenarde Thunderflash	D	Mrs D & Miss H Hamilton/Mrs M E Temple	6	1958–60

Name	Sex	Owner	No of CCs	Years of CCs
Depleach Kettledrum	D	C Pollard	16	1959–61
Armagh Biddy	B	W H Gillespie	3	1955–59
Ballymakenny Cora	B	H Fairtlough	3	1959
1960				
Oudenarde Irish Mick	D	Mrs D & Miss H Hamilton/Mrs M E Temple	3	1960
Breezy Red Sorrel	B	Mrs E Howard Jones	5	1957–60
Roeside the Colleen Bawn	B	C P Lynch	3	1960
Pathfinders Gypsy	B	Miss N Woodifield	4	1960
1961				
Pathfinders Dragonfly	D	Miss N Woodifield	3	1961
Roeside A Real Mick	D	C P Lynch	5	1961–62
Never Too Late	B	Mrs S Tongue	5	1961
Pathfinders Fantasy	B	Miss N Woodifield	3	1961
1962				
Chip Of Old Block	D	F Roberts	4	1962
Pathfinders Castaway	D	N Frost	10	1962–64
Roeside Pathfinders Stowaway	B	C P Lynch	8	1962–63
1963				
Lynphen Bloom of Tara	D	G B Brudenell	15	1962–64
Torstans Drumshaw Clover	B	A & Miss P Whalley	9	1961–65
Susan of Swinpen	B	T C Evans	5	1962–64
Ballinruan Belle	B	T K Loughrey	4	1963
1964				
Firethorn Red Robert	D	F Roberts	3	1964
Pathfinders Livthorpe Kerrymyne	B	Miss N Woodifield	3	1964
Swinpen My Choice	B	T C Evans	4	1963–64
Oudenarde Zelia	B	Mrs D & Miss H Hamilton/Mrs M Temple	11	1963–65
1965				
Begorra Dalriada Dariel	D	D B Aaron	4	1964–65
Lattenbury Dalriada Dennis	D	G B Brudenell	4	1964–65

Name	Sex	Owner	No of CCs	Years of CCs
1966				
Drumshaw Piper	D	W Tracey	3	1965–66
Lynphen Micky Finn	D	C Pollard	5	1965–66
Redneval Rose	B	F W Bell	6	1965–67
Duncairn Martha	B	J Farrell	5	1965–67
Tiobra Tina	B	W Tracey	3	19666
1967				
Teltown Skipper Jojo	D	T C Evans & J Sweeney	3	1966–67
Pathfinders Hoppitt	D	Miss M Dawes	3	1966–67
Pathfinders Hopscotch	D	Miss N Woodifield	7	1966–68
Pathfinders Craftsman	D	Miss N Woodifield	6	1966–68
Livthorpe Golden Casket	B	Mrs F O'Connor	3	1965–67
Pathfinders Dairymaid	B	Miss N Woodifield	3	1966–67
Ballymakenny Frankeen	B	H Fairtlough	4	1967
1968				
Chapelea Never Look Back	D	Mrs S Tonge	4	1967–68
Pathfinders Seirios One Bell	D	Miss N Woodifield	4	1968
Oudenarde Soldier	D	Mmes M Temple & S Tarry	6	1968–70
Swinpen My Girl	B	J Wilson/T C Evans	8	1968–70
Brackenwood Carousel of Medris	B	Misses G Harris, M Medcalf & M Abell	17	1968–72
1969				
Merrey Midshipman	D	Miss F M Simpson	4	1968–69
Gentleman Jim	D	F Roberts	3	1969
Arcroney Acrobat	D	W Tracey	8	1969–70
Pathfinders Seirios Three Bells	B	Miss N Woodifield	3	1967–68
Drumcorrie Nina	B	Miss M de Beaumont	3	1969
1970				
Pathfinders Leapfrog	D	Miss N Woodifield	3	1970
Redneval Ballinruan Beau	D	F W Bell	31	1970–73

Name	Sex	Owner	No of CCs	Years of CCs
Teltown Medley Tina	B	J G C & S O Sweeney	3	1969–70
Merrey Miss Muffet	B	Miss F M Simpson	4	1969–70
Ballinruan Sheila	B	T K Loughrey/S Eakins	3	1970
1971				
Drumshaw Lisa	B	Mrs I V Shaw	3	1968–71
Teltown L'Amour	B	J G C & S O Sweeney	3	1971
Carolmac Fancy	B	P J Carroll	3	1971
Ballymakenny Josephine	B	H Fairtlough	9	1971–72
1972				
Swinpen Dinah	B	T C Evans	3	1972
1973				
Breezy Cuchullin	D	Mrs E Howard Jones	3	1972–73
Teltown Dandy of Swinpen	D	T C Evans/J Sweeney	3	1972–73
Gedmorr Early Riser	D	G A Morrison	3	1973
Imperial Major	D	W T Watterson	5	1973–74
Breezy Garland	B	Mrs C S Jackson	5	1972–73
Carolmac Katy of Brackenford	B	J L Jones	4	1973
Carolmac This Time	B	F W Bell	5	1973–74
1974				
Merrey Malachi	D	Miss F M Simpson	11	1972–78
Camogie Conman	D	W Tracey	4	1974
Carolmac Saddletramp	D	P J Carroll	4	1974
Redneval Rifleman	D	F W Bell	10	1974–75
Medris Sea Ginger	B	Misses Harris & Medcalf/J Edmondson/ P J Carroll	3	1972–74
Happy Return of Halfacre	B	Mrs C Birch	8	1973–74
Imperial Molly of Esperons	B	W T Watterson	5	1973–74
1975				
Gnomeshalt Witching Hour	B	Mrs B Napthine/Miss J A Simcock	3	1973–75
Ballybrac Copper Coin	B	C Campbell	3	1974–75

Name	Sex	Owner	No of CCs	Years of CCs
Gedmor Crock of Gold	B	G A Morrison	5	1975
Woodville Narthern	B	M & Mrs G Bell	9	1975–76
1976				
Camogie Crusader	D	J Marland	6	1975–77
Teltown General McKee	D	J G C & S O Sweeney	3	1976
Duncairn Mirabelle	B	H A Davis	4	1976
Breezy Satisfaction	B	Mrs E Howard Jones	4	1976
1977				
Bonsire Major	D	H A Davis	3	1975–77
Conjola Ironbark of Breezy	D	Mrs E Howard Jones	5	1976–77
Esperons Bright Gold	D	W T Watterson	3	1977
Pathfinders Dressage	D	Miss N Woodifield	4	1977
Flypeg of Carolmac	B	P J Carroll	4	1976–77
Harvestime No Shade	B	Mrs C S Jackson	11	1976–81
Pathfinders Daffodil	B	Miss N Woodifield	3	1977
1978				
Carolmac Fiddlesticks	D	P J Caroll	7	1977–78
Esperons Hillside Sandy	D	P Dorrian	3	1977–78
Divine Emerald of Oudenarde	B	Mrs D & Miss H Hamilton	12	1977–79
Penwarne Love Girl	B	Mrs S Tarry	3	1978
1979				
Montelle Amber Tweed	D	Miss A Bradley	3	1978–79
Montelle Golden Rod	D	Miss A Bradley	5	1978–79
Ben's Heir The Bosun	D	H A Davis	3	1979
Breezy Delight	B	Mrs E Howard Jones	3	1978–79
Carolmac Fiddle De Dee	B	P J Carroll	4	1979
1980				
Ardgabha Mac An-T-Saoir	D	Mrs M Semple	3	1978–80
Oudenarde Only Derry	D	Mr & Mrs S Somerfield	4	1979–80
Ben's Heir Ramla	D	H A Davis	3	1979–80

Name	Sex	Owner	No of CCs	Years of CCs
Oudenarde Irish Tony	D	Mr & Mrs S Somerfield/A D Bell	6	1979–86
Oudenarde Ballyfinlake	B	S Somerfield	3	1979–80
Aran of Paddymack	B	Miss A Bradley	5	1979–83
Nic An-T-Saoir Ardgabha	B	Mr & Mrs W T Semple	5	1980
Esperons Dancing Amanda	B	W T Watterson	3	1978–80
1981				
Carolmac Music Master	D	J Crawley	3	1979–81
Enniskillen Dragoon	D	R Semple	24	1980–85
Ardgabha Shemil	B	Mr & Mrs W T Semple	3	1980–81
Tanwell Lucky Shamrock of Merrydais	B	Mrs E J Symonds/Mrs W A Moore	4	1980–81
Ben's Heir Liz	B	H A Davis	6	1981
1982				
Ben's Heir Ben	D	H A Davis/F Jones	3	1981–82
Fairywells Glensman	D	Miss A Traynor	3	1982
Pathfinders Smart Suit	D	Miss N Woodifield	5	1982
Ardgabha Tempo	B	W T Semple	3	1981–82
Ben's Heir Scarlett	B	C Campbell	4	1981–82
Lady Dinah of Montelle	B	Miss A Bradley	7	1982–83
1983				
Slemish Spokesman	D	R Grant/M McShane	3	1980–83
Ganjo of Ben's Heir	D	H A Davis	4	1982–83
Major General of Montelle	B	Miss A Bradley	3	1983
Modern Millie of Montelle	B	Miss A Bradley	5	1982–84
Breezy Briar Rose	B	S Docherty	3	1983
Riojem Paprika	B	Mrs J Livesey	4	1983–84
1984				
Robin Hood of Esperons	D	W T Watterson	3	1974–84
Montelle Gamblin Millar	D	Miss A Bradley	10	1984–85
Dragoon's Lady	B	R J Semple	10	1983–85
Carolmac Once Again	B	P J Carroll	7	1984

Name	Sex	Owner	No of CCs	Years of CCs
1985				
Riojem Thyme	D	Mrs J Livesey	7	1985–86
Teltown Margo Flash	B	B Moynihan	7	1985
Tubereasa Ben's Son	D	Miss A Dowell	3	1984–85
Nenu of Ben's Heir	D	H A Davis	13	1984–86
The Survivor	D	W McGill	3	1985
1986				
Ben's Heir Golden Lass	B	G Clarke	3	1985–86
Teltown Lucky Lass	B	P J Carroll/W Ryan	7	1986
Fairywells Brigadier of Blackdale	D	H O'Donoghue	3	1985–86
Tanwell Treasures Gift	B	Miss M J Higginson	3	1986
1987				
Yewood Ruby	B	S Brown	3	1986–87
Magill of Ben's Heir	D	H A Davis	3	1986–87
Tubereasa My Demerrera	B	Miss A Dowell	11	1986–89
Rastaman Autumn Gift	D	P Sweeney	3	1987
Josakas Sorley Boy of Jackmo	D	Mr & Mrs S Price/A Jones	18	1986–90
Ben's Heir Rambo	D	H A Davis	6	1987–88
Indian Spice of Montelle	B	Dr A Noonan/Ms L Williamson	5	1987–88
1988				
Kerrykeel Rose	B	K Anderson	3	1987–88
Esperons Mick	D	W T Watterson	3	1988
Mairi Bhan	B	S Docherty	7	1987–88
Red Rosette	B	Mrs M M E Lloyd	3	1988
Gatecrasher	D	N & D Cullen	3	1988
Rojem Pepper	B	Mrs J Livesey	4	1986–88
Josakas Rory McRory	D	Mr & Mrs S Price/A Jones	3	1988
Ben's Heir Martello	D	H A Davis	8	1987–90
1989				
Oudenarde Ragtrade	D	Maj S W Somerfield	4	1988–89
Rafferty of Yewood	D	S Brown	4	1988–89

Name	Sex	Owner	No of CCs	Years of CCs
Benslair Bright as Morn	B	J Thwaite	3	1989
Carolmac Pearly Boy	D	P J Carroll	4	1989
Shawgreen Ashley	B	Mrs S Saville/G Clarke	4	1989–90
Drumshaw Rosemary	B	C Aslam	3	1988–89
Yewood Gem	B	S Brown	4	1989–90
1990				
Teltown Mick	D	G Sweeney	3	1988–90
Ben's Heir Beauty	B	Mrs E Henry-Davis	10	1990–91
Trackways Booger Red	D	Maj S W Somerfield	11	1990–92
Carolmac Tareaway	D	M Gilbert	4	1989–90
Montelle Star Attraction	B	Miss A Bradley	4	1990
1991				
Edbrios Duplicate	D	K Anderson	3	1990–91
Faytyme Rising Star at Montelle	D	Miss A Bradley	3	1988–91
Yewood Murphy	D	S Brown	3	1991
Naranja Firedancer	B	Dr A Noonan/Ms L Williamson	4	1990–92
Ben's Heir Beau	D	H A Davis	15	1991–93
Carolmac Dolly Bird	B	H Atkinson/Mr & Mrs R Punter	11	1991–92
1992				
Montelle Sunarise	D	Miss A Bradley	3	1990–92
Lynphen Katie	B	C Pollard	11	1991–93
Tubereasa Ryans Daughter	B	Mrs A Smith	6	1991–95
Gamekeepers Fergie	B	Maj S W Somerfield	7	1992–94
1993				
Fairywells Sergeant Pepper	D	Mr & Mrs P Dorrian	3	1992–93
Rutlan Red Rum	D	Mrs J Livesey/H Kelly	3	1993–93
Tanwell Rainbow Quest at Helstonian	B	L Stevens	4	1992–93
Ben's Heir Ed	D	H Gruttner	7	1992–93
1994				
Micky Fynn	D	Mr & Mrs A Barker	4	1993–94
Maybe Red of Breezy	D	Mrs E Howard Jones	4	1993–94

Name	Sex	Owner	No of CCs	Years of CCs
Yewood Amethyst	B	S Brown	3	1993–94
Tubereasa Beau Venture Ardgabha	B	Mr & Mrs W Semple	14	1994–97
Montelle Star Return	B	Miss A & Mrs D Bradley	3	1994
Chanatalle's Tanya of Gabledown	B	Mrs E J Symonds	3	1994
1995				
Naranja Danse du Feu	B	Dr A Noonan/Ms L Williamson	3	1993–95
Kentee Begracefull of Fairywells	B	Mr & Mrs P Dorrian	8	1994–96
1996				
Chantalle's Gentleman Joe at Dehra	D	K Anderson/N Frost	4	1994–96
Fairywells Lass	B	P McQuaid	3	1994–96
Galway Gambler at Irvonhill	D	Mr & Mrs A Barker	8	1994–96
Tubereasa Fortune Teller	B	Mrs A Smith	3	1995–96
Shanvaus Ruar Colleen	B	Mr & Mrs D Croot	3	1995–96
Brazan Absolutely	B	Mrs M Lovelace	3	1996
1997				
Naranja Jumping Jack Flash	D	Dr A Noonan/Ms L Williamson	4	1996–97
Brazans Caramel	B	Mrs M Lovelace	3	1996–97
Lacus Party Piece	B	Mr & Mrs H Atkinson & R Punter	3	1996–97
Fairywells Golden Chance	D	Mr & Mrs Dirrian	3	1997
1998				
Ruffmar Flaithiulach of Inchicore	B	Mr & Mrs D Fegan	3	1993–98
Edbrios Gobnait of Brazan	B	S Price & A Jones	3	1997–98
Stanchills Tweed	B	A Barker & T Biela	3	1997–98
Brazan Riesling	D	Mrs M Lovelace & H Gruttner	4	1998
Montelle Wandering Star	B	Miss A Bradley	3	1998
Montelle Famous Star	D	Miss A Bradley	5	1998

Appendix C   Irish Breeders, Kennels and Champions

Ben's Heir

(Owned by Harry Davis – Northern Ireland)

Name	DoB	Sire/Dam	Breeder	Owner	Made Up
Ch Bonsire Major		Ch Imperial Major / Calamity Jane	Mr Magill	H A Davis	1977
Ch Duncairn Mirabelle				H A Davis	1976
Ch Ben's Heir The Bosun		Ch Redneval Ballinruan Beau / Limehill Liz	H A Davis	Breeder	1979
Ch Ben's Heir Ramla		Int Ch Ben's Heir Major / Limehill Liz	H A Davis	Breeder	1980
Ch Ben's Heir Liz		Int Ch Bonsire Major / Limehill Liz	H A Davis	Breeder	1981
Ch Ben's Heir Scarlett		Int Ch Bonsire Major / Limehill Liz	H A Davis	C Campbell	1982
Ch Ben's Heir Ben		Int Ch Bonsire Major / Limehill Liz	H A Davis	H A Davis/F Jones	1982
Ch Ganjo of Ben's Heir		Ch Ben's Heir Ramla / Fireball of Redcar	Mr Magill	H A Davis	1983
Ch Nenu of Ben's Heir		Ch Ben's Heir X-Lendi / Canadial Lass	Mr Magill	H A Davis	1985
Ch Ben's Heir Rambo	02.07.85	Ch Ben's Heir The Bosun / Ben's Heir Catherine	H A Davis	Breeder	1987
Ch Magill of Ben's Heir	02.06.85	Ch Bonsire Major / Fireball of Redcar	Mr Magill	H Gruttner	1987
Ch Ben's Heir Martello	02.08.85	Ch Bonsire Major / Ludy Mae of Ben's Heir	H A Davis	German owner	1988

Name	DoB	Sire/Dam	Breeder	Owner	Made Up
Ch Ben's Heir Beauty	15.02.88	Ch Nenu of Ben's Heir / Ben's Heir Fiona	H A Davis	Mrs E Henry-Davis	1990
Ch Ben's Heir Beau	02.08.89	Blackdale Golden Boy / Ben's Heir Megan	H A Davis	Breeder	1991
Ch Ben's Heir Ed	29.10.90	Ch Edbrios Duplicate / Ben's Heir Bonnie	H A Davis	K Kirch/H Gruttner	1993
Esperons (Owned by W T Watterson – Northern Ireland)					
Ch Imperial Major		Duncairn Matador / Clanleam Mandy		W T Watterson	1973
Ch Imperial Molly of Esperons				W T Watterson	1974
Ch Esperons Hillside Sandy		Ch Imperial Major / Esperons Maid Marion	W T Watterson	P Dorrian	1978
Ch Esperons Bright Gold	31.07.75	Ch Carolmac Saddletramp / Ch Imperial Molly of Esperons	W T Watterson	Breeder	1977
Ch Esperons Dancing Amanda		Ch Esperons Bright Gold / Esperons Maid Marion	W T Watterson	Breeder	1980
Ch Mystic of Esperons	15.08.78	Ch Esperons Terry Boy / Esperons Maid Marion	W T Watterson	Mrs A Watterson	1981
Ch Robin Hood of Esperons		Ch Imperial Major / Calamity Jane	Mr Magill (?)	W T Watterson	1984
Ch Esperons Mick	17.11.86	Esperons Irish Mist / Blackdale Sabrina	W T Watterson	Breeder	1988
Ch Esperons Terry Boy			W T Watterson	German breeder	

Name	DoB	Sire/Dam	Breeder	Owner	Made Up
Fairywells					
		(Owned by P Dorrian – Northern Ireland)			
Ch Danny Boy of Fairywells		Ch Robinhood of Esperons / Ch Esperons Dancing Amanda	W T Watterson	P Dorrian	1980
Ch Fairywells Glensman	20.09.80	Ch Danny Boy of Fairywells / Fairywells Irish Image	P Dorrian	Traynor	
Ch Fairywells Brigadier of Blackdale		Robin Hood of Esperons / Fairywells Irish Image	P Dorrian	H O'Donaghue	1986
Ch Fairywells Lady Luck	09.05.82	Mystic of Fairywells / Fairywells Irish Image	P Dorrian	Breeder	?
Ch Kentee Begraceful of Fairywells	12.02.93	Fairywells Sergeant Pepper / Fine Dish	D O'Reilly	Mr & Mrs P Dorrian	1995
Fairywells Lass	05.04.93	Ch Fairywells Sargeant Pepper / Fairywells Debonaire	P Dorrian	D McQuaid	1996
Ch Fairywells Sargeant Pepper	27.03.91	Fairywells Capable / Fairywells Lady Luck	P Dorrian	Exported	1993
Teltown					
		(Owned by the Sweeney family – Dublin)			
Ch Teltown Skipper Jojo			Sweeney	Sweeney/T C Evans	1967
Ch Teltown Medley Tina			J G C & S O Sweeney	Breeders	1970
Ch Teltown L'Amour			J G C & S O Sweeney	Breeders	1971
Ch Teltown Dandy of Swinpen			J Sweeney	J Sweeney/T C Evans	1973
Ch Teltown General McKee			J C G & S O Sweeney	Breeders	
Ch/Ir Ch Teltown Cover Girl	05.08.74	Ch Teltown Jojo of Swinpen / Teltown Roving Sue	Sweeney	Breeders (?)	1976
Ch/Ir Ch Teltown Commander Rolf		Ch Mister J / Ch/Ir Ch Teltown Cover Girl	Sweeney	Breeders (?)	

Name	DoB	Sire/Dam	Breeder	Owner	Made Up
Ch Teltown Margo Flash	21.08.82	Ch/Ir Ch Teltown Commander Rolf / Teltown Tina	Sweeney	B Moynihan	1985
		(This highly successful bitch combined breeding lines from Teltown, Swinpen and Slemish, especially through Ch/Ir Ch Teltown JoJo of Swinpen, Ch Teltown Skipper JoJo, Ir Ch Teltown Swinpen Top Note and Int Ch Susan of Swinpen.)			
Ch/Int Ch Rastaman Autumn Gift	29.06.83	Ch/Ir Ch Teltown Commander Rolf / Ir Ch Rastaman Shooting Star	Vaughn/McLoughlin	P Sweeney, then exported	1987
Ch Teltown Lucky Lass		Ir Ch Swinpen Bright Boy / Carolmac Silken Dalliance	Sweeney	P J Carroll/W Ryan	1986
Ch Teltown Mick	10.11.86	Ch/Ir Ch Rastaman Autumn Gift / Riojem Mint	G Sweeney	Breeder, then exported	1990
(BIS National Terrier 1992)					
Ardgabha (Owned by W Semple – Northern Ireland)					
Ch Ardgabha Mac An-T-Saoir		Slemish Smash Hit / Aine Rua	W Semple	Mrs M Semple	1980
Ch Enniskillin Dragoon	01.08.78	Ch Ardgabha Mac An-T-Saoir / Aine Rua	W Semple	R Semple	1980
		(Combination of Slemish, Teltown, Swinpen and Begorra lines. BIS at Bournemouth and Leicester Canine Show, 1981. First BIS for an Irish Terrier.)			
Ch Nic Ant-T Saoir Ardgabha		Ch Ardgabha Mac An-T-Saoir / Aine Rua	Mr & Mrs W Semple	Breeders	1980
Ch Ardgabha Shemil		Slemish Smash Hit / Aine Rua	W Semple	Marks	1981
Ch Ardgabha Tempo		Ch Enniskillin Dragoon / Ardgabha Lala	W Semple	Breeder	1982

Name	DoB	Sire/Dam	Breeder	Owner	Made Up
Ch Dragoon's Lady		Ch Enniskillin Dragoon Ch Oudenarde Ballyfinlake	S Somerfield	R Semple	1984
Ch Tubereasa Beau Venture Ardgabha			A Smith	Mr & Mrs W Semple	1994

Slemish
(Owned by R Grant – Eire)

Name	DoB	Sire/Dam	Breeder	Owner	Made Up
Ch Slemish Stormer			R Grant	Breeder	1935
Ch Slemish Splendid			R Grant	Breeder	1936
Slemish Sensation	04.06.76		R Grant	Breeder	N/A
Ch Slemish Spokesman			R Grant	R Grant/M McShane	1983
Slemish Statesman	31.03.88	Ch Slemish Spokesman Slemish Such A Girl	R Grant	Breeder	N/A

(In addition, 13 dogs exported to the United States of America from this kennel became American Champions.)

Mr Magill of Northern Ireland (No Affix)

Mr Magill bred several Champions, most of whom went to other kennels. For instance, Ch Bonsire Major, Ch Ganjo of Ben's Heir, Ch Nenu of Ben's Heir and Ch Magill of Ben's Heir all went to Mr Harry Davis; Ch Robinhood of Esperons went to Mr W T Watterson.

bibliography

Cooper, Jilly *The Canine Years*
Grambien Parry, *Maj* *Murphy – a Message to Dog Lovers* 1912
Haynes, William *Irish Terriers* 1921
Howard, Evelyn *The Dog That Went to Heaven*
Howard Jones, Edna *Irish Terriers*
Jackson, Lucy *The African Adventure of Finnegan O'Reilly*
Jackson, Lucy *For Irish Terriers and Other Dogs*
Jackson, Lucy *Jock of the Great War*
Jackson, Lucy *Miss Bunch and her Friends*
Jackson, Lucy *Stories of Breezy and Blarney*
Jackson, Lucy *Ted and his Teddy Bear*
Jowett, F W *Irish Terriers* 1914
Kidd, D *and* G *How to Raise and Train and Irish Terrier* 1965
London, Jack *Jerry of the Islands*
London, Jack *Michael, Brother of Jerry*
Richardson, *Lt Col* E H *British War Dogs*

abbreviations

BIS	Best In Show
BOB	Best Of Breed
BOS	Best Opposite Sex
BP	Best Pup
CC	Challenge Certificate
Ch	Champion (United Kingdom)
ITA	Irish Terrier Association
Ir Ch	Irish Champion
KC	Kennel Club
RBIS	Reserve Best In Show
RBOS	Reserve Best Opposite Sex
RCC	Reserve Challenge Certificate
WELKS	West of England Ladies Kennel Society

useful addresses

The Kennel Club
1–5 Clarges Street
Piccadilly
London   W1Y 8AB
Tel: 0171 493 6651

Breed Clubs

Because of all the pressure of the position, Secretaries of breed clubs change quite often. For this reason, I have simply listed the breed clubs below. The name and address of the current Secretary of the club you wish to contact can be obtained from The Kennel Club.

The Irish Terrier Association

The North of England Irish Terrier Club

Southern Irish Terrier Society

The Irish Terrier Club of Scotland

The All Ireland Irish Terrier Club

Others

Council of Docked Breeds
Secretary: Ginette Elliott
Marsburg Kennels
Whitehall Lane
Thorpe-le-Soken
Essex   CO16 0AF

index